D0734695

Union &
Emancipation

Union &

Emancipation

Essays on Politics and Race

in the Civil War Era

Edited by

David W. Blight

&

Brooks D. Simpson

PHILA. COLLEGE PHARMACY & SCIENCE
J. W. ENGLAND LIBRARY
RELEASED
4200 WOODLAND AVENUE
PHILADELPHIA, PA 19104-4491

The Kent State University Press

KENT, OHIO, & LONDON, ENGLAND

ACF-4774

© 1997 by The Kent State University Press, Kent, Ohio 44242
All rights reserved
Library of Congress Catalog Card Number 96-34978
ISBN 0-87338-565-9
Manufactured in the United States of America

04 03 02 01 00 99 98 97   5 4 3 2 1

Library of Congress Cataloging-in-Publication Data
Union and emancipation : essays on politics and race in the Civil War era
/ edited by David W. Blight and Brooks D. Simpson.
p.   cm.
Includes bibliographical references and index.
ISBN 0-87338-565-9 (cloth : alk. paper) ∞
1. United States—Politics and government—1849–1877.
2. Sectionalism (United States) 3. United States—Race relations.
4. United States—History—Civil War, 1861–1865.
5. Slaves—Emancipation—United States.
I. Blight, David W. II. Simpson, Brooks D.
E415.7.U55 1997   96-34978
305.8'00973—dc20

British Library Cataloging-in-Publication data are available.

E
4 15.7
U58

For

RICHARD H. SEWELL,

mentor and friend

Richard H. Sewell, Professor of History
Emeritus, University of Wisconsin–Madison,
author of *John P. Hale and the Politics of Abolition*
(1965); *Ballots for Freedom: Antislavery Politics in
the United States, 1837–1860* (1976); and *A House
Divided: Sectionalism and the Civil War, 1848–1865*
(1988).

CONTENTS

ACKNOWLEDGMENTS

WITHOUT the aid and encouragement of many people this book would never have come to fruition. We would first like to thank our fellow contributors for their splendid essays, as well as their patience and good humor. John Hubbell at The Kent State University Press has supported and encouraged us; his patience and advice have provided expert stewardship. Stanley Kutler was a guiding force behind planning the dinner and retirement celebration in Madison, Wisconsin, at which we presented this book of essays in Dick Sewell's honor. A special thanks to Stanley for not spilling the secret, an extraordinary example of self-restraint. Very special thanks are also due Eric Foner and Bertram Wyatt-Brown for delivering papers and helping us all to honor Dick in December 1994. We are further grateful to Ken Sacks and the University of Wisconsin history department for allowing us to participate in Dick's retirement banquet.

At Arizona State, Alice Valenzuela, Sharon Brockus, Carolyn Heath, Pat Nay, and Marlene Bolf contributed in ways large and small to finishing this volume. At Amherst, Nancy Board's expert assistance was indispensable for editing, revising, making computer conversions, and completing the manuscript for publication in its various stages. Brooks gives special thanks, as always, to Jean, Rebecca, and Emily. David salutes Karin Beckett, as always, companion and critic.

Finally, we would like to thank Dick Sewell. His guidance and inspiration made this book possible.

Union &
Emancipation

Introduction

DAVID W. BLIGHT & BROOKS D. SIMPSON

NOT long ago it seemed that American historians generally had moved beyond or around consideration of the Civil War as the pivotal event of the nineteenth century. A host of reasons and assumptions, methodological and ideological changes, accounted for such a turn in scholarly interest. The revolution in the study of social history, a de-emphasis on event-centered history, the search for the lives and values of ordinary people, the concentration on social structures and processes, and the emergence of whole new, richly active fields, such as women's history and African-American history, have all served at times to shunt the war—its causes, course, and consequences—to the background of research agendas. But over the past two or three decades all these questions depended on the position from which one observed these changes in historical interpretation. The tourists, the Civil War roundtables, the massive readership for Civil War literature and audience for films never went away. An intergenerational fascination on all levels with the Civil War era may be the most durable certainty we have amidst America's rapidly changing, multicultural demands for meaning drawn from our past. The Civil War has always been a key to understanding big questions about America, of seeking to know, or to avoid grasping, the "whole" of our history. Recent scholarship has opened up new worlds that have permitted us to understand the many "parts" that have fashioned our plural society. Collectively, we have become adept at *recognizing* our pluralism at the same time that we actively debate its *meaning* and its responsibilities.

All over the scholarly and pedagogical map these days, wherever the content and meaning of history matter to disparate American communities, historians are trying to be guides in the search for coherence. Such a challenge is, of course, riddled with traps and conflicts among historians themselves. Our debates are ultimately about what matters most in understanding history itself: great events? changing social structures over long periods of time? group cultures and identities? leadership? material interests? ideological interests? common experiences? Differences based on modes of empowerment? Such a list could continue. But as Eric Foner recently wrote, "the debate over difference and commonality today . . . threatens to become as sterile as that over conflict and consensus a generation ago. We can transcend it only by recognizing that these are not mutually exclusive categories."[1] As part of this process of understanding the mutuality of historical interests and methodologies, a broad spectrum of historians has once again come to embrace the centrality of the Civil War in the whole of the American experience. The *event* is back, treated now through the many lenses of political, social, and cultural history.

The seven essays in this volume address two major themes in scholarship concerning Civil War America: the politics of sectional conflict prior to the war, illuminated through ideological and institutional inquiry, and the central importance of race, slavery, and emancipation in shaping American political culture and social memory before, during, and after the war. Each focuses on a local or particular question in the sectional crisis, or on the meaning of the Civil War's character and outcome. But collectively, these pieces also reach for some careful generalizations about nineteenth-century American history. The public, national culture, the centrality of the nation-state in understanding a larger narrative of American history, the place of race in redefining what it meant to be an American, and, indeed, the way the coming and fighting of the Civil War helped to redefine the nature of the "political" and of "citizenship" are all major considerations readers will find in these essays. The significance of political parties—the ideas, interests, and slogans that motivate them—is also a central concern of this volume. Moreover, with differing conceptions of scale, some of these essays are concerned with understanding the idea of a "political generation," with the ways a public, national memory is shaped in relation to major events such as the war and emancipation.

The first three authors have addressed issues in traditional politics during the sectional crisis: each challenges a prevailing orthodoxy through careful reexamination of various texts and sources. Robert E. May demonstrates that Republican charges of a "slave power conspiracy" require significant modification when it comes to the dreams of a Caribbean slaveholding empire advanced by filibusters such as William Walker. May argues that American presidents gave no real aid to such adventurers, although he adds that their efforts to prohibit such activity did not always prove successful. That Zachary Taylor and Millard Fillmore kept clear of such enterprises is not surprising; however, their Democratic successors, Franklin Pierce and James Buchanan, also did not in the end assist such efforts, despite expansionists' expectations that they would do so.

Michael McManus's contribution demonstrates anew the fact that traditional associations between the South, slavery, and states' rights need reexamination. In Wisconsin, antislavery Republicans, convinced that the federal government was becoming an arm of the slaveholding South, employed states' rights justifications as a means of resisting enforcement of the Fugitive Slave Law of 1850; notions of federalism became a key and lasting part of the Republican appeal in the Badger state, a theme reflected in the postwar careers of James Rood Doolittle and Matthew Hale Carpenter.

Peter Knupfer examines in new ways another group of politicians closely associated with federalism, secession, and the character of the Constitution itself—the Constitutional Union party of 1860. Challenging portrayals of the leaders of this organization as little more than aging politicians out of touch with political reality, he demonstrates that party leaders were divided over the nature and future of their own movement. Suggesting that the Constitutional Unionists have been unfairly neglected by historians over the years, Knupfer analyzes how we come to define a "political generation," as well as why conservative political movements often fail in times of upheaval and radical change.

The four other essays in the volume address various aspects of the problem of race, slavery, and emancipation. The essays by Louis Gerteis and Ira Berlin take a broad and innovative view of the intersections among political, social, and cultural history. Gerteis explores the world of blackface minstrelsy, finding there an ironic, democratic, and mutual creation by performers and audiences, a distinctly American popular entertainment that both reinforced and challenged the prevailing white attitudes about race. Gerteis argues that mid–nineteenth-century minstrelsy was a combination of racism, racial masquerade, and wide-ranging parody of American politics. His multidimensional approach to blackface provides an intriguing window on the racial, instead of the sectional, divide; his critique of the idea of "authenticity" is useful to all considerations of American cultural history.

Berlin examines the old question of "who freed the slaves" in response to both public and scholarly imperatives. Using the results of his own magisterial project on the documentary history of emancipation, Berlin takes issue with those historians who continue to view black freedom in the Civil War primarily in terms of the Federal government's policy, and especially the singular role of President Abraham Lincoln. He reminds readers of the complexity of the story of emancipation, that many actors contributed to ending slavery, and none more significantly than the slaves themselves. Berlin sees Lincoln as both a reluctant and a decisive emancipator; his essay leaves us richly aware that the Civil War forged a crooked, tragic path to social revolution, and redefined the civic future of black people.

The final two essays, by the editors of the volume, focus on responses to the changes wrought by emancipation, its emergence from a military process, its aftermath and place in the historical memory of blacks and whites. Brooks Simpson examines Ulysses S. Grant's attitudes toward and use of black troops during and after the war. He suggests that Grant's decisions reflect deep ambivalence and conflicted priorities, born of the struggle of a commanding general to juggle and reconcile military imperatives with his own values and beliefs about race. Simpson's essay provides a treatment of what the architect of Union victory thought and did as he pondered how best to employ black soldiers to gain victory while remaining ambivalent about how their service as occupation troops defined the meaning of that victory.

David Blight's concluding essay examines the fifty-year process by which the memory of the Civil War became a struggle between the themes of race and reunion, each with its own hold on the American historical imagination. Blight analyzes why, by the fiftieth anniversary of the war and

emancipation in 1913, the spirit of sectional reconciliation had overpow-
ered any hope of racial reconciliation in the national memory. Blacks themselves struggled with how best to interpret and remember slavery and
emancipation, as white Northerners and Southerners found a new and
abiding unity in the memory of mutual valor on Civil War battlefields and
in the reunions after a family quarrel that had made the nation stronger, a
quarrel in which blacks were judged to have been passive spectators.

The seven contributors to this volume share more than an interest in
America in the era of the Civil War. They all completed their graduate
training in Madison at the University of Wisconsin. For each of them
Richard H. Sewell has been adviser, critic, colleague, and friend. Each
has been subject to his sharp editorial pen and quiet wit; each has been
the beneficiary of his tutelage and extraordinary kindness. We learned
from Dick in many ways. His own work on antislavery politics and the
coming of the Civil War demonstrated—at a time when methodological
innovation and a reliance on theory was receiving increased attention—
that one could still make a lasting contribution to scholarship by mining
the archives, pondering over what one found, and presenting one's findings in lucid prose accessible to all. Dick's *Ballots for Freedom: Antislavery
Politics in the United States, 1837–1860* (1976) remains the best synthetic
work on antislavery politics. Anyone who wishes to understand the centrality of slavery, expansionism, and abolition in American political culture from the 1830s to the Civil War, and how the fledgling Liberty party
evolved and transformed into the Republican party of 1860, must read
Sewell.

At the same time he reminded us of the importance of imparting historical knowledge and awareness in the classroom as well as in print, in-
stilling in each of us a belief that teaching is inherently part of scholarship. In the lecture hall, the seminar room, the office, and in the endless
exchanges of chapters, manuscripts, and correspondence, Dick Sewell has
been a great teacher. Embodying some older traditions with exemplary
grace, he has worn them well into new times. Unafraid to tell us when we
wrote badly or did not think clearly, he nevertheless rewarded and praised
us for some of the new directions we pursued. In a host of ways Dick
Sewell has taught us much about how to become scholars, about the character of research, about perseverance, about clarity of argument and good

prose, and, as he so often put it, about "the causes, course, and consequences" of the Civil War. With this volume we thank and honor him for all that and more.

Chapter One

❧

The Slave Power Conspiracy Revisited:

United States Presidents and Filibustering,

1848–1861

Robert E. May

Richard H. Sewell and other scholars of political abolitionism emphasize that from the 1830s to the Civil War the movement was charged by the conviction that a Slave Power conspiracy competed with liberty for control of the American future. Antislavery politicians believed that Southerners had initiated an unrelenting, ruthless campaign to impose proslavery policies on the federal government and that they had successfully enlisted many Northern public figures in their conspiratorial web. The Liberty and Free-Soil parties of the 1840s had only limited success convincing Northern voters that the Slave Power stood poised to take over the United States. However, the Republican party of the 1850s, aided incalculably by seeming evidences of an aggressive slavocracy such as the "sack" of Lawrence, Kansas, the caning of Charles Sumner, and the Dred Scott decision, made the charge stick. Electioneering rhetoric about the Slave Power helped produce Republican seats in Congress as well as the Republican presidential triumph that drove the South from the Union in 1860–61.[1]

Political abolitionism's indictment of the Slave Power included charges that slaveholders enlisted the federal government in schemes to strengthen their "peculiar institution" by extending its domain southward into Cuba, Nicaragua, Mexico, and other parts of the tropics. Antislavery politicians

and ideologues identified a number of foreign policy initiatives by the
Franklin Pierce and James Buchanan administrations, such as their efforts to acquire the slave island of Cuba from Spain, as confirmation of
their case.[2]

Antislavery figures further contended that several presidents, especially
the Democratic "doughfaces" Pierce and Buchanan, were so anxious to
appease the Slave Power that they tolerated and sometimes abetted illegal
"filibustering" expeditions designed to spread slavery southward. Between
the Mexican War and the Civil War, Americans raised a number of private armies to invade and conquer foreign states and dependencies—especially Cuba, Nicaragua, and Mexico—in defiance of the Neutrality Act
of 1818, which prohibited private military expeditions against nations with
which the United States was at peace. Filibustering was by no means an
exclusively Southern phenomenon. However, a number of the expeditions had blatantly sectional objectives. Former Mississippi governor John
A. Quitman, for instance, organized a primarily Southern force to invade
Cuba, in response to rumors that Spain intended to emancipate the island's
slaves. Quitman and his followers anticipated that a liberated Cuba would
follow Texas's precedent and enter the Union as one or more slave states.
The Gulf states, especially, rallied to William Walker's cause after the
Tennessean conquered and reestablished slavery in Nicaragua.[3]

Antislavery politicians almost invariably opposed filibustering expeditions into the tropics and condemned them as evidence of the Slave Power
conspiracy. Antislavery sentinels contended that such endeavors, in that
they required considerable advance planning and mobilization and were
often rumored in the press long before they departed, could never have
escaped federal interdiction without connivance by Washington. The *New-
York Daily Times* argued that the "business" was "winked at by the authorities." Theodore Parker informed an antislavery convention that President Pierce and his attorney general, Caleb Cushing, "encouraged"
filibustering. Free-Soil editor John Bigelow noted privately that it was
"well understood" that an invasion of Nicaragua had been "countenanced
in every practicable way by the [Buchanan] administration."[4]

Were political abolitionists merely shopping for votes with such charges?
Or did rhetoric echo informed conviction? David Brion Davis noted in
The Slave Power Conspiracy and the Paranoid Style that even the "wildest
theories of conspiracy" require some element of validity "to win the minds
of judicious men."[5] But *how much* truth was there to antislavery reports of

presidential collusion with filibusters? Recent research suggests that Abraham Lincoln and his fellow Republicans may have had legitimate cause for their alarm that the Dred Scott decision exposed Southern designs to impose slavery on the free states.[6] Perhaps their indictment of presidential complicity in filibustering had commensurate justification.

Although one scholar asserts baldly that the "White House . . . rarely discouraged filibustering," historians have yet to reach a consensus about presidential collusion with filibusters or even to provide sustained analysis of the question.[7] This essay investigates antislavery claims that the Slave Power successfully extorted profilibustering policies from the United States government. Clarification of the presidential record on filibustering serves two primary purposes: it informs debate on the role of sectional paranoia in the causation of the Civil War as well as facilitates a more accurate rendering of United States foreign policy in the age of Manifest Destiny.

At the outset, distinctions must be drawn between official and unofficial policy. There can be little debate about official policy in the post–Mexican War period. Every president from Zachary Taylor through James Buchanan issued formal and often vehement pronouncements that they opposed filibustering. Not only did all these chief executives criticize filibustering in messages to Congress, but each issued one or more proclamations to the American people warning them against participating in such endeavors. Taylor called filibuster invasions "criminal" to the "highest degree." Millard Fillmore described filibusters as adventurers bent upon "plunder and robbery" who deserved the "condemnation of the civilized world." Pierce stigmatized them as "derogatory to our national character." Buchanan said that filibusters were "reckless and lawless men" who violated the "principles of Christianity, morality, and humanity, held sacred by all civilized nations."[8]

Neither James K. Polk nor any of his four successors ever endorsed filibustering in an official document. This generalization even applies to Franklin Pierce, who advised the U.S. Senate to strike an antifilibustering provision from the Gadsden Treaty with Mexico. Since Pierce did not explain what prompted his request, one could infer that his recommendation derived from filibustering intentions. However, the provision would have committed both the United States and Mexico to pursuing and capturing filibusters on the high seas. Pierce may well have objected to the clause because it gave Mexico the right to judge the guilt or innocence of apprehended Americans without guaranteeing them a trial by jury. Rather, the provision defied the presumption that one is innocent until proven guilty by stigmatizing seized persons as "delinquents," and simply provided that such persons be "judged and punished" by the nation whose vessel effected the capture.[9]

Furthermore, American secretaries of state announced to foreign diplomats and governments with almost numbing repetitiveness that the U.S. government had always upheld and would continue to uphold the neutrality laws. Several secretaries of state even boasted that their country had an exemplary record regarding filibuster expeditions, and that other countries should respect its vigilance as a model of proper international behavior. Thus William L. Marcy told Costa Rica's chargé d'affaires in Washington that it would be "difficult to show an instance in which any other country, including his own, has done more by legislation than the United States to preserve with fidelity neutral relations with other powers."[10]

Unofficial policy, of course, is quite another matter. Contemporaries charged each of the presidents under scrutiny here with lax enforcement of the Neutrality Act. This criticism emanated not only from those opposed to slavery's territorial expansion but also from Americans of diverse partisan persuasions as well as many Latin American and European observers. The press printed rumors, for instance, that a U.S. army officer turned up at the White House on June 12 or 14, 1848, consulted with Polk and members of his cabinet, and gained the president's acquiescence in a scheme to invade northern Mexico and establish a Republic of the Sierra Madre, providing the invaders never publicly implicated the administration in their plot. Newspapers similarly claimed that members of President Zachary Taylor's cabinet condoned filibustering. In June 1850, after news arrived in Europe of Narciso López's recent landing in Cuba, U.S. Minister to France William C. Rives reported "illiberal and unfriendly insinuations" in the French press that the expedition had been "winked at" by the Taylor administration. Critics likewise deemed Millard Fillmore soft on filibustering. A correspondent of the *Baltimore Sun* attributed López's 1851 expedition to Cuba to "neglect of executive duty." Charges even circulated that the Fillmore administration repressed evidence against the filibusters that had been provided by Spanish officials because the administration did not want filibusters convicted in court.[11]

Partly because filibustering peaked during his administration, Franklin Pierce became a frequent target for accusations of presidential complicity with filibusters. Thus James Gadsden, who was trying to negotiate a land cession from Mexico at the very time that William Walker led some forty-five filibusters from San Francisco to Baja California and proclaimed a short-lived Republic of Lower California, complained to the Department of State about his difficulties convincing Mexican negotiators that the United States government did not "secretly" favor Walker's enterprise. Critics believed that Pierce encouraged John A. Quitman's Cuba plot, that he ignored the doings of Henry L. Kinney's Central American Land and Mining Company (a filibuster scheme based on a questionable land grant involving Nicaragua's Mosquito Coast) because his private secretary held a financial interest in the enterprise, and that he supported William Walker's invasion of Nicaragua. When Pierce recognized Walker's regime in May 1856, he seemed to confirm suspicions of his filibuster leanings.[12]

Reports circulated that James Buchanan would support filibustering even before the Pennsylvanian triumphed in the presidential election of 1856. After all, Buchanan had helped draft the "Ostend Manifesto" (1854) calling for American seizure of Cuba, and he had a considerable following in the South. Furthermore, Buchanan ran on a platform endorsing Walker's cause in Nicaragua. One paper supporting the candidacy of Republican presidential nominee John C. Frémont announced "Mr. Buchanan's devotion to the interests of Slavery and Fillibusterism." Such criticism did not abate after the election. Though expelled from Nicaragua in May 1857, William Walker mounted several subsequent expeditions to Nicaragua. The president was accused of encouraging these efforts. A British diplomat observed that Buchanan denounced Walker in public commentary, "yet his Government imbued with Southern ideas took no effectual means to prevent Vessel after Vessel crowded with armed men from leaving their Ports." The *New York Times* charged that Buchanan returned confiscated arms to the filibusters, that he refused to adequately empower the navy to apprehend filibusters, and that his efforts to prosecute Walker were a sham.[13]

One need not endorse State Department dogma as to the exemplary federal record on filibustering to dismiss collusion charges against Polk, Taylor, and Fillmore. That several expeditions evaded federal apprehension from 1848 to 1853 had nothing to do with connivance by these presidents. Throughout the antebellum period, federal administrations were hampered by the small size of the United States Navy and the disrepair of its vessels, the small size of the United States Army, obstructive acts by profilibuster mobs in port cities, profilibuster U.S. marshals, customs officials, and district attorneys, profilibuster juries, the clandestine nature of most filibuster operations, and a host of other circumstances that had little to do with presidential intent and decision making.

Polk confronted filibustering on several occasions during his last year in office and consistently opposed private expeditions despite his own expansionist sentiments. At the end of the Mexican War, Polk learned that discharged American volunteer soldiers planned to revolutionize Cuba during a stopover in Havana while on their return to the United States. In response, the administration diverted troop transports away from Cuba, ordered the United States consul at Havana to avoid even the semblance of revolutionary activity, and tipped off Spain to what it had learned about plans under way in the island for an imminent rebellion. Polk's secretary of state, James Buchanan, also sent antifilibustering instructions to United States district attorneys about both the rumored plot to create a Republic of the Sierra Madre in northern Mexico and complaints from the government of Venezuela that planning was in progress for a filibuster against that country. Buchanan called for the prosecution of filibusters and made it clear that he was doing the president's bidding. Furthermore, Polk's organ, the *Washington Union,* warned the American people that the administration would take all legal steps to prevent an expedition into Mexico. In his diary, Polk condemned filibustering as a violation of U.S. law and treaties, and confirmed his presidential responsibility to uphold the Neutrality Act. The president told the noted Democratic expansionist editor, John L. O'Sullivan, who was involved in the Cuba plot and visited the White House expecting support, that he would neither approve nor "wink" at such a scheme.[14]

President Zachary Taylor confronted a serious filibuster challenge soon after assuming office. In the late summer of 1849, Cuban exile Narciso López finalized preparations for an expedition to Cuba. López and his associates recruited hundreds of volunteers and acquired troop transports for an expedition designed to depart from mid-Atlantic coast cities and a point on the Gulf of Mexico. On the last day of July, the initial vanguard of a force which would grow to some five hundred men landed at López's rendezvous at Round Island, off the eastern Mississippi coast.[15]

The Taylor administration took effective preventive action against the scheme. On August 8, Secretary of State John M. Clayton forwarded available information about the expedition to Logan Hunton, U.S. attorney for the Eastern District of Louisiana (at New Orleans). Clayton quoted the Neutrality Act, told Hunton that Taylor was committed to upholding U.S. treaties with foreign nations, and ordered him to investigate filibuster operations within his jurisdiction and to do everything in his power to prevent an expedition. On August 11, Taylor approved a proclamation against filibustering that Clayton had drafted.

Though future Confederate spy Rose O'Neal Greenhow confided to John C. Calhoun from Washington on August 29 that the president had been enlisted in the Cuban invasion plot and that he had issued his proclamation solely for *"appearances,"* Taylor had actually been taking additional steps to stop the filibusters throughout the month. The president issued instructions that Secretary of the Navy William Ballard Preston immediately dispatch any warships necessary to prevent illegal expeditions. Preston ordered Commander of the Home Squadron Foxhall A. Parker to prevent filibuster ships from leaving the Gulf Coast. Should any vessels slip through this net, Parker was to proceed to Cuba and prevent a landing there. Later in August, the Department of War ordered the commander of the army garrison at Mobile to cooperate in the arrest of Cuba filibusters. The administration even hired a secret agent to visit Baltimore, Philadelphia, New York, and Boston to alert U.S. district attorneys, marshals, and customs officials about the plot and to make sure that they understood the provisions of the Neutrality Act. The orders emphasized: "The president demands of them a faithful execution of all laws intended to secure the faith of treaties." In early September, Clayton instructed District Attorney J. Prescott Hall in New York to arrest any expeditionaries against whom he had gathered "reasonable evidence" and to seize any vessel that had been engaged by the filibusters.[16]

This energetic effort repressed the expedition before it could sail. Hall confiscated several filibuster ships in New York harbor, earning praise from the president. The navy clamped an effective blockade on Round Island. Large numbers of adventurers began defecting in early September, accepting U.S. naval conveyance back to the mainland. The final filibuster remnants abandoned Round Island on October 11.[17]

In the spring of 1850, however, López effected the filibuster landing in Cuba that Taylor and Clayton had forestalled the previous year. On May 18, López and some five hundred men landed at the northern Cuban port of Cárdenas and defeated the Spanish garrison there, but fled to Key West after encountering delays and losses of munitions. That the administration failed to prevent this enterprise reflected López's enhanced sensitivity to American law rather than a change of policy or will by Taylor and Clayton. The administration actually took precautions against López as soon as reports surfaced that the filibuster was persisting in his design. Clayton, in January 1850, alerted district attorneys in New Orleans, New York, and Washington, D.C., that bonds had been sold and men raised for a new Cuban venture, and ordered that they "use every effort" to discover the identity of, arrest, and try the filibusters. The administration also detached three vessels from the West Indies Squadron to Cuban waters to forestall a landing on the island. What hampered the government was a lack of knowledge about where the filibusters intended to land as well as the filibusters' pretense that they were emigrants bound for the California gold mines. Some of the filibusters even procured passports from the Department of State for their supposed trip across Central America en route to the Pacific coast. Furthermore, López deferred military organization until his men landed at the island of Contoy off the coast of Yucatán, which he used as the immediate staging point for invading Cuba. This made it difficult for federal officials to prove hostile intent prior to the expedition's departure. Clayton, nonetheless, considered investigating several U.S. port officials for their inability to repress the expedition. The administration also took steps to prevent reinforcements of men and munitions from reaching the filibusters after the expedition was in progress.[18]

Following López's flight to Key West, the administration ordered his arrest and prosecution and instituted legal proceedings against some of his fellow officers as well as against the organizers of the expedition. In a dispatch to Hunton, Secretary of the Interior Thomas Ewing warned the district attorney that the administration was sending a police officer to help track down witnesses and that it would transport witnesses from Key West to fill any "blanks" in the case. Ewing noted that the filibusters had committed "no common crime and more than ordinary care" should be used to prevent its recurrence. Ewing and Clayton constantly invoked Taylor's name in their instructions. That they were not imposing their values on a profilibuster president is apparent from Clayton's obvious delight in informing Taylor on June 9, "I have nabbed López." "Rely on it," the secretary promised, "Hunton will now do his duty." Unfortunately, a profilibuster New Orleans grand jury let López and his accomplices off the hook more than a half year after Taylor's death.[19]

President Millard Fillmore and his secretary of state, Daniel Webster, proved themselves just as determined to enforce the Neutrality Act against Southern filibusters invading Cuba and Mexico as they were to uphold the Fugitive Slave Law of 1850 against Northern abolitionists. Shortly after assuming his duties, Webster served notice on District Attorney Hall in New York that the president expected him to make "immediate and strict inquiry" about rumors of filibuster preparations in his city. The administration tipped off other port officials to reports of filibuster preparations, urged federal officers to seize filibuster vessels and arrest "at least" the organizers of expeditions, promised to cover "all necessary expenses" incurred in antifilibuster efforts, authorized marshals to draw on army manpower to prevent filibuster departures, dispatched naval vessels on antifilibustering patrols, and warned federal officials that they would be held to strict accountability for expeditions effected within their jurisdictions. In April 1851, federal authorities in New York broke up an invasion of Cuba by detaining a vessel engaged for the expedition and arresting filibuster ringleaders. After the final—and fatal—López expedition left New Orleans in August 1851, an angry president fired the port's collector. Soon afterwards, the administration released orders to army generals and navy officers to prevent Texans from crossing the Rio Grande to join the revolutionary cause of José María Jesús Carvajal in northern Mexico. And in several instances, the administration rejected requests from its district attorneys that ongoing prosecutions of filibusters be discontinued because of the evident impossibility of procuring juries sympathetic to the government's position.[20]

During his last year in office, Fillmore recommended to Congress that legislation be drafted to tighten up the neutrality laws. Fillmore endorsed Daniel Webster's suggestion that Congress authorize federal authorities to confiscate vessels, arms, and ammunition assembled for illegal expeditions. He also sent a sharp warning to shipping magnate George Law not to proceed with his announced plan to create an incident in Havana harbor as a pretext for a new filibuster invasion of Cuba.[21]

Presidents Polk, Taylor, and Fillmore, therefore, demonstrated consistent opposition to Southern filibustering. The question, it must be remembered, is not whether the three presidents achieved success in repressing filibustering nor even whether they adopted the most effective means to that end. Rather, we are merely concerned with whether there is evidence that the Slave Power enlisted the chief executives in filibuster plots. Clearly, all three presidents wanted to stop filibustering. Unfortunately, their immediate successor presents a more muddled case.

There can be no doubt that the Southern filibuster community counted Pierce in its camp during his first year in office. The president's inaugural promise that he would be unrestrained by "timid forebodings of evil from expansion," his packing the diplomatic corps with notorious expansionists, and his appointment of Jefferson Davis as secretary of war encouraged filibusters to believe that they finally had a sympathizer in the White House.[22] According to J. F. H. Claiborne, who had close ties to John Quitman, Quitman left Washington, D.C., after a visit there in the summer of 1853, "with the impression . . . not only that he had their sympathies, but that there could be no pretext for the intervention of federal authorities" against his intended expedition to Cuba. Proslavery New York Congressman Mike Walsh told Quitman in May 1854 that he had made inquiries about Pierce's intentions, and had been assured by Senator Stephen A. Douglas and others that there would be "no active interference at all, if matters are only conducted with decent caution." Walsh meant that the filibusters would be permitted to carry out their scheme unimpeded so long as they did not draw so much publicity about their preparations as to make it politically embarrassing for the president to remain passive. Even after Pierce issued his May 31, 1854, proclamation against filibustering, some of the adventurers and their sympathizers assumed that the pronouncement represented merely Pierce's need to give the illusion that he was upholding the law.[23]

The administration's lethargic response to reports about the Kinney expedition strengthened impressions that Pierce condoned filibustering. From May to December 1854, Central American diplomats filed protests about Kinney's plans with the Department of State. Nicaraguan Minister to the United States José de Marcoleta maintained that Kinney's land grant was illegitimate and that his colonization project constituted aggression against Nicaragua. Rather than act upon these complaints, Secretary of State William Marcy defended Kinney's right to emigrate peacefully to Nicaragua and refused to pass judgment on the legitimacy of Kinney's title to the Mosquito Coast grant. The *Washington Union*, Pierce's news organ, affirmed the legitimacy of Kinney's title and defined his followers as colonists "voluntarily expatriating themselves." Marcoleta was so appalled by Marcy's attitude that he turned to former Secretary of State Clayton for help. Marcoleta complained that "filibustering persons of high standing" were involved in a plot to conquer Nicaragua, and expressed shock "that the American Government would act towards us in such a shameful manner." Meanwhile, Quitman's filibusters, encouraged by the same reports that Pierce had links to Kinney, considered using the Kinney project as a cover for their preparations to invade Cuba.[24]

Complaints from federal civil and military officers in the field reinforce the portrait of a filibuster president. Samuel D. Hay, U.S. district attorney for Texas, not only protested when the administration rejected his request to provide higher fees for private attorneys retained by the government to help prosecute officers of the Carvajal expeditions into Mexico, but he also complained of a general indifference in Washington to his antifilibustering exertions. Gen. John Wool, commander of the Department of the Pacific, feuded with Secretary of War Davis after Davis censured his arrests of filibusters in the San Francisco area. Davis contended that Wool had usurped the responsibilities of civil officials. Commanding General of the Army Winfield Scott became incensed when Pierce denied approval of his request in May 1855 to deploy the army against the Kinney expedition. The president professed anxiety that army artillery might be trained accidentally on innocent ships passing out to sea.[25]

Do such enforcement lapses, however, constitute proof that Pierce had been enlisted in a Slave Power conspiracy to spread slavery southward by filibustering? Had Pierce truly been in league with Southern filibusters, he would surely have supported Quitman's scheme against Cuba. Instead, the administration helped cause the expedition's demise. Rather than endorse Louisiana Senator John Slidell's bill to facilitate filibustering by suspending the Neutrality Act, Pierce issued his proclamation against filibustering to Cuba and sent word to Quitman through private channels that he was "determined to prevent any expedition." In June 1854, Pierce asked Slidell to telegraph the filibusters to call off the expedition. The *Washington Union,* moreover, ran a series of editorials denouncing the scheme. In January 1855, federal officials seized one of the expedition's ships, put a second filibuster vessel under close surveillance, and confiscated many of the supplies that had been assembled for the invasion. Finally, in March, Pierce and Marcy persuaded Quitman to disband his forces by convincing him at a White House meeting that a Spanish military buildup in Cuba spelled disaster for any invading force.[26]

The Pierce administration likewise opposed William Walker's invasion of Lower California. In 1853, Secretary of War Davis formally approved Gen. Ethan Allen Hitchcock's seizure in September of Walker's vessel in San Francisco harbor. That December, the administration sent a naval purser to California with instructions to Commodore Bladen Dulany, commanding the Pacific Squadron, not only ordering Dulany to prevent filibustering expeditions but also authorizing him to charter a private steamer if he felt his naval vessels were insufficient to enforce the Neutrality Act. When the administration learned that Walker had managed to launch his expedition in October, it dispatched additional instructions that Pacific Squadron officers "exercise all lawful means" against filibusters and that they take action promptly. In January 1854, when the administration sent Gen. John Wool to replace Hitchcock, it instructed him to use "the utmost" of his ability against filibusters—instructions that led Wool to interfere with Californians intending to join Walker as reinforcements. In March 1854, the Department of the Navy approved steps that Capt. Thomas A. Dornin, commanding the *Portsmouth,* had taken against Walker. In February, Dornin had put in at Ensenada, the capital of Walker's "Republic of Lower California," and offered to return Walker's adventurers to the United States if they would abandon the invasion. His presence had induced Walker to evacuate the town for fear that Dornin would intercept reinforcements arriving at that time. Secretary of the Navy James C. Dobbin authorized Dornin to take further steps to stop Walker short of invading Mexico with naval personnel. In April 1854, Davis approved Wool's transferring arms and ammunition to a U.S. naval vessel for the purpose of preventing a suspect ship from leaving San Francisco. Davis, to be sure, undercut the administration's credibility with his well-publicized attack on Wool for exceeding instructions when he arrested some of Walker's collaborators. But the administration, on balance, did far more to inhibit Walker's movement than to encourage it. There is no hard evidence to substantiate the charge of Alejandro Bolaños-Geyer that Pierce purposely deferred action against Walker until news arrived in Washington of the Gadsden Treaty with Mexico, because he (Pierce) hoped that Mexican fears of Walker would induce that country to make land cessions to the United States. The ultimate failure of Walker's invasion and the filibuster's return to American territory in May 1854 resulted, in part, from the administration's interference.[27]

While the Pierce administration took almost a year determining that the Kinney enterprise represented a filibuster rather than a legitimate colonization endeavor, it did, ultimately, make the latter determination and thereby caused Kinney's force to leave United States territory in a weakened condition. In February 1855, Marcy cautioned Kinney that his project appeared to be illegal and that Kinney would be liable for violating the Neutrality Act if that proved to be the case. In April, Attorney General Caleb Cushing asked John McKeon, U.S. attorney for the Southern District of New York, to take legal action against Kinney and his associate Joseph W. Fabens, U.S. commercial agent at San Juan del Norte, Nicaragua. Fabens was in the States recruiting for the expedition at the time. In May, Pierce alerted Capt. Charles Boarman, commanding the Brooklyn Navy Yard, to Kinney's intentions, and called upon Boarman to use the naval forces under his command to stop Kinney. The administration's instructions led to the arrests of Kinney and Fabens and a naval blockade of Kinney's vessel, then moored at an East River wharf in New York City. Marcy also dismissed Fabens from his post as commercial agent. Unfortunately, U.S. District Judge Charles Anthony Ingersoll required Kinney and Fabens to post only a $1,000 bond each in the case, thereby allowing Kinney the opportunity to trick federal officials and slip out of New York harbor in a small schooner. Kinney managed to reach Nicaragua and establish a regime at San Juan del Norte with himself as "Civil and Military Governor."

The Pierce administration's interference, however, had reduced Kinney's party from an intended several hundred men to an anemic group of nineteen adventurers. Pierce and Marcy, diverging from the position of other administrations during the antebellum period, took the position that it was "questionable" whether the U.S. Navy could legally seize filibusters on the high seas, and refrained from dispatching vessels to prevent Kinney's landing. But there does not seem to be any solid proof confirming the many reports that Pierce favored the expedition. In fact, William Sydney Thayer, secretary of Kinney's government, wrote a letter dated October 8 which makes it quite clear that the filibusters feared that Pierce and Marcy were on the verge of taking "hasty" action against Kinney's settlement. Thayer obviously did not consider the president an ally.[28]

Pierce's recognition of William Walker's regime in May 1856 represented a deviation in policy rather than an example of Pierce's servility to Slave

Power filibusters. Secretary of State Marcy rebuked John H. Wheeler, the American minister to Nicaragua, after Wheeler in October 1855 attempted the role of intermediary between Walker and his Nicaraguan antagonist Gen. Ponciano Corral. Marcy also reversed Wheeler's decision that November to recognize the filibuster regime in Nicaragua following an agreement by Corral and Walker to cooperate in a coalition government, with Walker as commander in chief of the Nicaraguan army.

During the winter of 1855–56, the administration issued directives to district attorneys that they prevent reinforcements for Walker from leaving American soil. Pierce's instructions led District Attorney Tom Clay in New Orleans to order a U.S. marshal to conduct a search of a suspect ship. They also induced McKeon, in New York, to delay the sailing of the steamer *Northern Light.* McKeon forced forty suspected filibusters to disembark from the vessel prior to its departure. McKeon's efforts eventuated in indictments in January 1856 of a number of filibusters and filibuster agents. McKeon warned the Accessory Transit Company that he would seize its vessel *Star of the West* if it tried to take arms to Walker. Further, Attorney General Cushing advised McKeon to warn Walker's appointed minister to the United States that he lacked diplomatic immunity should he raise men and arms in New York for the filibuster's cause, since the Pierce administration had never officially received him.[29]

That most reinforcements for Walker in the winter of 1855–56 eluded federal apprehension primarily reflected Walker's success at conforming to the letter of American law. Walker's filibusters, unlike participants in the López and Kinney schemes, traveled aboard commercial steamships rather than chartered filibuster vessels. It was extremely difficult for federal investigators to prove that such persons intended to join Walker's army because thousands of peaceful Americans traveled annually to Nicaragua for the purpose of crossing the Central American isthmus as a means of transit between the East, West, and Gulf coasts of the United States.

How could federal officials separate recruits for Walker from legitimate travelers unless they discovered evidence that intended ship passengers were organized into military companies and engaged in drill prior to their departure? Generally, Walker's reinforcements eschewed such organization until they were beyond U.S. jurisdiction. Furthermore, Walker's agents provided recruits with tickets for their passage, underscoring their pretense of legitimate travel. It is no coincidence that the filibusters ejected from the *Northern Light* were those passengers without tickets. It was so difficult, in fact, to distinguish filibusters from other passengers on Nicaragua-bound ships that even the filibusters themselves had trouble doing it from time to time! One filibuster captain complained in February 1856 that unscrupulous men had accepted free filibuster tickets to Nicaragua and once at sea "refused to consider themselves under any obligations" to join Walker's army. "Holding tickets . . . precisely similar to those held by men who paid their own way, I have found it impossible to separate them from other passengers," this officer lamented.[30]

Secretary of State Marcy emphasized the difficulty of distinguishing filibusters from genuine passengers when responding to complaints from foreign governments concerning the failure of federal authorities to cut off reinforcements for Walker. For instance, Marcy informed the Guatemalan and Salvadoran minister to the United States that most of Walker's recruits from San Francisco were probably miners returning to the Atlantic coast. In many instances, he suggested, they might not have had an "illegal design" in mind when they initially left California, but decided to join Walker while en route east.[31]

Pierce's recognition of Walker's regime in May 1856 requires interpretation as something other than a mere ploy for Southern support of Pierce's dwindling hopes for renomination. Filibustering did derive its greatest strength from the slave states, especially the Deep South, throughout the 1850s. Walker was immensely popular in the Gulf region in the spring of 1856. However, Pierce's recognition of Walker antedated the filibuster's reestablishment of slavery in Nicaragua by several months. And it should be noted that countless Americans throughout the nation that May perceived Walker as an agent of America's Manifest Destiny rather than as a tool of the Slave Power. Most important, Walker had repulsed a Costa Rican invasion in March and April of 1856, and had secured de facto control of most of Nicaragua prior to Pierce's recognition decision. The United States, throughout its history, has recognized odious foreign governments on the basis that they have established de facto control within their nations' limits. Furthermore, the administration was aware that Great Britain supported Costa Rica's war against Walker. Because the United States was engaged at this time in a bitter dispute with Britain over the Clayton-Bulwer Treaty and the status of British colonies in Central America, as well as over other matters including efforts by British Minister to the United States John F. T. Crampton to recruit Americans for service with British forces engaged in the Crimean War, many Americans, including the Pierce administration, came temporarily to regard Walker as an agent in the American struggle with Britain for hegemony in Central America.[32]

It is less significant that Pierce recognized Walker's government in May 1856 than that this recognition proved to be short-lived. When Pierce established relations with Walker's regime, he was dealing, technically, with Nicaraguans—Walker's provisional president, Patricio Rivas, and Rivas's appointee as minister to the United States, Augustín Vijil. After Walker in June 1856 declared Rivas a traitor and seized the Nicaraguan presidency in July in an apparently rigged election, Pierce reversed course. He never officially received Maine native Appleton Oaksmith, Walker's new minister to the United States. Furthermore, the administration recalled John Wheeler after he recognized Walker on his own initiative.[33]

Had Pierce truly been a Slave Power lackey, he would have stuck with Walker, especially after the filibuster, by decree of September 22, 1856, reestablished slavery in Nicaragua. Wheeler, prior to learning of his recall, in a dispatch to Marcy lauded Walker's decision as "necessary" since anyone residing in Nicaragua would realize that its "rich soil so well adapted to the culture of cotton, sugar, Rice, corn, cacoa [*sic*] indigo & c can never be developed without slave labour." The administration saw things differently.[34]

Of all the pre–Civil War presidents, James Buchanan was the one most unfairly stigmatized as a filibuster ally. Buchanan selected an apparent filibuster enthusiast as secretary of state; his choice, Lewis Cass, sent a telegram wishing William Walker success to a mass meeting in New York City in 1856. Cass, a longstanding apostle of Manifest Destiny, asserted that the filibuster's cause served the interests of the whole world. However, Pennsylvania's "doughface" president proved to be as intent on repressing Southern filibusters as any of his immediate predecessors had. Buchanan never gave his secretary of state an opportunity to make good on his profilibuster pronouncement.[35]

Just one-half year after assuming office, Buchanan confronted the first of William Walker's several attempts to reconquer Nicaragua. In September 1857, the Department of State alerted collectors of customs, marshals, and district attorneys at ports along the Atlantic and Gulf coasts to the pending departure of the filibuster, and urged them to take all lawful steps possible to prevent it. After the administration learned that Walker had selected either New Orleans or Mobile as his intended departure point, it authorized its district attorney in the former city to rent a private steamship at government expense to stop Walker. The administration also lauded federal officials whom it considered to be energetic against Walker, and deployed naval forces in American waters and off Central America with instructions to intercept any sighted filibuster ships.[36]

The administration's vigilance almost prevented Walker from sailing and led ultimately to the failure of the enterprise. Federal authorities in New Orleans put Walker under arrest on November 10. Unfortunately, Federal District Judge Theodore H. McCaleb set Walker's bond at only $2,000, low enough for Walker to risk its forfeiture by launching the expedition. Secretary of the Treasury Howell Cobb sharply rebuked the collector at Mobile for not stopping Walker's exit from that city aboard the steamship *Fashion* on November 19, all but promised that another such dereliction would lead to the collector's dismissal, and noted Buchanan's displeasure with the turn of events. Secretary of State Lewis Cass, likewise, informed District Attorney Franklin H. Clack at New Orleans that the administration was very disturbed by Walker's escape. The administration immediately took a number of steps to prevent reinforcements from reaching Walker.[37]

The administration's precautions caused Walker's downfall after he reached Nicaragua. In early December, Commodore Hiram Paulding surrounded Walker's camp on the Nicaraguan coast and forced his surrender and return to the United States. Buchanan, in a subsequent message to Congress, criticized how Paulding had handled the affair. But Buchanan's censure stemmed from Paulding's landing sailors and marines on the Nicaraguan coast in order to capture Walker rather than from presidential complicity with Southern filibustering. Paulding's intervention violated international law, since he had not previously secured permission from the government of Nicaragua. Buchanan, who had wanted the navy to take Walker at sea, was upset with Paulding's methods, not his purpose. Had Buchanan truly favored Walker's expedition, he would have rectified Paulding's error by having the navy return Walker to the Nicaraguan coast, a course of policy which Walker's proponents at the time were in fact demanding.[38]

Unfortunately, the navy's intercession failed to deter Walker from further operations. Within months, the administration had to confront the possibility of another Nicaraguan enterprise. In April 1858, the United States collector of customs at Mobile, Thaddeus Sanford, warned the administration that former filibusters were involved in the Mobile and

Nicaraguan Steamship Company, a firm incorporated by the Alabama legislature that had purchased Walker's recent vessel, the *Fashion*. The company had announced intentions to engage in trade with Central American and Texan ports. But the collector suspected a filibuster. Realizing that he had no legal authority to deny clearance to a "vessel proposing a legal voyage," Sanford solicited instructions from Washington. No more willing to ignore domestic than international law, the administration left things up to Sanford but warned that only "well grounded suspicions" or unmistakable attempts to violate the law would justify refusal of clearance to engage in the coastal trade.[39]

Buchanan took more pronounced steps against Walker once it became evident that a filibuster was truly in progress. In October 1858, Walker notified Sanford of his intentions to send between two and three hundred "emigrants" to Nicaragua. Walker promised that the travelers would be unarmed and that they intended to settle permanently in Nicaragua and seek Nicaraguan citizenship. According to Walker, each emigrant had paid $20 passage money. The next month, Walker's treasurer, Julius Hesse, formally applied to Sanford for clearance of the chartered barque *Alice Tainter*, carrying provisions, agricultural implements, household items, and three hundred or more passengers, for Greytown, Nicaragua. Sanford not only alerted the Department of the Treasury to these circumstances, but also informed Washington that he had learned from a reliable source that the vessel's passengers held passports furnished by the Nicaraguan minister to the United States. Sanford had seen some of these passports, and reported that they appeared to be authentic.[40]

Buchanan and his cabinet reacted quickly to this information. The administration discovered that only seventeen passports had been issued by the Nicaraguan minister, and informed Sanford that the Nicaraguan government had not authorized any American colonization projects and that any passports he had seen were either forgeries or fraudulently obtained. Cobb called on Sanford for "prudence and firmness" against filibusters, and instructed him to deny clearance to the *Alice Tainter*. Sanford complied with these instructions, forcing Walker's agents to cancel their charter of the vessel and to transfer operations to the schooner *Susan*. When the filibusters applied for clearance of the *Susan* to Key West as a "coasting" vessel, Sanford again refused to accommodate them. Infuriated, the filibusters threatened to slap Sanford with lawsuits. Cobb approved

Sanford's denying clearance to the *Susan* and promised that the administration would "sustain" Sanford if the filibusters took him to court.[41]

The administration also took legal and military action. Attorney General Jeremiah S. Black, invoking the president's desire to stop the filibusters, alerted district attorneys and marshals in Mobile and New Orleans to
the pending expedition. The administration pursued the two-pronged
strategy of authorizing Supreme Court Justice John A. Campbell (about
to preside over a circuit court session in Mobile) to offer the filibusters a
pardon if they would cease operations or to prosecute the filibusters if the
pardon were declined. To the latter end, the administration retained Robert H. Smith of Mobile to assist the district attorney in that port. It also
hired a special agent to go to Mobile under instructions to infiltrate filibuster circles there, make out affidavits so that warrants could be issued for
the arrest of incriminated persons, and help special counsel Smith's efforts
to get such persons committed to prison until their trials. Meanwhile,
Secretary of the Navy Isaac Toucey sent a copy of the president's October
30 antifilibustering proclamation to the commander of the Home Squadron, informed him that the Nicaraguan government required passports of
any persons claiming to be immigrants to that country, and instructed the
officer to "be vigilant" and to "intercept at *sea*" any filibusters.[42]

Given the administration's thoroughness, it would be absurd to blame
Washington for the expedition that left Mobile that December carrying
108 of Walker's followers (Walker intended to follow later). Judge Campbell
charged a grand jury to investigate violations of the Neutrality Act, even
though he felt that he lacked legal grounds for his charge since the congressional act of 1840 under which he was operating seemed to confine his
court's jurisdiction in that term to cases already pending before it. When
the grand jury adjourned without rendering true bills against the plotters,
the filibusters had the opportunity to press their luck one more time. They
boarded the *Susan* on the night of December 5, intending to sail without
the required clearance. Captain J. J. Morrison, commanding the U.S. rev-
enue cutter *Robert McClelland,* intercepted the vessel the next day, boarded
it, and demanded that the filibusters return to Dog River Bay, pending
further instructions from federal officials in Mobile. The filibusters refused to do so, denied that they had done anything illegal, threatened
Morrison with their bowie knives and revolvers, and anchored temporarily in the bay. A standoff ensued. Morrison left Lieutenant George F.

White aboard the ship and returned to his own vessel, which he then anchored abreast of the *Susan*. Amidst thick fog early the next morning, with White still aboard, the *Susan* slipped away. She made good her escape when the *McClelland* grounded in pursuit. Appalled by this turn of events, the administration planned to fire its marshal in Mobile. After the *Susan* grounded on a coral reef in the Bay of Honduras and a British ship returned the filibusters to Mobile, the administration exhorted its officials to prosecute the expedition's leaders.[43]

Buchanan's antifilibustering vigilance persisted to the end of his term. In an 1859 directive, Acting Attorney General Alfred B. McCalmont noted Buchanan's "deep solicitude" that such movements end, and again informed U.S. officials that the president wanted filibusters brought to justice. Throughout that year, cabinet officials issued a stream of instructions to prevent rumored filibusters not only to Nicaragua but also to Mexico. Federal authorities broke up Walker's annual adventure that year before it even left American soil. The president should not be held responsible for Walker's final expedition in 1860, because it was launched from the island of Ruatán in the Bay of Honduras rather than from U.S. territory. Walker's men traveled to Ruatán in small parties rather than as an identifiable military body. Buchanan certainly shed no tears over Walker's execution that September by a Honduran firing squad. Rather, in his final annual message to Congress, he expressed satisfaction that the filibuster era had apparently drawn to its close during his presidency.[44]

Little evidence exists, therefore, to substantiate antislavery charges that American presidents were locked in step with the Slave Power to conquer Latin countries by filibuster plots. The federal government sometimes took diplomatic action on behalf of filibusters taken prisoner by foreign powers. But such interventions were prompted by humanitarian and legal considerations, such as indications that some of the adventurers had been lured into expeditions under false pretenses, and were never intended as an endorsement of filibustering.

Franklin Pierce may have hinted during his first year in office that he would support filibuster projects. Historians will probably never know Pierce's private feelings regarding filibustering or whether he would have supported filibustering had not the passage of the Kansas-Nebraska Act put his administration on the political defensive in the North. Certainly Pierce could have exerted much more effort to dispel popular perceptions that he was under filibuster control. But, in the end, even Pierce did the movement much more harm than good. It is a mistake to project the undeniably expansionist ideologies of such presidents as Pierce and Buchanan, which did indeed include a willingness to tolerate slavery's extension, onto their responses to filibustering. In several instances, in fact, U.S. presidents and their cabinets opposed filibustering for the very reason that it seemed to jeopardize what they considered more promising means of territorial growth. This was especially the case regarding Cuba. Both the Polk and Pierce administrations suffered under the delusion that antifilibustering policies would pay off in the sale of Cuba by a thankful Spain.[45]

Certainly the filibusters themselves looked upon the nation's chief executives as antagonists; if the presidents were filibuster accomplices, few of the adventurers ever noticed their assistance. Rather, throughout the post–Mexican War years, except during the brief filibuster honeymoon with Pierce, the filibusters and their sympathizers regularly lambasted American presidents for interfering with their operations and destroying their dreams. "What does Police master-general Fil[l]more . . . mean by keeping a watch over our 'f[r]ee and enlightened citizens' and stopping them from making up little pleasure parties to go to w[h]ere they please by land or water?" exclaimed one Southerner anxious to filibuster. "The administration is bound to yield to the voice of the country in regard to our affairs," predicted William Walker in 1858 after James Buchanan's navy stopped his invasion of Nicaragua. The filibusters railed the loudest against Franklin Pierce, virtually charging that they had been double-crossed by the president. Walker observed that Secretary of State Marcy "set his face against the introduction of Americans into Nicaragua" from the inception of "the movement," and that Marcy's policies had triggered much of the Central American resistance to his government. John S. Thrasher, one of the key coordinators of Quitman's aborted movement, announced that he despised "Marcy and his crew." Pierce's "despicable administration" had dared oppose noble heroes trying to save Cuba from "social death."[46]

Ironically, in the light of abolitionist charges identifying filibustering as a component of the Slave Power conspiracy, the adventurers and their sympathizers concluded precisely the opposite: that presidential hostility derived from apathy about and sometimes even antislavery hostility to the South's desperately felt sectional needs. John Quitman assumed that Pierce turned against his Cuba expedition because he was afraid to offend an antislavery majority in Congress. Quitman and his accomplices sensed insensitivity in the executive department to Southern exigencies: neither Pierce nor his cabinet seemed to comprehend that a filibuster strike against Cuba offered the only way to ward off Spanish abolitionist intentions and to annex the island with its slave labor system intact. Using related logic, Alexander H. Stephens concluded that Buchanan and his cabinet opposed Walker "because if successful he would introduce American slavery" in Central America. Georgia congressman Augustus R. Wright attributed Buchanan's antifilibustering policies to pressure from "northern abolition" commercial interests intent on making money off isthmian transit across Central America once Walker was out of the picture.[47]

In the end, analysis of presidential policies toward filibustering reminds us how difficult it was, by the late antebellum era, for Americans, whatever their section, to truly understand what was going on across the Mason-Dixon line. Despite widespread perceptions to the contrary, America's chief executives maintained their distance from both the Slave Power and Northern abolitionists as they determined policies to repress their nation's filibusters.

Chapter Two

☙

"Freedom and Liberty First, and the Union Afterwards": State Rights and the Wisconsin Republican Party, 1854–1861

MICHAEL J. MCMANUS

SPEAKING to the Wisconsin legislature in 1856, Coles Bashford, the state's first Republican governor, gloomily noted that "slavery is the direct cause of the present exasperated state of feeling between the different portions of the Union.... It is the only brand of dissension which threatens permanently the peace of the country and endangers the perpetuity of our republican institutions."[1]

In the years since Bashford's statement, American historians have debated endlessly the role slavery played in exacerbating sectional discord and bringing on the Civil War. Out of these discussions, several schools of thought have emerged. Simply stated, one group of scholars agrees that slavery comprised the substance of the controversy. Without it, they insist, a resort to arms would have been unthinkable. Other writers disagree and minimize both slavery's significance and the Northern commitment to antislavery principles. Instead, they focus on either the profoundly different cultures or the economic systems that evolved in the North and the South during the first half of the nineteenth century. Historians who stress regional, social, and cultural dissimilarities argue that the incompatible nature of these civilizations, far more than quarrels over black servitude, triggered the bitter antebellum conflicts that ultimately led to war, while those offering an economic interpretation fix on the supposed battles that inevitably arise when competing interests struggle for political supremacy.[2]

In his *The Impending Crisis, 1848–1861,* the late David M. Potter attempted to reconcile these points of view while still insisting on slavery's centrality to the sectional controversy. In the half-century after the American Revolution, he wrote, slavery became the predominant force shaping the economic, cultural, and intellectual life of the Southern states, which consistently and stubbornly fought off all attempts to interfere with or to confine their "peculiar institution." In the North, meanwhile, slavery was increasingly viewed as fundamentally hostile to the republican ideals of individual liberty and political equality bequeathed by the nation's founders. Rather than a positive good, as the South maintained, slavery was an immoral institution that inhibited economic development, spawned authoritarian methods of social control, and reinforced the political power of an aristocratic planter elite. Moreover, it was believed, with the aid of obsequious Northern Whigs and Democrats, this Slave Power dominated political affairs in Washington and conspired to fasten slavery permanently on American soil. As such, growing numbers of Northerners, although bound to honor the constitutional promise to avoid meddling directly with slavery in the Southern states, yet uneasy about their own freedom, chose to agitate against it where it did not exist, in the national territories and in their home states. In time, they hoped, hemming slavery in would eradicate it. In this atmosphere of heightened tension and mistrust, according to Potter, slavery came to permeate every aspect of the sectional dispute.[3]

Potter describes the sectional split precipitated by slavery as a conflict of values, and it is this conflict, he cogently argues, that comprised the core of the controversy. It defined and exaggerated the cultural and economic divisions between the North and the South, minimized the values they shared, and deepened their isolation and estrangement from each other. From this perspective, the issue challenging Northerners was not whether they opposed slavery, since most certainly did, but how they measured their antislavery beliefs against other cherished values.[4]

Devotion to the Union, as formed by the Constitution, ranked high among these values, and in the years between the Revolution and the Civil War, two competing definitions of the Union vied for supremacy. One version maintained that liberty and Union were indivisible. Therefore, any attempts to separate must be blocked—if necessary, by force. The North eventually would embrace this notion of an absolute Union and crush the South's attempt to establish an independent nation. But prior to the war, many Northerners held the alternative view, that the Union was not an end in itself and had been established as part of the constitutional compact to help secure national freedom and safety.[5] To further these goals, the federal government had been granted certain specified powers, but all others were retained by the states, including the right to determine the conditions and extent of civil liberties within their jurisdictions and to check the unauthorized use of federal power. This interpretation recognized that states played a far greater role in the lives of their citizens than the federal government did in antebellum America, and that state-centered loyalty and identity prevailed among the people of both the North and the South. It also comprised a part of the detailed reasoning developed in favor of state rights and nullification, and would be used by proslavery Southern theorists to defend noninterference with slavery and to justify secession in 1861. But state rights cut both ways, and the idea that a state might nullify federal legislation it deemed unconstitutional or interpose its authority between the national government and the people had long found wide acceptance in the North as well. In the context of the antislavery controversy, state rights most often was employed in defense of individual freedom. Even secession, although an extreme step and approached with considerable caution, was considered by some to be a legitimate state prerogative.[6]

Northern abolitionists, who combined a profound distrust of government with a genuine anti-authoritarianism, were especially attracted to state rights principles. They held that government had no more right to limit the freedom of its citizens than slaveowners had to sovereignty over fellow human beings, and so ought to be limited, decentralized, and local. William Lloyd Garrison, the Boston abolitionist, stretched this principle when he condemned the Constitution and called for a breakup of the Union because both protected slavery and imperiled liberty.[7] Other abolitionists upheld the principles of limited government, including state rights and interposition, but they insisted that the Constitution was fundamentally a charter of freedom, not slavery, and stopped short of endorsing Garrison's call for disunion. Instead, they preferred to work within the political system, initially through the agency of the Liberty party, to deprive slavery of federal sustenance and to prevent it from expanding beyond its existing borders. This policy, Liberty men believed, would safeguard the Union and eventually force the South to abandon slavery.

Nevertheless, their Unionism came with qualifications. They would not sacrifice the principles of individual liberty and political equality, which were incompatible with and endangered by slavery, to preserve sectional peace; nor would they abandon antislavery agitation in their own states or drop their opposition to slavery's spread at the federal level to appease the Slave Power. As one Liberty party member put it,

> Instead of the Union first—the Union last—the Union forever, we should cry, Freedom first—Freedom last and Freedom forever! Freedom is the soul, the Union is the form, and we had better seek to preserve the soul pure, then we may rest with confidence that the form will correspond.[8]

Nevertheless, Northern Unionism as much as anything else acted to curb broad-based antislavery agitation until, in 1846, the question of permitting or prohibiting slavery's extension into the western territories recently acquired from Mexico unleashed an outpouring of moral indignation against the institution. The result was fifteen years of unrestrained sectionalism that persuaded Northerners to reevaluate the relative importance of slavery and the Union in their hierarchy of values.[9] As the events of the 1840s and 1850s lent credibility to the notion that slavery and the Slave Power jeopardized the very fabric of the nation's free institutions, the appeal to "Freedom and Liberty First, and the Union Afterwards" won many converts. Northern Whigs, who historically had been more receptive to measures against slavery than their Democratic opponents, saw their party wrecked and their loyalty to the Union weakened largely owing to the deepening sectional controversy. Most eventually found their way into the Republican party, despite Southern threats to secede, rather than see its antislavery platform set in motion. Conversely, a far smaller proportion of Northern Democrats joined the Republicans because their feelings against black bondage never displaced their fervent Unionism.[10]

As antislavery politics coalesced around the emerging Republican coalition in the mid-1850s, disaffection from the Union led many antislavery activists in the party to rely on state rights to counter the proslavery bias of the national government and to defend civil liberties. Personal liberty laws passed by nine Northern states in the prewar years represent the most prominent examples of this tendency. Designed to secure the fundamental rights of persons within their jurisdictions and to frustrate the effective enforcement of the Fugitive Slave Law of 1850, these laws were frequently cited by Southerners as a main cause of secession.[11]

Without question, Wisconsin's Republicans adopted the most unyielding stand on state rights in the 1850s, both as a means of defending civil liberties at home and a means of acting indirectly on their antislavery ideals. Ironically, they found themselves the object of bitter attacks by Southern leaders who, as spokesmen for the same creed, later became ardent proponents of secession. Moreover, as they firmly planted themselves upon state rights ground, and frequently demanded fidelity to the principle as a test of party loyalty and as a requirement for political advancement, their Democratic opponents, the traditional champions of state rights, wholeheartedly defended federal authority. This essay examines the nature of the state rights movement within the Wisconsin Republican party from its founding until the outbreak of the war, and includes the intraparty conflicts it produced and an analysis of the support it obtained from the party faithful. Wisconsin's experience, perhaps in an extreme form, sheds some light on Republican alienation from federal authority and the Union, brought on by the sectional controversy, which likely was shared in some measure by party members throughout the North, and suggests a topic in need of further study.

Wisconsin entered the Union as the nation's thirtieth state in 1848 after ten years of accelerating population growth. Restless Yankees from upstate New York and New England poured into southeastern Wisconsin during this period, laying claim to its extensive lakefront property and fertile prairie land. Huge numbers of foreign-born immigrants (most of them from Germany, but including many displaced Irish families and respectable numbers of English, Scotch, Welsh and Scandinavians) took up residence alongside the suspicious Yankees. By the end of the 1840s, native New Yorkers comprised nearly 53 percent of Wisconsin's adult population, the foreign born 36 percent.[12]

Among Wisconsin's Yankee population were natives of western New York's "Burned Over District." During the first four decades of the nineteenth century, this region had been swept by successive waves of religious enthusiasm that instilled in its people a passionate desire to build a society dedicated to advancing the physical, moral, and social well-being of all. Slavery presented a major barrier to the realization of this goal, because it stripped bondsmen of their humanity, desensitized slaveowners to human suffering, and prevented both from achieving their full potential.[13] Many of the territory's Yankee immigrants undoubtedly received their schooling in antislavery activism while residents of the "Burned Over District." Not surprisingly, it first found expression in their lakeshore and southeastern communities.[14]

Wisconsin's antislavery movement developed in much the same way it did in other areas of the North. At first, antislavery men adopted the tactic of moral suasion to win converts and influence local and national policy, but this strategy brought limited success and led to the formation of the Liberty party. Although its political achievements were modest, the Liberty party played a decisive role in broadcasting a specific legal and constitutional program for bringing about slavery's destruction.[15] In 1848, Liberty men merged with other Northerners seeking to keep slavery out of the western territories. The resulting Free-Soil coalition won more than 10 percent of the votes cast in the presidential contest that year. In Wisconsin, Free-Soilers gained 26 percent of the ballots, a percentage exceeded only in Massachusetts and Vermont, and succeeded in electing the ex-Liberty man, Charles Durkee, to Congress.[16]

Free-Soilers attempted to follow up their impressive showing at the polls by joining forces with one or the other of the major parties in the different Northern states. Most often, their efforts brought disappointment. Passage of the Compromise of 1850, hailed by many as the final solution to the slavery question, further damaged the party. Wisconsin's Free-Soilers suffered similar frustrations, but a hard core of party loyalists continued to agitate throughout those difficult years. Spurned by the well-organized Democrats, they worked instead with friendly Whigs, whose perennially weak state organization was slowly collapsing under the weight of sectional politics, the growing irrelevance of the issues that once had divided the two major parties, and the rise of ethnocultural concerns.[17]

The introduction and passage of the Kansas-Nebraska Act in early 1854 shattered the fragile sectional truce fashioned by the Compromise of 1850. The act repealed the "solemnly covenanted" Missouri Compromise of 1820, which had banned slavery north of the Mason-Dixon line, and permitted settlers in the newly organized territories of Kansas and Nebraska to decide on its status themselves. As a result, many concerned Northerners grimly concluded that slavery would likely take root in the West and eventually spread into the free states. Resistance to the measure, along with state and local issues, helped set in motion the political forces that ultimately would come together to form the Republican party.[18]

The union of state rights principles with antislavery politics in Wisconsin originated with the arrest of Joshua Glover near Racine on the evening of March 10, 1854. A Missouri runaway, Glover had escaped from his owner, Bennami Garland, two years earlier. Finding work as a millhand, Glover, by all accounts, was "a faithful laborer and an honest man." On the night of his capture, he had been drinking and playing cards with two black acquaintances, one of whom had betrayed his whereabouts to Garland. After a short but violent struggle, he was bound, thrown into a wagon, and carted off to the Milwaukee county jail.[19]

Glover had been seized on a writ obtained under the Fugitive Slave Act of 1850. Its provisions denied alleged runaways the right to a trial by jury, to sue for writs of habeas corpus, and to bring witnesses to testify on their behalf. Moreover, federal judges were authorized to appoint commissioners to try cases under the law, and they in turn were empowered to command the citizens of any state to assist in its execution.[20] Much of the North broadly condemned the Fugitive Slave Act. Not only could whites be enrolled as slave hunters against their will and prosecuted for obstructing its enforcement, but free blacks were stripped of all protection against false claims and unjust enslavement. In Wisconsin, whose black citizens possessed greater legal rights than they did in most Northern states, cries for repeal came from men of all political persuasions. Milwaukee's blacks also publicly displayed their anger and vowed to come to the aid of any fugitive. As evidence of their intent, one Free-Soiler noted approvingly, the city's "colored people are armed to the teeth, and go armed about their daily work. . . . The first kidnapper who lays hands on one of them, we expect will be shot dead."[21]

In addition to robbing citizens of basic civil liberties, the law was considered by many Wisconsinites as an unconstitutional encroachment upon the reserved rights of the states. They contended that the Constitution committed the free states to act in good faith in the recovery of fugitives, and empowered them, not the federal government, to set the terms of compliance.[22] Free-Soilers and Whigs had endorsed this interpretation of the fugitive slave clause as early as 1851, unlike Democrats, who consistently upheld federal authority in the matter of black escapees.[23]

On the morning after Glover's arrest, citizens of Racine held a mass meeting on the public square. They passed resolutions demanding a fair trial for Glover, and promised to use force if necessary to free him. In the meantime, word of the capture reached Milwaukee's Sherman M. Booth, a longtime abolitionist agitator and Free-Soil party leader and editor. Acting quickly, he rode through the city's streets screaming that slave catchers were in town and that an indignation meeting would be held that afternoon at the Milwaukee County Court House. Booth then persuaded a county judge to issue a writ of habeas corpus on the fugitive's behalf, but the sheriff refused to serve it, on the grounds that Glover was held in federal custody and not subject to local authority.[24]

Later that day, more than five thousand people jammed the court house grounds to protest Glover's arrest. As the day wore on, the mob grew restive. About 5 P.M., Glover's self-appointed attorney spoke to the crowd and suggested that perhaps it was time to take the law into their own hands. Booth advised against a forcible release, but after local officials refused a demand to deliver Glover, the crowd rushed the jail, smashed in the door, and carried the jubilant escapee to freedom. One reporter was moved to write of the affair, "We regret to . . . inform the friends of Glover that it was deemed unsafe for him to remain in this Republican country, and that by this time he is safe in Canada, under the protection of a monarchy."[25]

For his alleged role in the rescue, a United States commissioner had Booth arrested on March 15. Two days later, at a preliminary hearing, he was released on bond for later trial, but not before he regretfully denied taking a direct hand in liberating Glover. Booth immodestly claimed that the need for his voice against the Kansas-Nebraska bill, then being debated in Congress, had restrained him. Amidst wild cheering, he went on to say that rather than see any fugitive in Wisconsin returned to slavery, he would prefer that every federal official in the state be hanged.[26]

Coming amidst the tumultuous congressional contest over the Kansas-Nebraska bill, the Glover affair brought the slavery controversy closer to home and intensified the growing distrust of federal authority. At a crowded "'Anti-Slave Catchers' Mass Meeting," convened in Milwaukee on April 13, the attendees revived the argument that the Fugitive Slave Act was an unjust seizure of power by the national government and a threat both to individual liberty and to state sovereignty. They also endorsed the famed Virginia and Kentucky Resolutions of 1798, composed by James Madison and Thomas Jefferson, which had provided a thoughtful defense of state prerogatives, as well as of civil liberties believed to be under attack by the administration of President John Adams. These declared that whenever the federal government transcended its constitutional mandate, "its acts are unauthoritative, void and of no force."²⁷

On May 26, Booth, still free on bail, disclosed his intention to challenge the Fugitive Slave Law when he turned himself in to federal authorities and was returned to jail. His attorney, the twenty-six-year-old Byron Paine, then applied to state supreme court judge Abram D. Smith for a writ of habeas corpus. The timing of Booth's move was purely tactical, since on two earlier occasions the opportunity to apply for a writ and to receive the judgment of the full court had been available. He seems to have waited until intersession, hoping that Smith, a Democrat and well-known opponent of the act, might be persuaded to pronounce against it. On May 29, Booth's counselor made his case to the judge.²⁸

In a lengthy argument, Paine asked the court to overturn the Fugitive Slave Act because the Constitution did not grant Congress the power to legislate on the matter. Furthermore, the law condemned alleged fugitives to slavery without a jury trial, and it vested judicial power in court-appointed commissioners unrecognized by the Constitution. Paine also presented an exhaustive refutation of the 1842 United States Supreme Court decision in the case of *Prigg v. Pennsylvania,* which strongly affirmed federal jurisdiction in the execution of the Constitution's fugitive slave clause and, in his view, improperly transferred control over these cases from the states to the national government. He further insisted that state courts could intercede on behalf of citizens imprisoned under national authority, and denied that the federal government was the final judge of the limits of its own powers. To concede these points would inevitably lead either to unspeakable tyranny or to the "terrible ordeal of revolution."²⁹ One week later, to the delight of most of Wisconsin's antislavery men, Smith sustained Paine's reasoning, discharged Booth, and declared the law unconstitutional and void.³⁰

Stunned federal officers then applied to Smith for a writ of certiorari, hoping that the full court would reverse his ruling. Instead, on July 19, it affirmed his decision. Two days later, acting under an order of a United States district court judge, federal officials rearrested Booth.³¹ Paine again applied to the state supreme court for a writ of habeas corpus. This time the justices denied his request, asserting that there was a major difference between a warrant issued by a federal court and one by a commissioner exercising extrajudicial authority. They acknowledged that the federal judiciary had assumed jurisdiction in the case and that they would await the outcome.[32]

In January 1855, after a controversial trial, a federal grand jury found Booth guilty of abetting Glover's rescue and violating the Fugitive Slave Act.[33] The state supreme court now granted the editor's application for a writ of habeas corpus. On February 3, the state judges reaffirmed their earlier judgment and overturned the federal court decision.[34] All three justices agreed that Wisconsin possessed the right to inquire into the reasons for the imprisonment of its citizens and to release them if they were found to be held illegally. Otherwise, they argued, the state would be powerless to safeguard their individual liberty and have no claim upon their loyalty. This ruling was consistent with current legal thinking, since the issue of federal judicial supremacy as it related to the powers of the states on questions of habeas corpus jurisdiction remained unsettled and controversial.[35] In the case of Booth, the judges claimed that his discharge was required because the warrant made out for his arrest contained deficiencies, in that Garland had not laid title to Glover in precise accordance with the act's provisions. As Smith noted, the act operated in restraint of freedom; therefore its application required "strict technical exactness," including the issuing of warrants. Consensus did not extend beyond this one issue, though; on other questions, the justices expressed widely divergent opinions.[36]

Associate Justice Samuel Crawford declared himself satisfied that the Constitution empowered Congress to legislate upon the matter of fugitive slaves. He based his conviction on the Supreme Court's ruling in *Prigg* and on the belief that the High Court possessed ultimate authority over all constitutional issues. As such, the Wisconsin bench had "to yield obedience . . . for upon such questions we are subordinate."[37]

Chief Justice Edward Whiton also bowed to the Supreme Court's superiority and acknowledged the right of Congress to enact fugitive slave legislation. But, he maintained, in the *Prigg* case the Court neither entrusted specific legal powers to commissioners appointed by federal officials to hear fugitive slave cases, nor did it directly refuse jury trials to alleged escapees. Lacking federal guidance, it fell to the state supreme court to judge the constitutionality of these two provisions of the 1850 statute.

Moved by this logic, Whiton concluded that Congress had exceeded its mandate and proclaimed the Fugitive Slave Act void.[38]

Smith delivered a far more sweeping opinion than that of either of his colleagues. Influenced by the state rights philosophy expounded in the Virginia and Kentucky Resolutions and, although never directly cited, by the writings of the South Carolinian John C. Calhoun, he found that the Fugitive Slave Act violated the Constitution and that Congress lacked authority to legislate on the subject.[39] The American people, Smith argued, operating through their states, had forged the constitutional compact, which clearly specified all powers delegated to the federal government and reserved to the states all powers not expressly bestowed. This system of divided sovereignty permitted both federal and state authorities, as co-departments in a unified system of government, to fully exercise their rights and to act as checks upon each other. And, according to Smith, a careful reading of the fugitive slave clause, one of the comity provisions of Article IV of the Constitution, disclosed nothing that either inferred or implied a grant of power to the federal government in this matter. Besides, he asked: did anyone really believe that the nation's founders would have adopted this provision without opposition or debate if, in its enforcement, they thought the national government would be allowed to appoint officials in every county in every state invested with judicial prerogatives, and answerable neither to state courts nor to local police regulations? Smith also queried whether federal lawmakers would be permitted to suspend the writ of habeas corpus and the right to a jury trial, and to send "the whole military and naval force of this Union" uninvited into any state in pursuit of a runaway Negro. "The idea is preposterous," he insisted. "The Union would never have been formed on such a basis. It is an impeachment of historic truth to assert it."[40]

In regard to the *Prigg* case, Smith bluntly declared that the Supreme Court had overstepped its constitutional grant and should reexamine its 1842 decree. He also criticized the Court for urging the need for a federal statute to force the Northern states into compliance with the fugitive slave clause, assuming that they would otherwise neglect their obligation, solely for the convenience of slave owners and the safety of their economic interests.[41]

Although Smith went on to encourage state officers to cheerfully acquiesce in every privilege constitutionally exercised by federal officials, he likewise exhorted them to resist every assumption of power "not expressly granted or necessarily implied in the federal constitution." Like Paine, Smith flatly rejected the notion that any branch of the national government, including the judiciary, could define the extent of its powers. Each could operate only within confines precisely spelled out in the Constitution. As such, state judges, bound to resist federal intrusions upon the reserved rights of the states and to guard the liberty of their citizens, could invalidate both congressional laws and judicial determinations that violated the constitutional compact.[42]

In order to calm the fears of those who imagined that his states' rights philosophy would lead to "dissension, disruption and civil warfare," Smith emphasized that the collisions inherent in a system of divided sovereignty signified strength and vitality, not weakness. They encouraged investigations into the correct and legitimate boundaries of federal and state sovereignty, and served to restrain both, "quietly and almost imperceptibly . . . within their true and proper limits." Indeed, submission to unconstitutional enactments posed a far greater danger to national peace and unity, Smith warned, than resistance to the unlawful manipulation of power. If left unchecked, the abuse of power soon would become "so deeply and firmly rooted that the only remedy is revolution."[43]

The decision of Wisconsin's supreme court to release Booth from custody after he had been tried, convicted, and sentenced before a federal tribunal for violating a federal law was unprecedented. It represented a bold act of defiance to the national government and to the still-controversial doctrine that the United States Supreme Court was the final arbiter of constitutional questions. Moreover, Smith's opinion embraced a form of state rights and nullification that few Southern zealots had ever contemplated. As one antislavery editor chuckled, "we shall be curious to see how this new application of an old doctrine will be relished by the ultra states' rights men of the South." The new application he referred to was "judicial *nullification*," which was distinctly different from Calhoun's position that only a state convention, as the original contracting party to the Constitution, could resort to nullification when the general government exceeded its powers.[44]

Wisconsin's invocation of state rights also differed from the South's in another important way. South Carolina had originally embraced state rights principles to safeguard its economic interests. Thereafter, the South took up state rights to block national interference with slavery within the slaveholding states, and state sovereignty, with decrees such as the Fugitive Slave Act, began to demand federal protection for the rights of slave owners outside the state jurisdictions in which they had been granted.[45] To counteract Southern aggressiveness, Wisconsin, along with other Northern states, employed state rights to defend individual liberty from legislation regarded as unconstitutional. Most often, resistance took the form of personal liberty laws designed to thwart enforcement of the act. To many antislavery men, this form of state interposition represented a middle ground between revolution and absolute submission to a proslavery federal law that overturned fundamental civil rights.[46] Consequently, Wisconsin's use of state rights to secure personal liberty more truly represented the philosophy embodied in the Virginia and Kentucky Resolutions than did the South's, which, in increasingly provocative ways, shaped the doctrine to justify perpetuating and expanding slavery.[47]

Paine's brief and Smith's opinion won praise in antislavery circles throughout the North. Both were reprinted in pamphlet form and enjoyed brisk sales, particularly in the East. Paine received congratulatory letters from antislavery advocates such as Charles Sumner and Wendell Phillips, while Smith was invited by "numerous and prominent citizens of New York" to attend a banquet in his honor. One of them, Horace Greeley, editor of the influential *New York Tribune*, headed his account of the court's decision with the words, "Glorious Wisconsin."[48] Similarly, most members of Wisconsin's newly formed Republican party championed Smith's pronouncement as evidence of their resolve to take on the Slave Power, both at home and in Washington, whereas the state's Democrats condemned it with equal fervor.[49] Still, a determined Republican minority rejected Smith's case for the supremacy of the state judiciary, and in the years before the onset of war, this principle split the party leadership and became the litmus test for political preferment.

The Republican coalition that had been formed in the wake of the Kansas-Nebraska Act and the Glover rescue won two of Wisconsin's three seats in the House of Representatives in November 1854. Two months later, its unity was tested for the first time in the balloting for United States senator. The choice fell to a joint vote of both houses of the state legislature, where the Republicans, in league with a few holdover Whig senators and a handful of anti-Nebraska Democrats, commanded a razor-thin majority. Senate Democrats, with nothing to lose, at first refused to consent to a joint session, chancing that delay might help their favorite if the opposition failed to unite behind a candidate.[50] The strategy nearly worked as erstwhile Free-Soilers and Whigs stood fast behind their own nominees. Just when it appeared that the coalition would fly apart, with a number of Free-Soilers threatening to side with the Democratic aspirant, the Whigs gave in and former Liberty man and Free Soil congressmen Charles Durkee received the caucus nod. On February 1, the joint session finally convened, and Durkee, after a tough fight, secured the necessary majority.[51]

Two days after Durkee's election, Wisconsin's high court overturned the decision of the federal district court in the Booth case. With Justice Crawford up for reelection in April, former Whigs saw an opportunity to assert themselves after the rebuff they had received in the senatorial contest. They likened the election to a referendum on the state court's decision and inferred that the Democrat Crawford's return would be construed as an endorsement of the Fugitive Slave Act. Thus, although Crawford was a competent judge, Republicans had to field a candidate against him. Other party chieftains agreed and also promised to name a Whig.[52]

With the judicial election scheduled for April 3, there was no time to convene a nominating convention, so the Republican caucus in the state legislature assumed responsibility for choosing a candidate. Ex-Whigs Timothy Howe and Orsamus Cole competed for the appointment. A former state legislator and circuit court judge, the highly regarded Howe was suspected of upholding the final authority of the national Supreme Court on constitutional questions, and therefore was unacceptable to Booth and the state rights faction, while Cole's appeal straddled both partisan and ideological lines. As a one-term congressman representing Wisconsin's conservative southwestern district, the lifelong Whig had voted against the Fugitive Slave Act. Furthermore, he had forthrightly backed Smith's state rights position from the beginning, and just days before had been the losing choice of Whig Republicans to represent Wisconsin in the United States Senate. In closed-door meetings, Republican lawmakers debated the merits of both men, finally settling on Cole and rejecting Howe because of his supposed "federal views."[53]

Campaigning on behalf of "State Rights, State Sovereignty, and the personal liberty of all our citizens," the popular Cole received enthusiastic support from most Republicans. Democrats rallied behind Crawford and criticized their adversaries for opposing him because of "his opinions upon *one political question*," and for introducing partisan issues into a judicial election. But their efforts were unavailing; Cole won a surprisingly easy victory, picking up 55 percent of the vote. Not unexpectedly, Crawford picked up most of his support from voters who had supported Democratic congressional candidates in the previous year's balloting, but the unusual cohesion of the still-new Republican coalition provides striking testimony of the extent of popular party support for the state rights position. With good reason, Republicans cheered Cole's election and declared the Fugitive Slave Act dead in Wisconsin.[54]

For the remainder of 1855 and most of 1856, Know-Nothingism and preparing for the 1856 presidential contest held the attention of Wisconsin's Republicans. Warfare in Kansas between proslavery and antislavery settlers, and the brutal beating of Massachusetts Senator Charles Sumner by a Southern congressman on the floor of the United States Senate, exacerbated sectional tensions and boosted the party's organization efforts.[55] And although the Republicans failed to gain the White House in 1856, in Wisconsin they swept to an impressive triumph, rolling up huge majorities in the legislature and bringing the state rights issue back to center stage.[56] Once again, a joint ballot of both houses would choose a United States senator, but this time Republican control assured an easy victory, or so it was thought. Timothy Howe, hoping to avenge his earlier defeat, was the clear front-runner. Horace Rublee and Rufus King, both past Whigs and editors of influential party newspapers in Madison and Milwaukee, were rumored to be working quietly on his behalf. Old-line Whigs and the few Know-Nothings in the legislature also favored him. Equally auspicious, opposition to Howe was scattered over no fewer than eight other candidates, only one of whom, the former Democrat James R. Doolittle, commanded any meaningful support; but he was a recent convert to the Republican cause and thought to be constitutionally ineligible for the post. So all appeared bright for Howe's chances on the eve of the party caucus, with one keen observer claiming that two-thirds of its members were ready to endorse him, and another that his "election seemed a near certainty."[57]

Only Sherman Booth and the state rights bloc stood between Howe and a Senate seat. Recognizing his strength, and conceding that "on the Slavery question he is a decided Republican," Booth at first seemed willing to endorse Howe if he would stand by the principle of the state court's preeminence. But he warned that Howe's refusal to bend to "the sentiment of the . . . party on this vital issue" would kill his chances.[58] Two weeks before the scheduled caucus gathering, the two men met privately in an attempt to avert a split, but Howe steadfastly denied the authority of state courts to issue writs of habeas corpus on behalf of residents charged with violating federal law. Moreover, on the question of the appellate jurisdiction of the national judiciary, he feebly claimed that he had not yet formed an opinion. Howe's rejection of this "well defined and clearly expressed doctrine of the party," Booth reported, should eliminate him from consideration.[59]

Howe's stand seriously hurt his position within the party and induced Booth to actively oppose his election. Equally damaging, it forced many of his Whig allies to reluctantly abandon him. "The time has come when I see no middle ground on the issue before the country," one wrote. "We must either acquiesce in federal usurpation and passively yield our rights to the dictation of the slave power, or we must assert the Jeffersonian doctrine of state sovereignty and actively sustain our rights as a free people."[60] Caucus members gathered on the evening of January 15, and their disarray became apparent on the first ballot. Howe received a mere twenty-two votes. Nearly sixty more were scattered among five other hopefuls. Disturbed at this turn of events, Howe partisans warned that to make state rights a test of Republican orthodoxy imperiled party unity. They agreed that most Republicans stood by the doctrines and the decision of the state tribunal, but these were not contained in the national party platform and could not arbitrarily be added by the Wisconsin organization.[61] Caucus members thought otherwise.

After another poll revealed that an impasse had been reached, the caucus adopted three resolutions and asked the candidates to respond to them.[62] The first pledged the party to revitalize the republican creed bequeathed by the founding fathers and to resist unjust seizures of power by the federal government; the second endorsed in full the state rights precepts of the Virginia and Kentucky Resolutions. The last and most important declared the need to sustain the right of Wisconsin's court to shield its citizens from the application of unconstitutional enactments, such as the Fugitive Slave Law, free from federal judicial scrutiny.[63]

Two days later the caucus reconvened and examined the candidates' replies. In a curious attempt to placate state rights men and party nationalists, Howe heartily approved the Republican mission statement, the constitutional doctrines of the Virginia and Kentucky Resolutions, and the authority of state tribunals to render final judgment on the reserved rights of the states in order to safeguard their citizens from unauthorized national legislation and judicial decrees. But he also cautioned against an overly zealous regard for state rights that elsewhere had bordered on treason,[64] reiterated his belief that writs of habeas corpus issued by state courts on behalf of federal detainees were unlawful, and once again excused himself from offering an opinion on whether the Supreme Court could review the decisions of state judges.[65]

The caucus then reviewed Doolittle's response. Endorsing the first two resolves without qualification, he also championed liberal accessibility to habeas corpus and declared that the failure of the Fugitive Slave Law to provide alleged escapees a jury trial clearly violated the Constitution. Doolittle went on to expressly repudiate the idea that "the decision of one supreme court is absolutely binding upon another supreme court," arguing that all jurisdictional disputes between state and federal authorities ultimately must be resolved peaceably by an appeal to the people, "the highest of human tribunals." He took it for granted that the national government would respect state decrees backed by public opinion, and that it never would attempt to enforce its will by a resort to arms.[66]

Howe's stand on the habeas corpus issue and his attempt to dodge the question of the appellate jurisdiction of the federal courts failed to satisfy state rights men and doomed his candidacy. His remaining supporters made strenuous efforts on his behalf, but to no avail. The scattered forces of the remaining candidates coalesced around Doolittle instead. On the sixth ballot, he received a bare majority of the caucus votes, and later was elected by the Republican-dominated legislature to the Senate.[67]

After naming a United States senator, Republican lawmakers tackled the state rights issue again in the form of a proposed personal liberty law. Its aim was to give effect to the decision of the state supreme court in the Booth case and to make the Fugitive Slave Act all but unenforceable in Wisconsin. Free-Soilers first forced a debate on this question during the 1853 legislative session, when a committee report argued that Wisconsin's citizens needed an ordinance to shield them from the unjust application of the 1850 act and other proslavery measures enacted by the national government. The majority Democrats, however, frustrated this early effort, as well as others made in 1855 and 1856.[68] In control of both houses of the 1857 legislature, Republicans now confidently expected to put a law on the books. Their proposal would require state officers to do everything in their power to obtain the freedom of all men or women arrested or claimed as runaways; this included granting writs of habeas corpus and jury trials. In addition, anyone making false accusations or submitting inaccurate testimony would be subject to stiff fines and a minimum of one year in prison, and depositions presented by the prosecution would be inadmissable as evidence.[69]

A Senate majority of twelve to seven passed the bill in mid-February. Republicans cast all twelve favorable votes and only one against it.[70] The Assembly amended the Senate's handiwork to include a provision (dubbed the "Booth Relief" provision) directing the state to fully reimburse any citizen of Wisconsin prosecuted under the Fugitive Slave Act, and banning the sale of any real or personal property to enforce a judgment secured under it. Fifteen Democrats joined forty-eight Republicans in approving the amended version, hoping to embarrass their opponents with the "infamous clause . . . to pay Booth for breaking the law."[71] But Senate Republicans refused the bait. They struck out the relief clause and returned their original bill to the Assembly, where it passed 47 to 31.[72]

Most Republicans praised the personal liberty law for erecting the barrier "of State Sovereignty to protect citizens of Wisconsin from the aggressions of the Slave Power," although a few, most notably Timothy Howe, groused about it in private. Predictably, the state's Democrats denounced the law as an act of treason against the constitutional compact between the states.[73] As chance would have it, Chief Justice Whiton's term of office was coming to an end in April 1857, and in his bid for reelection, Wisconsin's voters once again would be given an opportunity to express themselves on the state rights issue. Interest in the contest intensified greatly when, one month before the election, the United States Supreme Court delivered its judgment in the case of *Dred Scott v. John F. A. Sanford.*[74]

Two weighty questions were before the federal judges in this case. Could Dred Scott bring suit in a federal court? And was Scott, a Missouri slave who had temporarily resided in Illinois and Wisconsin, made free as a result of their prohibitions against slavery? The Court majority ruled that American blacks were ineligible for United States citizenship or any of its rights and privileges. This included the right to sue. Further, they declared unconstitutional the Missouri Compromise restriction on slavery north of the Mason-Dixon line.[75]

The Dred Scott decision outraged Republicans. They condemned it as an unjust abrogation of the sacred accord reached in 1820 and a monstrous injustice to the nation's free blacks. It now permitted slaveholders to carry their bondsmen into all the territories, they cried; next they would demand entry into Wisconsin and the other free states.[76] The judgment also reinforced the Republican conviction that the Slave Power controlled all branches of the national government, and lent added importance to Chief Justice Edward Whiton's bid for reelection. If they wished to protect the individual liberty and basic civil rights of all their citizens, and check the growing centralization of power in Washington, wrote one routinely temperate Republican editor, Wisconsinites should stand behind their court and their legislature and return Whiton to his post. This would show the rest of the nation that they at least "remain a free people."[77]

Democrats depicted the contest for chief justice as a referendum on the "dangerous doctrine of nullification" and a test of the state's devotion to the Union.[78] But Whiton's personal popularity and the broad Republican regard for the court's stance and the personal liberty law led to a smashing victory. Attesting to the widespread interest in the contest and its significance, the incumbent received 57 percent of the ballots cast amidst a record turnout for a state election. The vote also reveals that crossover voting was insignificant; public party positions accurately reflected and reinforced the opinions of the electorate.[79]

In his evaluation of the election, Horace Rublee reported that "every friend of state rights, every opponent of slavery extension, of the nationalization of slavery, of the recent daring encroachments upon the reserved rights of the states," could take great satisfaction in Whiton's triumph.[80] Rublee's good friend Timothy Howe did not agree. From his Green Bay home, he looked with increasing displeasure at the direction the Republican party was taking. Booth's success in engineering his defeat was especially galling, although he readily admitted that most Republicans backed the party's unofficial state rights position. Nevertheless, in early March, Howe publicly declared his intention to steer the party away from state rights and nullification, if possible, at its fall convention. He also threatened to abandon the organization if it continued to proscribe men from high office who rejected the doctrine.[81]

Most Republican leaders resented Howe's threat to desert the party and vowed to resist him at the state convention.[82] Not unexpectedly, Booth plotted to foil Howe's plan "to take over the party." He advised summoning a mass meeting on June 17 both to protest the Dred Scott decision and to show support for Wisconsin's judiciary and legislature. In the weeks before the gathering, Booth and other organizers worked hard to obtain backing for the meeting from the state's leading Republican officeholders and editors, and to bring in nationally known speakers. In both efforts, they were successful.[83]

The weather on June 17 was terrible. Rain blocked travel in the rural districts, and towns such as Fond du Lac reportedly were under water. Nonetheless, between eight and twelve hundred enthusiastic convention-eers jammed into the Madison meeting hall to hear the wealthy New York abolitionist Gerrit Smith and the grim-faced Kansas "freedom fighter" John Brown give well-received speeches. Nearly every Republican leader in the state attended, although Howe and Rublee were conspicuously absent.[84] The meeting proceeded without a hitch and unanimously endorsed distinct antislavery and state rights resolutions denying that the Constitution sanctioned slavery or gave Congress any power to legislate on its behalf. They also expressed alarm at the Slave Power's domination of every branch of the federal government, most recently displayed in the Dred Scott decision, the principles of which, "if carried out, would introduce and perpetuate slavery in every free state in the Union." The concluding resolutions affirmed each state's obligation to guard the liberties of its citizens, and pledged Republicans to stand by Wisconsin's judiciary and legislature in the legitimate exercise of their reserved rights, "at all hazards and in all emergencies." In keeping with the spirit of these sentiments, the delegates denied that the states were obliged to return fugitive slaves, and asserted that, in Wisconsin at least, all people were presumed free. For this reason, slave catchers could expect to be prosecuted as kidnappers and to suffer the severe penalties prescribed in the state's personal liberty law.[85]

The convention adjourned in good spirits. Harrison Reed, an influential Republican editor from Menasha with keen political instincts, probably spoke for most when he wrote that its success should remove any doubts about the resolve of the Republican party to defend the people of Wisconsin from acts of "federal aggression and official usurpation." Even Rublee, who claimed that the press of business had prevented him from attending, deferred to popular sentiment and backed the resolutions. And while Booth disputed charges that political considerations had inspired him to call the meeting, the tone of the resolutions clearly indicated that Howe's bid for ideological and political control of the party faced tough going.[86]

In the weeks prior to the state Republican convention, scheduled for September 1, Howe continued to caution the party against taking a stand that would force him and his supporters out.[87] The meeting began inauspiciously when Booth's allies joined with the friends of gubernatorial candidate Alexander Randall and nominated the former Free-Soil Democrat to head their ticket over Howe's favorite. Matters did not improve when, in his acceptance speech, Randall resolved to "resist to the extreme limit of the executive power of the state, each and every attempt at aggression or usurpation by the federal government upon the reserved rights of the states."[88] Satisfied that his position within the party was secure, Booth, in a show of party unity, then agreed to Howe's appointment as chairman of the Resolutions Committee.[89] This harmonious facade crumbled, however, when the committee delivered its report. In addition to reaffirming the party's antislavery principles and its opposition to the Dred Scott decision, Howe insisted on inserting a resolution binding the party to "maintain this creed—this whole creed—and nothing but this creed" in order to protect him and his partisans from being proscribed from future political favor because of their refusal to endorse Smith's state rights position. Booth exploded at this blatant attempt to back away from a principle supported by most Republicans and declared that his followers would quit the party if it adopted the Creed Resolution. They were willing to forego formal approval of the state rights faith, he explained, but they demanded the right to continue publicly to advocate the doctrine and to withhold or grant political preferment to anyone based on it. Realizing that his resolution would lose badly if it came to a vote, Howe wisely retreated, seemingly content that the party, at least officially, had not gone on record in favor of state rights and nullification.[90]

During the next year, Republicans in Wisconsin and the other Northern states watched with excitement as continuing troubles in Kansas and differences over the doctrine of popular sovereignty tore apart the national Democratic party, and with grim foreboding as a peaceful resolution to the slavery controversy became increasingly remote. "The future certainly looks dark and I fear there is no light except through the flames of civil war," one wrote, somberly confessing that "I am ready for the worst."[91] One furious Green County Republican even looked forward to a bloodletting. "This nation has become so corrupt in the administration of its general government," he fumed, "that nothing but the cleansing influence of a sacrifice of blood will purify its political elements" and bring about a reaffirmation of the principles of human equality and individual liberty handed down by the founding fathers.[92] In the midst of this growing pessimism, and nearly five years after Glover's rescue, Chief Justice Roger B. Taney, on March 7, 1859, delivered the decision of the United States Supreme Court in the Booth case.

Taney first upbraided Wisconsin's court for its unprecedented refusal to provide federal authorities with a copy of its decision to liberate Booth, for boldly asserting its domination over federal tribunals in constitutional disputes, and for placing the state in direct conflict with the national government. If sustained, the Wisconsin ruling would "subvert the very foundations of this government." He went on to affirm the preeminence of the national judiciary in unambiguous terms, insisting that its jurisdiction covered "every act of Congress, whether it be made within the limits of its delegated powers, or be an assumption of power beyond the grants in the Constitution."[93]

The chief justice followed his thorough affirmation of federal judicial supremacy with a succinct repudiation of the decision of Wisconsin's court in the Booth case. States were not empowered to conduct investigations into the imprisonment of persons held for violations of national law or to issue writs of habeas corpus on their behalf, he argued, so the decision of the federal district court regarding Booth was final. In essence, the Court's ruling annulled the right of a state to protect the liberty of its citizens. As for the closely reasoned and well-documented arguments of Judge Smith and Byron Paine respecting the constitutionality of the Fugitive Slave Act, the chief justice decreed in one sentence that "it is, in all of its provisions, fully authorized by the Constitution of the United States."[94]

Taney's proclamation electrified the state. Wisconsin's legislature immediately took up and passed a joint resolution denouncing the Supreme Court's assumption of sovereignty as an unconstitutional and arbitrary abuse of power which, if left unchecked, placed the liberties of the people in grave danger. As such, the ruling was "without authority, void, and of no force."[95] The lawmakers went on to adopt almost verbatim the Kentucky Resolutions of 1798, arguing that the states brought the Constitution and the federal government into being, so they alone possessed the right to adjudicate disputes over the powers granted and reserved to each, and to interject "a positive defiance . . . of all unauthorized acts done or attempted to be done."[96]

Wisconsin's Resolves of '59 represented yet another rebuke to federal authority. Republican legislators maintained strong support for the state's position when they cast all sixty favorable votes and only four of forty-eight no votes on the measure in the Senate and Assembly. Most party men cheered on their lawmakers and urged them to stand fast against this latest manifestation of federal tyranny, although Timothy Howe, not surprisingly, denounced the resolves and asserted that "they are copied mainly from Mr. Calhoun."[97]

The Supreme Court's decree also enlivened the campaign to replace Justice Smith, whose term of office as a member of the state judiciary was coming to a close in early 1859. Elected as a Democrat in 1853, the Republican hero had fallen on bad times. Implicated along with numerous Wisconsin politicians and other men of influence in a massive bribery scandal involving land grants to railroad promoters in 1856, Smith had failed to secure renomination to his seat.[98] Ironically, his downfall had been engineered by Sherman Booth, who convinced a reluctant Byron Paine to accept the nomination, contending that the Republican masses would reject the discredited incumbent.[99]

Four days after Paine's selection, the Supreme Court ruling reached the state. Angry Republicans enthusiastically took up Paine's cause and looked to his election as a sign to the rest of the nation that Wisconsin would stand by the rights of each state to safeguard individual freedom from federal authorities devoted to the interests of slavery.[100] In a long and stirring address delivered in Milwaukee and warmly received by Republicans throughout the North, the German-born Carl Schurz declared that the sweeping decision of the national court served to remind the people of Wisconsin of the main issue at stake in the upcoming judicial election: "It is the question of State Rights." Citing the doctrines of Jefferson, Madison, and Calhoun, Schurz warned that, in the absence of any curbs on federal power, political control inevitably would accumulate in the hands of a centralized and despotic state, and result in the elimination of individual liberty and constitutional government.[101] He also dismissed dissenters such as Howe, who referred to state righters as upholders of lawlessness and disunion, asserting that conspiracies against freedom could not be displaced without a struggle. If the Union could not withstand the scrutiny of a liberty-loving people, then it would be better to disband. Schurz concluded with a fiery exhortation urging Wisconsinites to defend their rights with a vote for "STATE RIGHTS AND BYRON PAINE."[102]

And vote they did. In an exciting contest, Republican editors from all corners of Wisconsin took up Schurz's cry, and voters once again turned out in record numbers to give Paine an easy victory. As in the previous judicial contests, the Republican vote came largely from party loyalists, augmented by a few ballots from Democrats and nonvoters. The Democratic turnout, however, deviated somewhat from prior elections. Identifiable party members cast only 55 percent of the total Democratic vote, with nonvoters and Republican defectors making up the rest. Indeed, about 15 percent of the men casting ballots for Paine's Democratic opponent seem to have supported Randall's reelection in the governor's race nine months later. These defectors numbered perhaps 7,500, but they constituted no more than 10 percent of the total Republican constituency, indicating that the state rights position continued to find widespread support within the party, and that the Howe faction remained a distinct minority. The drop-off in Democratic turnout also suggests that disenchantment with the federal government and disgust with the national organization were beginning to have negative political consequences for that party.[103]

The Republican party's state rights faction retained broad popular backing and clearly dominated Wisconsin politics in early 1859, just as it had for most of the past four years. Yet Paine's triumph would prove to be its high point. Soon thereafter, circumstances began to erode the control of Booth and his adherents. Timothy Howe, for one, remained an irritating spokesman for a small but powerful group of Republican leaders and editors who acknowledged the popularity of the state rights position among the party rank and file even as they opposed it. Publicly, some of these nationalists toed the state rights line, although, like Howe, they despaired of the party's involvement in "the enormous lie of nullification" and often talked of abandoning it if it became part of official Republican doctrine.[104]

The problem of Howe's disaffection increased when a number of state rights leaders took issue with Randall's appointments to state office, and then attempted to displace the furious incumbent as the party candidate for reelection in 1859. The cagy Randall, with the backing of Howe and influential former Democrats, responded by using the state patronage to undercut his opponents and gain the support of local party leaders. As a result, Randall easily won renomination, and the standing of several state rights leaders, particularly the ambitious Carl Schurz, suffered temporary setbacks.[105]

Sherman Booth's fall from power dealt the state rights cause its most serious blow. More than anyone else, Booth had kept the Republican organization true to its antislavery origins and the state rights position, although his blistering pen, arrogant self-righteousness, and imperious tactics had made him many enemies who looked forward to a day of reckoning. Booth's undoing stemmed from the fierce attacks he made on Judge Smith while working against his renomination in 1859, as well as from his disputes with and later attempts to dump Randall. These shocked many of his supporters and alienated others who shared his views but were growing tired of his dictation.[106] Booth's influence declined further when he was hauled into court on a charge of having had sexual intercourse with the fourteen-year-old daughter of one of his Milwaukee neighbors. In a sensational trial, Booth won acquittal, but irreparable damage was done to his reputation and to his cause.[107]

Randall's appointment in 1859 of Luther S. Dixon to complete Edward Whiton's term as chief justice of the state supreme court represented yet another reversal for state rights. Whiton had died on April 12, and the governor chose Dixon after supposedly receiving assurances that he was sound on the matter.[108] It therefore came as a surprise when in December the new chief justice acquiesced in a motion filed by Wisconsin's federal attorney directing the state judiciary to reverse its decision in the Booth case and accept Taney's ruling. Dixon agreed that Congress had overstepped its authority in passing legislation regarding runaway slaves, but he also maintained that the United States Supreme Court possessed the final say on constitutional questions. And since the Court had come down in favor of Congress, he concluded, "I am bound to regard its decision." Although the motion failed because Cole voted to refuse the recommendation and Paine disqualified himself for having represented Booth, Dixon's opinion lifted the spirits of party nationalists. It also forced defenders of state rights to contend with the difference between challenging a local federal court and theorizing about the dangers inherent in unchecked federal power, and the reality of actually combating a decision of the national Supreme Court. Three months later, cautious but newly confident federal authorities rearrested Booth, who promptly requested a writ of habeas corpus. In another split decision, the court rejected the application and Booth was returned to jail.[109]

Dixon's seeming duplicity outraged most Republicans. Many accused him of misleading state rights men into believing he backed the position of Wisconsin's court and legislature in order to obtain the judgeship, and looked forward to contesting his candidacy for a full term in the Republican state convention scheduled for March.[110] Others were divided over the wisdom of naming a candidate. Randall and Howe, now openly allied and backed by the *Milwaukee Sentinel* and the *Wisconsin State Journal*, argued against a partisan nomination, claiming that the likely selection of "an out and out State rights man" would only intensify party divisions at a time when the impending presidential contest required the united energies of all Republicans. Lacking Booth's leadership, state righters vacillated at first, but when it became clear that the Democrats would line up solidly behind Dixon, support for a party choice rapidly gained favor.[111]

At the convention, Howe attempted to turn back the growing sentiment in favor of a nomination. He praised Dixon's stand as principled and bold, and urged delegates to forego tying Republicans to anyone by naming a candidate. Opposing Howe, Carl Schurz pressed them to run a state rights man but to avoid taking any public stand on the question.[112]

Schurz carried the day, with 137 votes in favor of making a nomination against 84 opposed. Afterwards, on the first nominating ballot, Dixon failed to receive a single vote out of the 221 cast, his few followers electing to sit out the process in frustrated silence.[113] A. Scott Sloan, a former circuit court judge, then received the nomination after his followers vouched for his reliability on the state rights question.[114]

As agreed, Sloan ran without a platform in order to downplay state rights and to conciliate all party members as they prepared for the pending presidential contest. This especially pleased Governor Randall's supporters. They claimed that the issue would cease to be of any practical importance if the Republican party won the White House and hoped to focus only on issues that Wisconsin's Republicans had in common with the party in other states. Moreover, it was even hinted that William H. Seward, a leading contender for the Republican presidential nomination and Wisconsin's favorite, had ordered several party chieftains to drop state rights immediately.[115]

But Dixon's December opinion and his refusal to grant Booth's request for a writ of habeas corpus, along with the Milwaukee editor's subsequent arrest, made any show of party unity unlikely. Relations continued to deteriorate after Dixon was persuaded to run against Sloan as an independent at the behest of Democrats and a few dissident Republicans, solely on the basis of his decision in the Booth case.[116] A number of party men then renounced the policy of noncommittalism and pressured Sloan to spell out his position on the state rights question.[117]

Sloan meanwhile had been corresponding with Republican leaders around the state, expressing his puzzlement at the demand for an "authorized avowal of my sentiments on State Rights." He had voiced his agreement with Smith and the state legislature at the convention and acknowledged that most Republicans shared his view. Otherwise, it would have been an act of bad faith for him to have accepted the nomination. Nevertheless, although he did not think it fitting to issue a public statement, in mid-March the reluctant candidate gave in and allowed one of his letters to be published. Within days, satisfied state rights men happily endorsed the harassed nominee.[118]

Unfortunately for Sloan, the strategy failed. In a close election, he lost by 395 votes out of a total of 116,621 cast. Turnout declined to 61 percent of Wisconsin's eligible voters from 65 percent in the previous year's judicial contest. Unwilling to support their party's nominee or Dixon, perhaps as many as 7,000 Republicans from the 1859 judicial contest sat out the 1860 election and cost Sloan the victory. Otherwise, surprisingly little crossover voting occurred in spite of the efforts of a few Republicans to swing votes to Dixon. Despondent state righters railed against the treachery of Dixon Republicans, but Sloan's defeat signified the end of their controlling influence within the Republican party.[119]

Before long, caught up in the excitement of the 1860 presidential contest, Wisconsin's Republicans patched up their differences and rallied behind the candidacy of Abraham Lincoln. Their commitment to the Union and federal supremacy was born in the secession crisis and war that followed his election. In time, they would attenuate the state rights principles that had served them so well in defense of civil liberties in the last half of the 1850s. Less than one year after Dixon's victory, they elected Timothy Howe to the United States Senate; in 1862, somewhat grudgingly, they repealed the Personal Liberty Law; and in 1863, again with some reluctance, they rescinded the spirited Resolves of '59.

Before the war, Republicans from Wisconsin and other Northern states embraced state rights in order to defy federal legislation that stripped people of their personal freedom and constitutionally guaranteed rights. After the war, they nationalized civil liberty with the adoption of civil rights legislation and the Thirteenth and Fourteenth Amendments, thus making freedom a concern of both federal and state authorities, and dividing a power once almost exclusively exercised by the states.[120] In both cases, they shared the common goal of protecting and expanding individual liberty.

Today, many Americans understandably fear state rights because of their association with the Southern defense of slavery and later forms of discrimination against blacks. Wisconsin's positive application of the principle underscores the need for a vigorous balance of power between federal, state, and local governments, coupled with a generally accepted partiality to whichever promotes liberty against those who would impose sweeping restraints on personal freedom in order to achieve their version of a just society.

Chapter Three

૪

Aging Statesmen and the Statesmanship of an Earlier Age: The Generational Roots of the Constitutional Union Party

PETER KNUPFER

A prominent Southern Opposition member of Congress met one of the returning delegates from the Baltimore [Union] Convention. "Well," said he, "who did you nominate?"
    "We nominated Bell and Everett."
    "What!—Bell and Everett?"
    "Yes."
    "Why didn't you nominate Choate?"
    "Choate!—why, he is dead!"
    "Oh, I know it, but he has not been dead a very long time."
                        New York Daily Tribune, May 22, 1860

ABOUT a week before Christmas 1859, a band of conservative political leaders met in Washington, D.C., to lay plans for the coming year's presidential election. Almost three weeks had passed since the hanging of John Brown at Charlestown, Virginia. The House of Representatives remained deadlocked in a violent conflict over the election of a speaker. Up from the South rumbled clear warnings that a Republican victory (already forecast in several Northern state elections two months before) would signal the disruption of the Union. Serious and ultimately unreconcilable fractures had appeared in the Democratic party, as rivals for its nomination clogged the Senate calendar with speeches and recriminations. The chairman of the meeting, seventy-two-year-old Senator John Jordan Crittenden of Kentucky, surveyed the assembled leaders from the old Whig and American parties and called them to order as a newly christened National Union Executive Committee charged with launching a third, Union party for the election. Assuming his accustomed role as "Nestor of the Senate," Crittenden issued a prophetic warning: "Let us rest assured that once destroyed this Government can never exist again. We can restore nothing that we have once broken." Pointing to a water pitcher on the table in front of him, he continued: "Break that pitcher and you can never have it the same again. You may patch it and mend it, you may put all the pieces together, but it cannot be the same. It will have its former ring no more forever. And so if we destroy this Government we can never have the same feeling for any we may reconstruct. The ring and the charm will be lost."[1]

Crittenden might well have been speaking of his old Whig party as of the old Union. For the previous ten years, Crittenden and his fellow conservative Whigs had been striving to reglue the shards of their old organization as a national Union party in order to counter the rising sectionalism of the Democratic and Republican parties. Like his mentor, Henry Clay, Crittenden concluded in the aftermath of the Compromise of 1850 that any resurgence of sectional feeling in the country would force conservatives to reorganize their forces to stop the twin threats of Northern abolitionism and Southern disunionism. The divisive aftershocks of the Kansas-Nebraska Act in 1854 had prompted a flurry of such efforts, resulting in the abortive candidacy of old Whig Millard Fillmore as the American party candidate in 1856. Fillmore's overwhelming defeat at the hands of the Democratic and the new Republican parties disheartened old Whigs, but did not dim their sights. By 1858 they were active again, sometimes seeking an alliance with conservative Republicans in the North and national Democrats in the South. Buoyed by a surge of anti-Democratic sentiment in border state elections in 1858 and 1859, and encouraged by the apparent sympathy of leading abolitionists and Republicans for John Brown's raid on Harpers Ferry, they would try again in 1860. Party leaders met in Baltimore on May 5 and 6 to nominate John Bell of Tennessee and Edward Everett of Massachusetts on a short, simple platform proclaiming their adherence to maintaining "the Constitution of the country, the

Union of the States, and the Enforcement of the Laws."² The ensuing
Union effort was an utter failure. The votes of conservatives were divided
in 1860 among four candidates, each claiming to be the moderate, "safe"
alternative to the other: Bell, Vice President John Cabell Breckinridge
of Kentucky, Senator Stephen A. Douglas of Illinois, and Abraham Lincoln of Illinois. Bell fared worst of the four, garnering about 3 percent of
the popular vote in the North, 13 percent nationally.

The reaction of contemporaries to the creation of the Constitutional
Union party set the tone not only for the campaign but also for subsequent assessments of the Union effort by historians, by pointing to the
party's shopworn, graying image. Writing about the Union platform in
his *New York Tribune* soon after the party's convention, Horace Greeley
remarked:

> Like some of its authors, it is a fossil dug up from the remains of a
> past age. It belongs to the year 1830, and not the times in which we
> live. It ignores all that has transpired in the most animated and preg-
> nant period of our history. The contests, the triumphs, the prin-
> ciples, the convictions, the interests, the passions, the still palpitat-
> ing and unsettled questions of a quarter of a century are all carefully
> shut out of sight by this platform, as if they had never existed and
> had no right to exist. In this point of view the platform is almost
> comical. Who can seriously propose to shove aside and ignore the
> questions of the power and duty of Congress as regards the Territo-
> ries, of the nature and rights of property in slaves, of the Dred Scott
> decision, of reopening the African slave trade, of acquiring new slave
> States in West India, Mexico, and Central America? The people of
> this country have done very much and suffered very much in order
> to bring these questions to a final settlement. There is a very earnest
> and almost universal desire for a decision respecting them. But here
> comes the Old Gentlemen's party with this mild suggestion that the
> case shall be abandoned and all records wiped out, leaving the con-
> troversy to be renewed at a future day, under aggravated circum-
> stances. We think the decision of all sensible people, belonging to
> the present geological epoch, will be that the matter had better be
> adjudicated and settled now, so that we can afterward attend to other
> business without danger of being interrupted and disturbed by this.
> The Old Gentlemen's platform, then, will never do.³

The "Old Gentlemen's" label stuck. The party's opponents ridiculed it as "fossilized" "old fogies" left over from "dead Whiggery" and "rotten Know-Nothingism," riddled with internal disputes and doubts over strategy and general objectives, and led by a gerontocracy of decrepit, timorous statesmen. James Gordon Bennett hooted from the *New York Herald* that the National Union Convention was "a Great Gathering of Fossil Know Nothings and Southern Americans."[4]

Constitutional Union leaders tried to make political capital from their apparent seniority, if not senility, by cultivating the party's image of statesmanlike experience and longevity. Crittenden himself thought that the "great many of the experienced & distinguished statesmen" attending the party's nominating convention "will be our security against any foolish or unadvised course. Guided by their counsels, our party may probably be made available for great public good."[5] Naturally, Bell agreed. In his acceptance speech, he praised the "gentlemen, who had retired long from public affairs, of able and large experience, of comprehensive and sagacious views," and who "have proved themselves worthy of great trusts by a long public service," for going to Baltimore to nominate him.[6] Party newspapers harped on the theme of stability and wisdom that long political experience had bred in its candidates. "We cannot resist comparing [Lincoln's] nomination with that of the Constitutional Union Convention," the *Baltimore American* sniffed in late May. "Only think of it—John Bell, the educated statesman, the experienced statesman, the man who has brought ability and dignity to the discharge of important official duties; and 'Abe Lincoln,' the disputatious village politician, the stump orator, whose highest qualification has been an offhand popular manner and a rough wit, and whose public life is as obscure as it is unmeritorious."[7]

Historians have picked up on these themes, but without pursuing their roots in the civic culture. The Union party's "evasion of the real issues gave it a real fossil look," Allan Nevins has observed; "it would have done better for 1824 than for 1860."[8] David Potter's account of the convention studiously marks the advanced age of each aspirant for its favor. James McPherson stretches the point further: "Few delegates," he notes, "were under sixty years of age."[9] Old men used old tricks, apparently; the party's strategy and tactics, resulting in part from its myopic diagnosis of the nature of the sectional crisis, made it a forlorn venture. Its only hope of capturing the presidency lay in a replay of another infamous election back in 1824; the fact that Union leaders looked forward to such a scenario, while most of the country prayed it would never happen again, says a great deal about the party's generational roots. In addition, several scholars have pointed to the party's paranoid rhetoric and opportunistic "anything-to-beat-the-Democrats" mentality, which permanently alienated potential friends among Douglas or Breckinridge supporters in the South.[10] And the party's failure to grow beyond its Upper South base (where it was more preoccupied with beating Democrats than with building a national coalition), combined with a milk-and-water platform that ignored the most pressing issue of the day, doomed its prospects in 1860. Most observers seem to accept the postmortem that here lay old Whiggery, resting in pieces as the country stampeded ahead to secession and civil war. Indeed, the party has suffered the fate reserved for third parties, according to the political scientist V. O. Key, who observed that "though [third parties] may move onto the political stage as a prairie fire running ahead of a strong wind, they die out after an election or so and are remembered principally by historians."[11] Its obscurity has been perpetuated by the absence of a full, published study.[12]

The feebleness of the platform and the prominence of former Whigs in the leadership of the Constitutional Union party have obscured the larger generational and ideological themes suggested by these assessments of the party's character and program. The historical literature's misreading of the significance of the debate about the age of the party's leaders is evident both in its overemphasis on the party as a form of "persistent Whiggery" and in the implication that very old men lacked the requisite character or flexibility to grapple with intractable public issues like slavery. If the Constitutional Union party was but a recrudescence of persistent Whiggery, then one wonders what elements of the old party the Unionists hoped would persist. Certainly not its antislavery wing, to which Unionists had bidden good riddance when it permanently defected to the Republicans. And the fact was that antebellum public culture still respected leaders who had had long experience in public affairs. On the latter point, no one seriously questioned John Bell's fitness for public office; fears for his health and doubts about his preparation for national office are absent from the extant record of the campaign.

Nor is there an empirical basis for the common assumption that generational themes in politics necessarily stem from an age skew in the population at large. The 1860 census reported that barely 8 percent of the population was over fifty years of age, hardly a swing bloc of voters worth fighting over. In effect, we have no straightforward demographic evidence of a clear generation gap in the late 1850s. There was no party of youth, nor a party of old age. Democrats, the Opposition, and Republicans appealed to the spirit of Young America, conveying contrasting messages in similar tones of urgency, impatience, and alarm that resonated with a restless population grappling with major domestic crises. In the aggregate, rough correlation estimates of relationship between census age cohort and votes for the four candidates in 1860 indicate weaker correlations between membership in the 50 to 59 age group and votes for Bell than in the 20 to 29 category, for instance, while the positive correlations across all age groups for Lincoln and Douglas are clear and strong.[13]

Nor can we say that Greeley's characterization of the Constitutional Unionists was entirely on the mark. Greeley was forty-nine in 1860; the Bell party's national chairman, Representative Alexander R. R. Boteler of Virginia, was forty-five. In fact, of the ninety-four Union leaders tracked for this essay, the mean age was fifty-three (the median fifty), and the mean age of the most influential members of the party's high command was closer to Boteler's than to Crittenden's. James and Erastus Brooks, editors of the Know-Nothing organ *New York Express* and major figures in the New York Union movement, were fifty and forty-five. A key Union organizer in Philadelphia, Edmund Pechin, was twenty-six in 1860. Considering the high entry rates of new voters at each presidential election (the electorate's rate of increase between 1840 and 1860 was 95 percent), one wonders if the "old gentleman's party" was "old" and if its platform and campaign strategies were in truth shaped by notions common to a bygone age.[14]

"Old fogyism" in 1860 raises some intriguing questions about the nature of generational rhetoric in an era not noted for age-consciousness.[15] The evidence of generational rhetoric in the 1860 campaign and the persistent appeals by all the parties to the conservative sentiment of the country, when considered in light of the realignment of political forces that marked the demise of the second party system, also raise questions about underlying shifts in late antebellum political culture. What were conservatives in 1860 seeking to conserve? Was there a relationship between the self-styled conservatism of Unionists, the generational tone of campaign rhetoric, and the political customs and assumptions that had undergirded the decaying second party system? If there was no demographic foundation for generational rhetoric in the age structure of the electorate, how do we explain contemporary evidence of generational themes in the 1860 campaign?

One possible explanation can be found in recent research on the nature and behavior of political generations. Generational theory, a staple of political science and demography, has received respectful but generally scant attention in historical circles, largely owing to skepticism about its possible deterministic implications and especially the difficulty of distinguishing generational, maturation, and period effects when assessing political behavior.[16] Social scientists in this field generally agree that the primary problem when sorting out relationships between age and voting behavior is separating the varying influences on the socialization of specific birth cohorts, the process of biological maturation, and historical events that might alter the normal transmission of political orientations through familiar institutions such as the family, the school, the church, and the press.

The vast literature on aging, generations, and political change has revealed a number of important themes in the study of historical generations. First, a historical generation need not be formed by a searing event such as the Great Depression, the Civil War, or World War I, all of which in one way or another marked a generation that had already undergone formative stages in the development of its political ideas and identity. It is formed, rather, when its members undergo the same basic historical experiences during their formative years. In effect, the story of generations has boiled down to the formation of generations during late adolescence, usually seen as being between the ages of 17 and 25. Beyond that point, aging and maturation tend to consolidate and entrench political attitudes and attachments, a process that antebellum politicians knew only too well.[17] In politics, this means that a political generation is most likely to develop a distinctive self-identity when its members enter politics, either as voters or as participants in significant political movements or organizations.[18] Membership in a historical generation is rarely stronger than class, ethnicity, or gender in determining political motivations. But generational attachment is just as durable as these other factors and clearly plays a role in the individual's filtering of political information and understanding of the ways of the political world.

Finally, the research on generational development has noted the salience of generational themes in "founded" societies: those with a birthday as a benchmark for future generations. Americans in particular have measured the march of generations from July 4, 1776; and the generations immediately following the founding were especially sensitive on this point. Historians have picked up on this theme when they have noted the passing of an older generation and the emergence of a new one in politics. The "old revolutionaries" who opposed the new Constitution in 1788; the youthful "War Hawks" who defied the previous generation's appeasement of Great Britain; the Jacksonians who developed new political institutions and celebrated a mass democratic culture at variance with traditional republican notions of deferential, paternalist behavior in politics—all of these cases suggest generational themes in early American politics.[19]

Intuitively, historians of the 1850s have understood this. Surveys of the Jackson era routinely conclude in the late 1840s. The Young America movement's mixture of youth and acquisitiveness bespoke a restless and aggressive spirit that contemporaries identified with the adolescent stage of the country's development.[20] Histories of the Compromise of 1850 commonly note that the congressional elections of 1848 brought to Washington a flood of novices—a "blundering generation" deaf to the swan song of the so-called "postheroic" generation of Clay, Webster, Calhoun, and Benton and who recklessly hurtled the country into civil war. And the successful enactment of the Compromise is regarded as the last act of a generation noteworthy for its sectional compromises.[21] Reid Mitchell has noted that during and after the Civil War, Union veterans associated the war with the nation's "coming of manhood" after an "adolescent" period of innocence.[22]

Political parties in the Jackson period contributed to this generational consciousness by intensifying group loyalties and channeling them through a furious electoral cycle that emphasized the martial virtues of organizational cohesion and offensive tactics in the face of a political opponent. As the primary agents of political socialization, parties captured the young and transmitted newly formed loyalties through them to successive generations of voters. Yet it is possible to argue that the uneven development of the system—that is, the head start obtained by Democrats in organizing their party, plus the recurrence of third-party movements that tended to sap the Whigs more than the Democrats—influenced the socialization of party members in different ways. One wonders, in short, how long it really took for a young Whig to become an old Whig if the party proved unable to outlast its first generation of leaders.[23] The dissolution of the Whig party into third-party movements whose strongest units eventually congealed into the Republican organization might very well have been a formative experience even for "older" Whig politicians who raised such third-party movements as the Antimason and Liberty parties, just as it could have provided future members of the anti-Republican opposition the opportunity to revitalize Whiggery on a conservative basis. Realignments, involving the severing of traditional associations and the forging of new ones, might create political generations.

Socialization and maturation theory can help us explain this kind of realignment. For example, William Gienapp has argued that the Republican strategy recognized how partisan affiliations are determined in youth and become ingrained through the continued practice of voting over time. Older voters have firmer partisan attachments than do younger ones; in the search for votes in 1856, then, the Republicans targeted a natural constituency of new and young voters by running a new and young candidate on an assertive, clearly defined, and, for the day, radical platform. Presumably, according to this model, voters socialized into the party in the mid-1850s would remain firmly in Republican ranks throughout their remaining civic lives, but without time-series analyses through the subsequent two generations of voters, we cannot tell if this was the case.[24] Recent research indicates that, in fact, partisan affiliation is not frozen early in the citizen's civic life cycle and may undergo significant and permanent alterations in response to critical historical circumstances—precisely the kind of circumstances that brought Democratic defections to the Republican camp in the aftermath of the Kansas-Nebraska Act.[25]

All this is to suggest that appeals to the voters on the basis of age-related issues need not stem from demographic shifts that place an older generation athwart the path of a younger one seeking to take power. Instead, the huge size of youth cohorts in the electorate could stimulate attempts by members of both the new and previous generations to make age-related appeals to youth, the former stressing the senility, and the latter the "safety," of experienced politicians and statesmen. The issue, then, was not the age but the Age—the *generation*—of the Constitutional Union party. The party's opponents and defenders were arguing about the failure or success of the Jacksonian party system in resolving the great issue of the day.

By 1860, thoughtful observers noted that the disruption of the old political parties, the growing acceptance of disunion sentiment in the South, and the irresistible groundswell of Northern support for the Republican party presaged a new age marked by the eclipse of an older generation's power and influence. "Not even the youngest man, now just embarking upon the ocean of life for himself, but must feel that a great change has taken place in the relations between the Slave States and those of the North and West," the *New York Express* observed on the day before John Brown's execution. "He can but go back to his school days, his boyhood, as he reflects upon the altered condition of the country, ere he can be convinced that he is really living under the same government that existed then, so different is the speech of people, and so changed are the politics of the country." The "aged and gray-haired" should be especially shocked at the "selfish spirit of sectionalism" fostered by Christians who "have joined, or sought to join, a fanatical religion with politics, and have abandoned the wholesome doctrines taught them by the Great Master." Failure to correct this "disastrous mistake" would bring civil war.[26]

James Buchanan agreed, lamenting after the Civil War that in 1860 "an entire new generation had now come upon the stage in the South, in the midst of the anti-slavery agitation. The former generation, which had enjoyed the blessings of peace and security under the Constitution and the Union, had passed away. That now existing had grown up and been educated amid assaults upon their rights, and attacks from the North upon the domestic institution inherited from their fathers."[27] Buchanan's accusatory tone warped an otherwise pertinent observation: the perilous condition of political affairs in 1860 stemmed from the indoctrination of a new generation in the "modern" idea that slavery was a legitimate political issue. In the view of conservatives like Buchanan, the abolition societies of the North had abandoned their private campaign of moral suasion and entered politics, sweeping aside the traditional parties and creating the Republican organization. Contemporary thought about the nature of political parties accorded them a vital role as barometers of institutional cohesion and as "conservators of the Republic," as William Henry Seward had put it in 1848. Parties socialized citizens as voters and prepared them for civic life. When restrained, parties protected the Union by establishing limits to political activity and by directing local and sectional pressures into productive channels. As private, civic associations unrecognized in law and organized along principles similar to those governing the behavior of businesses and voluntary societies, political parties promoted the public welfare.[28] The second party system was associated in the public mind with a set of customs about partisanship that made parties the temporary servants of overarching principles of constitutional interpretation and public administration.[29]

The tremendous influence of parties as mediators of public life made their condition and prospects a staple of public comment before the Civil War. Defenses of party were coupled with dire warnings about the excesses of party zeal. Third-party movements in particular had to justify their intrusion into the normal rhythms of two-party politics, and the Constitutional Unionists were no exception to this rule. Bell was an apostate from the Democratic fold; his supporters dusted off his previous rationales for switching parties and broadcast them around the country. "The first great duty of an American Statesman," he intoned in 1836, "is to guard against the excesses of party."[30]

Ritual denunciations of party spirit took on a more frightful and urgent tone during the 1850s as the old national organizations corroded. Conservatives in particular had been calling for a national union party to counter sectionalism and its partisan outcroppings in the major parties. Seeing themselves as defenders of institutions that were supposed to harmonize, not destroy, diverse social, political, and economic arrangements, conservatives hoped that a union party would revive national feeling and suppress dangerous extremes. The public culture and party politics mirrored this concern, as the decade witnessed a growing conservative reaction against lawlessness, violence, vigilantism, and rampant spoilsmanship in office.[31]

Republican generational rhetoric seemed to confirm these fears. For at least the previous five years, Republicans had attacked the "old fogies" in the Democratic high command, especially James Buchanan, the self-described "old public functionary" who presided over the most corrupt and faction-ridden administration in recent history. Running a youthful and dynamic candidate on an aggressive antislavery platform in 1856, the party was attempting to draw rough-and-tumble nativists from the rival Know-Nothing order into a new coalition.[32] In 1860, although the party had moderated its choice of platform and candidate, the appeal to young voters went forth again. Military-style Wide Awake Clubs coopted Know-Nothing lodges and attracted legions of youthful supporters; Lincoln, although himself fifty-one years old, was packaged as a self-made man in tune with the optimistic, ambitious *Zeitgeist* of the 1850s, a fresh alternative to the stale and shopworn politics of the "old fogies" in the Bell and Douglas ranks.[33]

Republican generational rhetoric ranged from the crude to the respectful, but always pointed to the outmoded attitudes of a previous generation. The Boston correspondent of the *New York Daily Tribune* ridiculed the Massachusetts delegation to the Baltimore Union convention as "a dozen frightened old fogies, . . . effete and obsolete old fellows, with whom, as substitutes, are joined a lot of purchasable Know-Nothings, like those who were in the pay of the Buchanan party in 1856, and were employed in keeping the Fillmore party alive."[34] Mainstream Republicans noted the difference but understood that the party's need of old Whig votes mandated a mixture of respectfulness and gentle chiding. Lincoln, for instance, judged "old fogies" as counter to the spirit of the age, a spirit of Young America that was overly boastful, aggressive, and proud, but that also better appreciated the expansion of learning and material prosperity than did old fogies.[35] As historian George Forgie has pointed out, even though Republicans like Lincoln persistently and faithfully argued that their party was in fact acting in the spirit of the founding generation, they could not escape being seen as contradicting the force of the compromise tradition associated with that older generation. For however much the party had been called into existence by the repeal of the Missouri Compromise, its rejection of the restoration of the Missouri line and its forceful denunciations of slavery stood in real contrast to the conciliatory and pragmatic tradition of sectional compromise.[36]

Perhaps the widest point on the generational divide was defined by the Republicans' belief that a sectional party could still be a national party. The party made no claim to "nationality" on the basis of incorporating geographically diverse constituencies, but instead put forth its claim on the basis of free labor principles that, as Lincoln pointed out forcefully in his Cooper Union speech in February 1860, did not vary with location or geography. "Nationality," which before the Civil War connoted a cross-sample of the nation's economic and social interests, therefore underwent a wrenching transformation. As heralds of a new party system, Republicans opened up the possibility, regarded for three generations as the prelude to disunion and war, that sectional parties no longer presaged national disintegration. If political arithmetic and Southern hostility forced Republicans to abandon a Southern strategy in 1860, the party quickly came to accept the fact and to celebrate its benefits. "So far from a 'sectional' victory being an evil," one Republican argued, "it will, in my estimation, be a positive benefit to the country, strengthening it at home and abroad. It will put a stop forthwith to the noisy gabble of the fire-eaters about disunion, and the disgusting cant of the fogies in the Northern cities, who seem to believe that our Government is so shaky that it cannot stand the free discussion of the Slavery question."[37]

The Democratic party was dead, its fundamental issues having been resolved and its leadership disgraced by corruption, the Republican *Hartford Evening Press* announced as the election, and victory, neared:

> The spirit of radical democracy will always exist and work in the country. That spirit has passed out of the old democracy into the new. To many the republican party looks radical, but it cannot look more so than the old democratic party did twenty five years ago when it had a life, a soul, and a purpose.... But it is not necessary to the point we are now making to claim that the republican party is better, except in consequence of its being younger; it is better because any young party is better than any old one.[38]

These statements indicate that some Republicans, at least, equated the party's radicalism with its youthful tone, not its platform. Having successfully attracted large numbers of Know-Nothings into its ranks, the party had as its objective in 1860 to mesh its assertive and muscular Unionism with a platform loaded with old Whig policies and proclamations of conservative, "safe" intentions. Lincoln's inexperience, humility, and self-made fame were joined with assurances of his firm faith in constitutional traditions. He was, in short, a prudent conservative leading a new party into power. As a coalition of sometimes-conflicting interests and social groups, the party had to mingle generational rhetoric with professions of conservatism.[39]

The Constitutional Union party's defense of old-school politics obscured differences within its ranks; like the Republicans, the Constitutional Unionists also were a coalition, even though the "old gentleman" moniker treated them as a compact, small, and ineffectual coterie of aging statesmen. On the one hand, ambitious politicians like Boteler, the Brookses, and A. H. H. Stuart sought to create a new party based in the border regions and dedicated to fostering a mixed economy of slave and free labor. Jettisoning the old Whig assessment of slavery's limited economic prospects, these men celebrated the integration of free and slave labor systems that would develop the country's existing resources without risking war over expansion into new territory. "Communities are controlled by their interest," Stuart told the Richmond Agricultural Society in October 1859. "The Northern and Southern divisions of the Union constitute no exception to this rule. . . . They are mutual benefactors instead of antagonists. The relations between the two systems have become so intimate and so interwoven with each other that they can no longer be regarded as separate, independent systems, but are in fact harmonious elements of one great system of American labor."[40] Stuart's interest in political economy bespoke a larger Constitutional Union outlook on the importance of economic issues in the campaign. Although the Union platform said nothing about the tariff, internal improvements, finance, or commerce, Union supporters and officials certainly did. Union meetings, campaign literature, and editorials in American and Union party papers argued that the sectional quarrel was diverting the country from serious fiscal and economic issues that had resurfaced in the aftermath of the Panic of 1857. New York American and Union leaders, in calling for a union party, declared their hope that the new organization would adopt protectionist, nativist, and antimonopoly programs.[41]

Emboldened by the appearance of great influence in the fight over the House speakership, in which Boteler distinguished himself as spokesman for Southern American holdouts against any coalition with the major parties, the younger members of the party foresaw not a revitalized Whig party but a union party that combined aggressive entrepreneurial values with touches of the old Whig nationalism. One can include in this group members of the Northern commercial and professional classes who profited from the sale and distribution of slave-made produce and who admired the orderly rhythms of a well-regulated labor force, North and South.

A strong example of this outlook can be found in the pages of the *New York Express*. Editors James and Erastus Brooks had been campaigning since early 1858 for a fusion of Republicans and Americans against the Democrats. Claiming that the two groups had a common interest in defeating Democrats and in promoting the development of business and commerce, the Brookses coyly admitted the prevalence of antislavery sentiment in the North while they defended the institution as a safer and more profitable use of black labor than what they called the North's "social slavery" of free blacks. The pages of the *Express* do not support the contention that Know-Nothingism and antislavery sentiment went hand in hand in the North. Anticipating the populist racism and xenophobia of Reconstruction-era politics, the *Express* moved easily from the bare-knuckle street violence of urban nativism to race-baiting demagoguery in search of working-class votes:

> The only reason why the Democracy here is not as black, as it is in some other Northern States, is that Seward now has the monopoly of the nigger here, and runs him as a monopoly on election day. All *professions* in the North, ultra pro-slavery, or pro-slavery, are hypo-critical, fraudulent, and never to be trusted in the least,—and only blockheads can be imposed upon by them. We are all an anti-slavery people,—from beginning to end—from Alpha to Omega,—without stop or halt by the way,—and the Democracy is just as anti-slavery as the Republicans. But, in the North, there is a constitutional, conservative opinion—largely in the majority here, when we can get at it,—which, under the Federal compact, means to execute any, and every article of that solemn agreement, in sound, good, honorable faith,—whether it is pro-slavery or not, and whether we may like it or not. The exclusive claim of the Southern Democracy to the ownership of the Northern Democratic nigger is a great bar and stump in the way of the utterance of that opinion; for when we see the negro ridden, as a sham, and as a hobby, as he is Southward, for politicians to ride to Congress upon, or to plunder the General Treasury therewith, we naturally get on the Northern negro's back, and whip away lustily here. Between the contentions of the two sectional niggers, there is little or no chance for the utterance of the sound conservative constitutional sentiment of the people, at the ballot box.[42]

Calling on Republicans and Democrats to "smash the machine politicians," the *Express* hoped that the people would "restore once more the good old feeling,—when we were ONE PEOPLE though of two parties,—ONE COUNTRY,—WITH ONE DESTINY,—the *E pluribus Unum* of our flag, that embraced both parties from the Rio Grande to the Passamaquoddy."

The success of an American/Republican "balance of power" ticket in state elections in October 1859, along with the furious aftermath of the John Brown raid, encouraged the Brookses in the belief that tens of thousands of Republicans were closet conservatives anxious to bolt to a law-and-order union party. Seeing their opportunity, the Brookses abandoned the idea of fusing with the Republicans, and took the lead in organizing the Constitutional Union party in December 1859. Opportunists to the hilt, these men looked forward to building a third, balance of power party, as the springboard for launching a major union party in the 1864 election. Here one sees an important congruence of racism, nativism, slavery, and commercial interests that carried through from old Whiggery to Know-Nothingism to the Constitutional Union party.[43]

What distinguished this group within the party was not only the sharper edge of its defense of slavery but also the political generation from which it sprang. Ranging in age from their late twenties to their mid-fifties, these men had entered politics at the birth of the Whig party. Boteler and Erastus Brooks were first eligible to vote in 1836, James Brooks in 1831, Edmund Pechin in 1855. First associated with the Whigs, they had arrived at political maturity and influence as the Whig party reached its peak and then went into decline as a national organization. Nothing better illustrated to them the ephemeral nature of political parties than the demise of that party and the speed with which other parties were established. Many of the Southern American contingent in the House, for instance, had become political has-beens with the demise of the Whigs and now looked desperately for new party digs. James Brooks first went to Congress as a Whig in 1849. He failed at reelection in 1852, entered the Know-Nothing/American movement while editing the *Express*, backed the Constitutional Union party, returned to Congress as a Democrat from 1863 to 1865 (when he was denied his seat in a contested election), and again returned to serve from 1867 until his death in 1873. Boteler did not run for office until 1858, as an American party candidate from his Shepherdstown, Virginia, district. He led Southern Americans in the House and was their leading candidate for speaker in 1859. Once Virginia seceded from the Union, he joined Stonewall Jackson's staff, served in the Confederate Congress, and became a vocal advocate of total war against the North.[44] This Upper South Unionist was no reluctant Confederate; and his former allies in the North were prominent in the Democratic and peace opposition in that section as well.

Other Constitutional Unionists, however, did see the movement as an opportunity to revive the Whig party. This group comprised the "old gentlemen" Greeley and his friends carped about. Old Whigs like Washington Hunt of New York, Crittenden, Bell, John P. Kennedy, Millard Fillmore, Marshall Wilder, and Nathan Sargent, among many others, hearkened back to Henry Clay. Their correspondence and rhetoric brimmed over with nostalgia for dead men, a dead party, and a dead party system. "Who could say whether a glorious dawn was not about to break for the Old Whig party, and that a great light was about to shine upon them which would repay them for all the past?" Crittenden asked a gathering of New York Whig leaders two weeks before he presided over the founding of the Union party. He then regaled the assemblage with wistful remembrances of the nonpartisan glory days of the Washington administration.[45] Crittenden, more so than Bell, stood for the older generation and made much of his reputation as an aging statesman. "When yr. name was proposed" at the Massachusetts Union state convention, Amos Lawrence told Crittenden, "it was received with singular enthusiasm; the severe decorum of the assembly completely broke down; the old men behaved like boys."[46]

At most, this group hoped to keep old Whig principles alive. Having entered politics well before the younger members of the party had, they yearned for the stability of national organizations that had fostered their long careers and had protected the established authority of experienced statesmen trained in the postheroic age of Jackson and Clay. Whereas Boteler, Stuart, and the Brookses looked forward to a commercial republic of mixed labor systems, Crittenden, Bell, and Fillmore hoped to preserve a wholly federal system in which slavery could meet its inevitable fate without forcible interference from outside its present limits. Hoping to restore the old party system, with its emphasis on economic issues and the suppression of slavery agitation, they saw political parties as working civic institutions worth preserving and controlling in the public interest.

Crittenden placed great hope in the creation of a national conservative party when he first threw himself into the effort during the Lecompton debates of 1858.[47] Over the next year, overtures from conservative Republicans and signs of a growing opposition in the South encouraged him to believe that a Union party might emerge. The Harpers Ferry raid and the fight over the speakership, which highlighted weaknesses in the Republican camp, and the vicious feuding among congressional Democrats over their presidential nomination encouraged him to make his move and call the national committees of the American and Whig parties into joint deliberations in mid-December, 1860.[48]

But within a month after this his friends were warning of impending disaster. "I do not see very clearly how a third party will relieve us or succeed," a New Jersey Unionist pointed out to Crittenden in January. "After years of hard fighting in our state, every thing enures to the benefit of the Republicans."[49] Word from the South was equally depressing. Two weeks before the party's national nominating convention, Charles Magill Conrad, one of the party's founders, wrote Crittenden that in Louisiana "organized opposition to the Democratic [party] is not only impossible," but "is considered impolitic even if it were practicable." It looks too much like "coinhabiting with the enemies of the South, giving them aid and comfort."[50] Some urged that the presidential nominating convention be set before the Republican meeting in Chicago so as to force the Republicans either to adopt a conservative Republican candidate (such as Edward Bates of Missouri) or to converge on a Union candidate (such as Crittenden).[51]

From spring 1860 on, Crittenden saw the party not as the prelude to a greater union movement at a later time but as the last attempt to prevent the dissolution of the government.[52] "A fair opportunity is now presented, for our friends at Baltimore to gather together, under the folds of the Constitution & the Union, all the conservative elements in every party of the nation, and to form them into a great *country party,* whose high office it will be, by frowning upon every form of sectionalism & by showing a catholic & equal regard for the rights & interests of every portion of the Confederacy, to restore health & harmony & happiness to the Republic," William Cabell Rives told Crittenden in May. By adopting the name "Constitutional Union party," Rives advised, the Union movement would reassure nervous Southerners of its fidelity to the old Madisonian system of divided sovereignties and congressional discretion on slavery expansion.[53] Men such as Crittenden and Rives did not look ahead to 1864, although many advised them to do so by forming fusion tickets as a prelude to a permanent coalition of anti-Republicans; by mid-summer 1860 they were arranging strategy simply to prevent Lincoln's election and keep the country together. Bell wrote Boteler:

If the wheels of government are permitted to move at all, under the rule of a sectional President, *which some doubt,* it is almost certain that,

that will be all, that will be permitted by the Opposition to the administration of such a President. No matter how National, or moderate, or conservative he may profess to be in his messages &c. The Opposition to such an administration *will be the whole South*—yes the whole South, in 30 days after the election of "Lincoln," would feel his election to be an *insult* to them—except for a few *Abolitionists* (not emancipationists—they would sympathize with the majority of their fellow citizens) & not a single member of Congress, from the Slave States, (St. Louis Mo. only excepted) whatever may have been his former party associations, but would obey the dictates of his resentments & join in making the most furious & bitter opposition.[54]

Here lay the defining characteristic of old fogyism in 1860: the continued fear that sectional parties would destroy the Union, a fear inculcated by a political system designed to avoid such a calamity. An examination of Constitutional Union appeals in 1860 suggests that Unionists identified the party not so much with an old party as with an old party *system* organized and led by a generation dedicated to sustaining the political arrangements bequeathed by their fathers. Believing that the mass of citizens had traditionally acted in good faith by attaching themselves to either of the "old" Democratic or Whig parties, Union party activists appealed to the long-standing consensus that the agitation of the slavery question should remain outside the limits of partisan warfare.[55]

The Union that conservatives sought to preserve had been defined by the previous political generation as a federation of public and private institutions that fostered a hierarchical, harmonious, commercial civilization. However much the Constitutional Unionists responded to Republican criticisms by emphasizing the experienced, safe qualities of their candidate and platform, however much they portrayed the Republicans as harbingers of disunion, they could not shake the image of being shopworn, anachronistic holdovers from a dead age. "Nationality," the essential ingredient of political parties in the second party system, required continuing compromise; but by 1860 the advocates of compromise appeared as ghosts of the past, apparitions easily dispersed by the volleys of sectional declamation.

And they knew it. Crittenden's old friend Samuel Smith Nicholas wrote him:

The incentives to your new organization *are the excess of partyism &*
danger to the Union. No one has plied those topics so industriously
as myself & no one can have had better opportunity for judging
their value in an effort to sever men from their party ties & to enlist
them in a conservative movement. The disastrous defeat in behalf
of Fillmore & equally disheartening defeat last election in Ky &
Tenn have satisfied me that they are wholly insufficient to induce
any considerable body of men to leave their parties pending the very
battle in an excited conflict like the present.

The only possible reason for continuing, Nicholas thought, was to preserve conservative strength from absorption into the major parties, a purpose he thought counterproductive. A third-party bid would merely ac-
celerate the erosion of conservative strength and help the Democrats.[56]
    Thus, although the Bell men closed ranks and sought coalition with
any Northern Democrats to fight the common Republican enemy, the
party did have its own internal, generational differences. The political generation of the old fogies—of Bell, Crittenden, Everett, and John Pendleton
Kennedy—had arrived at political maturity during the era of good feelings as the country was making the transition from the founders'
antipartyism and ambivalence about slavery to an activist democratic political culture that celebrated parties as agents of sectional as well as of
national interests. In their minds, the overriding issue of 1860 was not
slavery expansion but political abolitionism, secession, and disunion. The
political generation of the Brookses, Boteler, and Stuart came to political
maturity with the onset of the second party system. Their concern in 1860
was the preservation of a national economy of integrated, regulated, yet
diverse labor systems. In a very real sense, their political futures rested on
the success of a new political party, while the political futures of senior
citizens Crittenden, Kennedy, Everett, and Bell did not.
    Both groups shared a commitment to white supremacy, federalism, and
a party system that defined nationality in terms of harmonized geographi-
cal, social, and economic interests. Both issued appeals to the public on
the basis of the old second party system, recalling "the spirit of Washington and Jackson, Webster and Clay, to cherish and defend the Union, and
transmit it with augmented glories to future generations."[57] Both of them
fully subscribed to the party's slogan, coined by Henry Clay, who in 1850
had spoken favorably of a national Union party dedicated to "the Union,

the Constitution, and the enforcement of the laws."[58] Both groups were particularly alarmed by the declarations of prominent Republican leaders that slavery and freedom were on a collision course—that a house divided could not stand in the face of an irrepressible conflict between the sections. Their differences were not enough to split the party. But their common ground was easily traversed by conservatives in other parties, parties that provided a better chance of success in 1860 than did the Constitutional Union party. And the generational differences in the leadership left the party's image to aging statesmen whose aura of timidity, irresolution, and evasion was out of touch with a population yearning for decisive men of action after a decade of sectional warfare. When old fogy John Pendleton Kennedy was too ill to compose the party's national address, Crittenden turned to Erastus Brooks of the *Express*. Brooks's draft was "too party-like," Crittenden concluded, and lacked "stateliness and dignity."[59] Kennedy was persuaded to make the attempt. Edmund Pechin hoped to build up the same young men's Union organization in Philadelphia he had wielded for Fillmore in 1856, but substituted a more "general" association. In the end, the "strong, national, protective platform, with this cursed question of slavery ignored" never emerged, as Pechin had hoped, to call forth "a young giant" in the North "that will equally astonish the factious spirits of the North & the South."[60]

If the Constitutional Union party did indeed evoke customs and sentiments identified with an earlier political generation, the Republicans were hardly the shock troops of a new generation seizing power. In the aftermath of Lincoln's victory, the party did not embark upon a radical program. Republican assurances to conservatives had marked the campaign, while the party's leading lights, Lincoln and Seward, both sought to avoid antagonizing the South. Lincoln appointed prominent Union men to his cabinet and Seward conducted a feverish campaign to conciliate border state sentiment. Later, Lincoln changed the name of his party, briefly, to the Union party for the 1864 election in order to attract old Union men away from the Democrats. But the Republicans had set the basic conditions for a sea change in American politics by questioning the old notion that national parties must straddle the Mason-Dixon line. That new, Civil War generation would not identify so much with the Republican triumph in 1860 as with the Union triumph in 1865.

Perhaps, then, the emerging picture of politics in the 1850s bids us look at the socialization and maturation effects of realignment on older as well as younger voters. It could be that the relationship between generations and politics in the 1850s is but marginally explained by the size of birth cohorts and more fully by the onset of political maturity. The tribal attachments fostered by mass political parties, intensified by the parties' critical importance in maintaining the legitimacy of the regime, helped to create political generations accustomed to political methods and rhetoric that limited political action to narrowly defined, "safe" issues. In the second party system, the frequent appearance and disappearance of third parties raise intriguing questions about the socialization of voters in a highly volatile party system. If, as Michael Holt and others have argued, the relatively low barriers to entry in American politics encouraged the rise and decline of political parties,[61] and if the concept of political generations has any application to this scenario, then we need to examine the socializing of voters through third parties, extrinsic institutions like the militia and the judiciary, as well as major parties. The Constitutional Union party was not simply the product of conditions peculiar to 1860. It was the culmination of a decade-long attempt by conservatives to form a national opposition on the basis of alignments generated in and sustained through the height of the second party system. Its failure marked the final departure of the Clay and Jackson generation, a passing remarked frequently in the press when the great triumvirate of Clay, Webster, and Calhoun died early in the decade. And its failure also lends weight to the observation of historian J. Mills Thornton, that the Civil War was the great "catastrophe of Jacksonian America, the denouement of the Jacksonian drama."[62]

Chapter Four

Blackface Minstrelsy and the Construction of Race in Nineteenth-Century America

Louis S. Gerteis

In the first half of the nineteenth century, two developments transformed the construction and representation of race in the United States. First, a racial hierarchy that had been constructed by Enlightenment-era natural science gave way to Darwinian-era evolutionary theory. During the same decades, blackface minstrelsy achieved wide popularity in theaters across the land, marking the emergence of an American popular culture rooted in racial representation. The purpose of this essay is to trace the course of these parallel developments and to suggest some points of interaction between them.

THE SCIENTIFIC CONSTRUCTION OF RACE

In Enlightenment-era natural science, "race" described a hierarchy of human types that ranked Europeans at the top and the "Negro" at or near the bottom of a Great Chain of Being. The concept of racial hierarchy lent legitimacy to empire by linking the dominion of Europeans over dark-skinned human breeds to a status of superiority and inferiority imposed by nature.[1] In the structure of empire, moreover, race served to distinguish the citizens of the mother country, and its settlers abroad, from the subject peoples over whom they ruled.

Although the most famous and influential of the Enlightenment-era taxonomic systems of classification, developed by the Swedish scientist Karl von Linne, never specifically imposed hierarchy on its racial categories, the categories themselves strongly suggested hierarchy. Native Americans appeared before Europeans in the Linnaean list, but they were described as "red, choleric, erect"; they were said to be "*Regulated* by habit." Europeans appeared next on the list but were described as "white, sanguine, brawny"; they were said to be "*Governed* by customs." Asiatics, listed after Europeans, were "yellow, melancholy, rigid" and "*Governed* by opinions." Africans, listed after Asiatics, were "black, phlegmatic, relaxed" and "*Governed* by caprice." Whether or not a special category should be reserved within the species "homo sapiens" for the ape was never wholly agreed upon. In 1758, however, when Linne revised his original system, he divided genus "homo" into two species to distinguish "Orangutans" from the rumored wild men who were speechless like the apes.[2]

By the early nineteenth century the idea that distinctions of race were (as Jefferson had insisted) "fixed in nature" began to lose its Enlightenment-era clarity. The scientific understanding of nature entered a period of radical transformation. In the new understanding of nature, race would be distinguished from species and both monogenesis and polygenesis arguments would be displaced by evolutionary theory. In this new intellectual climate, the Enlightenment-era construction of racial hierarchy steadily lost its cohesiveness and persuasiveness.

By the 1830s the Linnaean system of classification (and the hierarchy of races that had become associated with it) seemed artificial. As the new science of morphology distinguished itself from traditional taxonomy, the "artificiality" of the Linnaean classification system gave way to structural groupings that were deemed "natural" because they defined the sexual border of species. Studies in plant geography by the American botanist Asa Gray advanced this empirical study of species borders and moved steadily away from the theoretical structures that linked existing species to a divine creation or creations. By the late 1830s Gray's empiricism had led him to disassociate himself from the Chain of Being theory. That theory had come to be associated with Romanticism—with German Idealism and American Transcendentalism—and with the work of Louis Agassiz, who became Gray's scientific rival in antebellum America. The popularity of Agassiz's arguments left Gray isolated and frustrated. "A species is a thought of the Creator," declared Agassiz in popular lectures, insisting as well that the "Negro" and "Malay" races were not the descendants of the sons of Noah (including Ham) but were separate creations. In 1854, Agassiz joined Josiah Nott and George R. Gliddon to produce a collection of essays intended to demonstrate the inferiority of the Negro. That volume sustained proslavery arguments, although Agassiz's views on race did not disturb his close social relations with Ralph Waldo Emerson and other Transcendentalists, nor did they affect his popularity among Boston's Brahmin elite.[3]

Gray labored in the shadow of Agassiz's popularity in antebellum America, but his association with Charles Darwin soon changed matters. Darwin saw Gray as an ally and confided to him the central themes of his emerging theory of evolution, a theory that dramatically extended the genetic definition of species to which Darwin and Gray adhered. The races of man, as Gray described them in the new Darwinian theory, were "the longest-domesticated of all species." With all of humanity contained within a single species, it was but a small step "backwards" in Darwinian terms for the Anglo-Saxon to discover his humble "blood relations" with the Negro and the Hottentot.

While Agassiz continued during the Civil War to warn against the dangers of racial amalgamation, Gray's advocacy of Darwinian theory shifted the ground of debate in the scientific construction of race. Racial superiority no longer rested on divine creation but on emergent qualities of evolutionary advantage—preeminently the reflective powers of self-consciousness—that placed the Anglo-Saxon race (through long domestication) in the lead in the scramble for advantage in the marketplace of human survival. It was Gray's close associate, Chauncey Wright, who synthesized the Utilitarian political economy of John Stuart Mill with Darwinian evolutionary theory, securing elite discussions of political economy and race on a reconstructed foundation of nature. "Intelligent self-consciousness," argued Wright in 1871, represented the "greatest of human qualities" in evolutionary terms and distinguished the "inferior and savage races of men" from the superior and civilized. Similarly, Wright observed of John Stuart Mill's writings on political economy, "The prospects of mankind are not hopeless, so long as men are capable of aspirations, foresight and hope." It was man's capacity for abstract thought, freed of the restraint of custom, that pointed the way to material prosperity and to the evolutionary progress of the races.[4]

BLACKFACE REPRESENTATIONS OF RACE

As the market revolution of the early nineteenth century knit together cities and towns along burgeoning avenues of commerce, the American inability to distinguish metropole from colony assumed heightened importance. The impersonality of the marketplace did not obviate distinctions of race, but it did erode the colonial legacy of racial hierarchy and promote representations of race that reflected new and more complex American realities. A central American reality was the permeability of the racial border, not simply in terms of sexual propagation, but more profoundly in the emergence of a popular culture. In the early nineteenth century, the permeability of the American racial border became the central theme in what might be called an American crisis of social representation. In a world in which continuous competitive exchange displaced hierarchical order generally, the Enlightenment-era scientific construction of race underwent a fundamental change. The collapse of hierarchy in the construction of race brought to traditional perceptions of race the same fluidity and uncertainty that had long characterized the interaction of individuals in commercial society. In America, as in Britain and Europe, individual identity and interaction followed theatrical patterns of representation in which "authenticity" referred not to a fully revealed self but to an observer's response that seemed appropriate to the portrayed self.[5] Blackface theatricality emerged as a distinctly American theatrical form in which European and British blackface folk traditions, already abstracted on the stage in a comedy of misrepresentation, suddenly flourished within a widening sphere of popular culture.

The crisis in scientific thought that framed the Agassiz-Gray debate contributed as well to the American crisis in social representation. Beyond hierarchy, in the ever-shifting realm of genetic evolution and commercial exchange, how did individuals represent themselves to others and to themselves? Blackface made a humorous virtue of uncertainty and of misrepresentation, and it did so amid a scientific reconstruction of nature and a market revolution in commercial relations.[6] A growing and mobile population made possible for the first time a popular theater across America. Northeastern theaters (in Boston, New York, and Philadelphia) provided the longest engagements and the most profitable houses, but theaters and theatrical companies also proliferated in the South (in Baltimore, Washington, D.C., Charleston, Mobile, and New Orleans) as well as in the West (in Louisville, Cincinnati, and St. Louis). Blackface emerged with this popular theater in the 1820s, drawing its original materials from the low comedy tradition of Anglo-American theater. Theater managers and performers catered to the tastes of every stratum of society—to blacks and whites, men and women, masters and apprentices, cabmen, firemen, and prostitutes—all the while striving to draw ladies and gentlemen from the traditional elite and from an expanding business class to the theaters' expensive private boxes. Blackface performers, too, found favor with all levels of the audience: in the boisterous pit and gallery, as well as in the decorous boxes.[7]

The popularity of blackface entertainment derived in part from its capacity to repackage familiar theatrical fare in distinctive American wrappings. The low comedy tradition drawn upon by nineteenth-century blackface performers had deep roots in English and European folk culture and in traditional blackface rituals associated with public masquerade. Blackface had existed in commedia dell'arte, which gave life to English "Punch and Judy" slapstick; it had existed in the even older traditions of popular masquerade, including those of the English Morris dancers whose antics accompanied May Day celebrations as well as the Christian holiday of Whitsunday (or Pentecost). Closely related to the Morris men were mumming plays representing St. George's legendary struggle with the dragon. The blackface elements of mumming plays and Morris dancers have been traced to the fifteenth century, but they undoubtedly had far earlier origins in popular representations of Christian conflicts with the Moorish invaders of Europe, conflicts that began in the eighth century. Like the blackfaced English Morris dancers and mumming performers (and their counterparts throughout Europe), the blackened Harlequin in commedia dell'arte was agile, acrobatic, and witty. The Harlequin was also childlike in his amorous affections, and, as commedia dell'arte spread from Italy through Europe and Britain in the sixteenth and seventeenth centuries, the association of blackface with dance and slapstick comedy matured and formed the direct antecedents of nineteenth-century uses of blackface in a distinctive comedy of misrepresentation.[8]

The linkages between public masquerade and popular theater are evident in a widely performed low comedy farce, *The Irishman in London,* a play first performed in England in the early 1820s and frequently staged in America thereafter. Written by the English actor William Macready, *The Irishman in London* illustrated the changing theatrical uses of blackface and provided a model for American adaptations of the genre. The plot of the farce, moreover, would be continuously recast on the Jacksonian-era stage in comedies of misrepresentation that developed older blackface traditions and soon dramatically expanded upon them. In the play, a West Indian planter arrives in London with his daughter whom he hopes to separate from an ardent suitor, a dashing ship's captain, and marry to a wealthy but dim-witted and foppish Irish gentleman. The Irish gentleman visits his prospective bride and her father in the company of his manservant, Murtoch Delany, whose character becomes the comic centerpiece of the farce. Delany is a rake and a wit who helps to deceive the father and his master and permits the daughter to wed her true love.

Delany was irresistible to women of his class—not to the planter's daughter, significantly, but to the female servants of the London household—and his comic role was enlivened by the character "Cubba," a black female servant accompanying the father and daughter from the West Indies. Cubba represented race and empire: played in blackface by a white actress, Cubba spoke in West African Pidgin, the lingua franca of the Atlantic slave trade. "Ah! poor missa," declared Cubba of her lovelorn mistress, "she be so good; still she cry great deal. Bocro [Cubba's master] do wrong, laugh and be happy—nobody ought to be merry when missa frettee." When Cubba, in the comic climax of the piece, tells Delany of her love for him she also tells him that her father is a king. In an aside to the audience, Delany jokes about her revelation: "Oh! it's King of the Morice-dancers she means; ay, ay, that fellow had a black face—I saw him yesterday."[9]

There is a lot going on here. The comic interaction of Cubba and Delany evoked a venerable folk tradition that itself associated blackface masquerade with frivolity and ribaldry. *The Irishman in London* then linked the Morris dance tradition to new theatrical representations of race encompassing slavery and empire. This content was clearly consistent with the popularity of *The Irishman in London* as a stock piece in Britain and in theaters across America in the first half of the nineteenth century. Far more popular in the United States, however, was an American variant of Macready's farce, a play called *The Forest Rose*, written in 1825 by the American master of popular fare, Samuel Woodworth. In Woodworth's play, the role of the Irishman Delany became that of Jonathan Ploughboy, a Yankee, whose comic role featured the tag line "I wouldn't treat a negro so." As with *The Irishman in London*, the plot of *The Forest Rose* developed around a series of mistaken identities through which the comic roles of Jonathan and the play's principal blackface character, "Lid Rose," developed. *The Forest Rose* was punctuated not only with comic delineations of Yankee and Negro characters but with romantic and sentimental songs, a feature that led the theater historian Richard Moody to describe the play as the *Oklahoma!* of the early nineteenth century.

In addition to black Rose, *The Forest Rose* featured the "little blackey" Caesar, who played the fiddle while the cast danced at the close of Act One. Caesar had no lines in the play and Rose had only a few, which, like Cubba's, were delivered in dialect—in Rose's case it was the dialect of an emerging American black vernacular English with a lingering trace of Pidgin: "Yes, Massa . . . me lubber you berry bad"; and "Oh you, Massa . . . you kissee me so sweet. . . ."[10] But Rose's role was central to the play's comic theme of misrepresentation.

Indeed, the juxtaposition of blackface comedy and romantic duets in *The Forest Rose* may have inspired the comic song "Coal Black Rose," the performance of which marked the beginning of a rapid proliferation of blackface entertainment in the Jacksonian era. According to the English comic actor Joe Cowell (who enjoyed a successful career in the United States during the 1820s and 1830s), "Coal Black Rose" was the creation of the New York actor Tom Blakeley, who originated the piece at the Bowery and Park theaters in the late 1820s. Cowell sang the piece himself (as did his son), but he thought Blakeley had been "the first to introduce negro singing on the American stage" and credited his "Coal Black Rose" with setting "the fashion for African melodies which [Thomas D.] Rice for years has so successfully followed."[11] "Coal Black Rose" may well have set the fashion for Rice's legendary blackface character, "Jim Crow," but others had preceded Blakeley in the introduction of blackface singing on the American stage. The theatrical manager Sol Smith, for example, claimed to have heard the actor Andrew Jackson Allen sing the Negro song "Backside Albany" in a play called *Battle of Lake Champlain*, performed in Albany in 1815. Allen, who acquired his middle name after staging a particularly effective performance celebrating the Battle of New Orleans shortly after news of Jackson's victory reached Albany, performed the song in blackface employing a dialect that illustrated several nonstandard black English forms characteristic of Pidgin and black vernacular.[12] The humorous appeal of this "Comic Ballad"—the lithographic cover of the sheet music version of the song depicts ragged black folk dancing in front of a shack[13]—seems to have derived from its use of dialect in a narrative celebrating the American victory over the British near Plattsburg, New York, during the War of 1812.

A mock heroic ballad, "Backside Albany" had a story to tell. In September 1814, an invading British army commanded by a Canadian general, Sir George Prevost, halted before the American fortifications at Plattsburg awaiting the defeat of the American fleet protecting Plattsburg harbor and endangering the British line of supply along Lake Champlain to Canada. Although outnumbered, the American fleet, commanded by Thomas Macdonough, decisively defeated the British and forced Prevost to retreat to Canada. The blackface performance of "Backside Albany" may have been a direct appropriation of an African American folk song; if it was not, it made accurate and effective use of African American dialect, as the song's first and third verses illustrate:

> Backside Albany dar Lake Shamplain,
> One leetle Pon haf full a water,
> Plattburg dar too close upon de main,
> Town small he grow bigger doe here arter,
> On Lake Shamplain
> Uncle Sam set he boat
> An Massa Macdonough he sail 'em,
> While Gen'ral Maccomb,
> Make Plattburg he home,
> Wid he army whose courage nebber fail 'em
> . . .
> Bow wow wow den de cannon gin't roar,
> In Plattburg an all 'bout dat quarter,
> Gub'ner Probose try he han pon de shore,
> While he boat try he luck pon de water,
> But Massa Macdonough,
> Kick he boat in de head,
> Broke he heart, broke he shin, tove he caf in;
> An Gen'ral Maccomb
> Start ole Probose home,
> Tort me soul den I muss laffin.

"Coal Black Rose" incorporated elements of Pidgin and black vernacular similar to those in "Backside Albany," but did so in a comic context replete with the slapstick elements of commedia dell'arte. In "Coal Black Rose," aspects of African American culture were for the first time fully integrated with the carnival and theatrical traditions of blackface. In "Coal Black Rose," moreover, blackface traditions began to interact with elements of African American culture to inaugurate a distinctly American form of popular culture.

"Coal Black Rose" featured an exchange of verses between Sambo and Rose. When sung by a single performer it undoubtedly featured two tones. It was also sung as a duet and in those instances probably offered an early opportunity for blackface gender masquerade. In 1829 and in 1831, for example, male performers (a Mr. Hamilton and a Mr. Sloman in the first instance, a Mr. McDougal and a Mr. Kreass in the second) performed the "Comic Duet, Coal Black Rose" at Philadelphia's Chestnut Theatre (the latter performance, incidentally, shared the bill with the famous Siamese Twins Chang and Eng).[14] The song may not always have been performed in blackface (Cowell recalled singing Negro songs in whiteface, for example). Moreover, the gender masquerade implicit in the two voices, when both were sung by men, need not have involved cross-dressing. Nevertheless, "Coal Black Rose" emerged in an American theatrical context, shaped in large part by *The Forest Rose,* that opened a new comic arena of racial masquerade. "Coal Black Rose" stands as an early example of the American fusion of a comedy of misrepresentation with blackface songs and musical performances.

The song tells the story of Sambo and his unfaithful lover Rose.

> Lubly Rosa Sambo cum,
> don't you hear de Banjo tum, tum, tum,
> Lubly Rosa Sambo cum,
> don't you hear de Banjo tum, tum, tum
>
> *Chorus:*
> Oh Rose de coal black Rose,
> I wish I may be cortch'd [scorched] if I don't lub Rose
> Oh Rose de coal black Rose.

Rose answers in the next verse, "Dat you, Sambo? yes I cum"; and, after hearing him complain—"Make haste, Rosa, lubly dear,/I froze tiff as a poker waitin here"—she encourages him to warm himself by the fire in the back room. Sambo tells Rose how he would provide for her "if you was mine":

Ob possum fat and hominey, and sometimes rice,
Cow heel and sugar cane, and every thing nice.

But Rose's deception is revealed and the chorus, always sung by Sambo, takes on a negative tone.

SAMBO:
   What in de corner dare, Rose, dat I py?
   I know dat nigger Cuffee by the white of his eye;
ROSE:
   Dat not Cuffee, 'tis a tick of wood, sure
SAMBO:
   A tick of wood wid tocking on, you tell me dat pshaw.

Chorus:
   Oh, Rose, take care Rose!
   I wish I may be burnt if I don't hate Rose,
   Oh, Rose, you blacka snake Rose!

With that, Sambo grabs Cuffee, knocks him to the floor and chases him from the room:

He jump up for sartin, he cut dirt and run—
Now, Sambo follow arter wid his tum, tum, tum,
He jump up for sartin, he cut dirt and run—
Now Sambo follow arter wid his tum, tum, tum,

Chorus:
Oh Rose curse dat Rose
I wish Massa Hays [New York City's sheriff] would ketch dat Rose,
Oh Rose, you blacka snake Rose.[15]

This song, popular in theaters around the country in the late 1820s and early 1830s, gave broad expression to black vernacular English and introduced a comic situation—the ardent Sambo, the fickle Rose, and the confrontation between Sambo and his rival, Cuffee—that soon became the plot of Thomas D. "Jim Crow" Rice's first "Ethiopian Opera," a blackface skit called *Oh! Hush! or, the Virginny Cupids! An Operatic Olio.*[16]

The Irishman in London and *The Forest Rose,* together with "Coal Black Rose," were the first entertainments featuring blackface to be performed frequently and widely across the country. ("Backside Albany" and other early Negro songs seem to have had a largely local appeal.) This theatrical fare, together with another work by Samuel Woodworth, a poem called "The Hunters of Kentucky," were the progenitors of Thomas D. Rice's celebrated "Jim Crow."

Woodworth's "The Hunters of Kentucky" offered patriotic praise for Old Hickory and attributed Jackson's triumph to his confidence in and reliance on the prowess of Kentucky riflemen. The western theatre manager Noah M. Ludlow (who, together with his partner Sol Smith, made St. Louis the center of their western theatrical operations) put Woodworth's words to music and performed the piece for the first time in New Orleans in 1822.[17] Ludlow's act and variants of it became enormously popular. In November 1829, Ludlow and his company opened a "season" in Louisville. Although Ludlow no longer advertised the performance of "The Hunters of Kentucky," the theme of the boastful western hero remained popular, and "Thespis," writing in the Louisville *Public Advertiser,* encouraged the town's citizens to attend Ludlow's performances and give full support to "the proud *national* impulse which excites in every bosom a noble sympathy in favor of *native* genius."[18] Ludlow, whose season extended through the winter, served up a theatrical fare heavy with low comedy and farce: he presented a Woodworth-style blackface comic in the character "Sambo, (a black man)"; presented another blackface actor "in the character of a Negro" to sing comic songs; and, as the *Public Advertiser* filled its pages with the speeches of Daniel Webster and Robert Y. Hayne, Ludlow himself took the stage as "Restive, the Politician" in an afterpiece entitled TURN OUT—*Or, The Enraged Politician.* For the price of admission of seventy-five cents ("Colored people, 50 Cents"), Ludlow and Company offered Louisville audiences what they presumably wanted, a playful portrait of a heterogeneous population and a restless democracy.[19]

A week after Ludlow left Louisville in March 1830, his chief rival, Samuel Drake, arrived in town. Drake managed a theater company that included an as-yet obscure actor named Thomas D. Rice, who played minor roles and sang comic songs. In May, in a production that Drake must have hoped would replicate Ludlow's success by combining Woodworth's blackface and Kentucky Rifle material, Rice appeared as "Sambo, (the Negro boy)" in a new melodrama entitled *Kentucky Rifle— or, A Prairie Narrative*. It was a "home-bred piece," Drake wrote in his advertisement, "it is a Bantling, born in Kentucky, and can only receive its nurture from the smiles of its inhabitants." "The story from which the Drama has been taken," Drake continued, "may be found in the souvenir of 1828." The principal memory of that year, of course, was Jackson's election as president. "In the course of the piece," Drake promised, "*Mr. Rice, in character, will sing the comic Negro Song, of Jim Crow.*"[20]

Rice, who had already sung "Coal Black Rose" in Louisville, became an instant success as "Jim Crow." Throughout the 1830s and 1840s, Rice played regularly in theaters from Boston to Mobile and from Baltimore to St. Louis, plying his trade among a group of performers who billed themselves as "comic delineators." The delineators, drawing their inspiration from English low comedy portrayals of Irishmen, Yorkshiremen, and Negroes, offered staged representations of distinctive American types. The group included Irish delineators, whose performances had originally been shaped through the character Murtoch Delany in *The Irishman in London;* Yankee delineators, who took their inspiration from Jonathan Ploughboy in *The Forest Rose;* and delineators of the western hunter and braggart, who followed the lead of the character Nimrod Wildfire in the melodrama *The Lion of the West*. Rice, in his "Jim Crow" act, shared with these and other delineators an attire distinctive to his character (in Rice's case it was the ragged dress of a "cornfield negro") and a humor that relied heavily on dialect. In addition, of course, Rice's Negro delineations required blackface makeup. But what quickly distinguished "Jim Crow" from the Irish, Yankee, and western delineators was the association of racial masquerade with a wide-ranging parody of American politics and culture. A close look at a series of Rice's performances in Washington, D.C., in the midst of the Nullification Crisis, suggests the nature of the emerging blackface genre.

Newspaper advertisements for Rice's performances in January 1833 listed the individual songs that he would sing "Between Play and Farce." They were: "Gumbo Chaff," "Clare de Kitchen," "Jim Crow's return to Washington," "The Evacuation of New York by the British," "Description of Boston," "The Burning of the Rail-road baggage Car," and "The Jim Crow of all the States."[21] The advertisement for his performance three days later indicated that Rice appeared as Jim Crow between a staging of Shakespeare's *Richard III* (in which Rice played the role of Henry VI) and a farce entitled *Wedding Day* (in which he played "Lord Rakeland," the groom). This structure of theatrical performances, with song and dance acts appearing between play and farce, was typical of the early American theater, and characteristic of the theatrical roles of delineators. What was as yet relatively new was Rice's performance in blackface as Jim Crow, offering comic commentary on the events of the day. For Rice's second performance the newspaper announced a new list of songs: "Jim Crow's Trip to the Capitol," "The New Road," "Philadelphia Nigges," "Trip to Washington," "New-York Trip," "Dandy Ball," and "Jim Crow Varieties."[22]

Some of the songs performed by Rice in Washington during the Nullification Crisis survive as published pieces of sheet music. Published versions of "Gumbo Chaff,"[23] for example, tell the tale of a comic blackface rogue, a character ready to roam the Ohio and Mississippi rivers after his master's death. Gumbo Chaff's adventures took him to New Orleans and back upstream to Louisville and to his old home on the Ohio bluff in Indiana. The first verse identified Gumbo Chaff as a riverman:

> On de Ohio bluff in the state of Indiana,
> Dere's where I live up to de Habbanna,
> Ev'ry mornin early massa gib me licker,
> I take my net and paddle and I put out de quicker,
> I jump into my kiff and I down the river driff,
> And I cotch as many cat fish as ever nigger liff.

"Habbanna" is probably a reference to the Havana cigar and thus to tobacco cultivation; the reference to "massa" in the free state of Indiana is perhaps inadvertent (inasmuch as Indiana rhymes with Habbanna), or it may reflect the reality that slaves worked on the "free" as well as on the slave sides of the Ohio and Mississippi rivers.

The second verse introduced Gumbo Chaff's comic adventures as he battled an alligator in the style of a western "roarer" only to discover that he had confronted nothing more dangerous than a pine knot on a stick:

> Now dis morning on a driff-log tink I see an Alligator,
> I scull my skiff around and chuck him sweet potato,
> I cratch him on de head and try for to vex it;
> So I picks up a brick an' I fotch'd him such a lick,
> But twant nothin' but a pine knot 'pon a big stick.

In succeeding verses, Gumbo Chaff's master's barn floated off in a flood after which massa died and went to hell: "An' I do believe sure enough he's gone to de debil,/For when he live you know he light upon me so./But now he's gone to tote de firewood way down below."

Massa's widow married "Bill de weaver . . . a gay deceiver." Bill robbed the widow of her money and abandoned her: "And de way he did put out was a sin to Davy Crocket." Gumbo Chaff is then off to New Orleans, where "de niggers laff" to see him try to haul bales of cotton. In New Orleans he learned French and took on some characteristics of a dandy:

> I learn'd to talk de French oh! A la mode de dancy,
> Kick him shoe, tare him wool, parle vo de Francey,
> Bone jaw Madamselle, Stevedors and Riggers,
> Apple jack and sassafrass and little Indian Niggers;
> De natives laff'd an swore dat I was corn'd [drunk]
> For dey neber heard such French since dey was born'd

Parody in this piece is a function of Gumbo Chaff's perspective on a world of expanding social and commercial relations. Freed of an abusive master, Gumbo Chaff is footloose and fancy free for a time, traveling the river highways that carried people and goods in a ceaseless flow of exchange. Gumbo Chaff would soon settle down, but his brief fling was both exhilarating and illustrative of the American crisis of social representation. A masterless man, Gumbo Chaff enjoyed physical mobility and could play with his identity, albeit within the theatrical confines of blackface racial representation. Like other blackface performers, he was neither black nor white—or both black and white—and his popularity (among whites and blacks in the audience) was tied directly to his ability to flout the standards of propriety, and even the proprietary claims, of the dominant culture. Blackface representations of race literally danced across the racial border. Rice's intent may have been to make his blackface character appear ignorant, as in a verse about Gumbo Chaff's efforts to learn to "read write and cifer," but the character's lack of formal education was offset and made humorous by his cleverness of language and undoubtedly by Rice's dancing skill as well. Only in the last verse is the issue of race directly raised as Gumbo Chaff returned to "de Ohio bluff" to amuse white folks with his music and to laugh with the "niggers" when he introduced them to "Mrs. Gumbo Chaff," presumably the deceived and impoverished widow:

> So we'd music all night and day set up sich a laff
> When I introduced de niggers to Mrs. Gumbo Chaff.

A sheet music version of "Clare de Kitchen" permits a similar analysis of another song performed by Rice in Washington, D.C.[24] "Clare de Kitchen" offered an assortment of unrelated rhymes that told no story but demonstrated the manner in which Rice borrowed from African American folk music. The song is the sort that Dena Epstein described being sung by groups of African Americans in a style of dancing called "patting juba," in which the participants used words, foot tapping, and body patting to create patterns of rhythm that accompanied banjo or fiddle music, or took their place when instrumental music was not available.[25] Some of the verses of "Clare de Kitchen" were of the sort that seemed to be "nonsense" to white visitors to the South, although one bore some resemblance to the English folk song "The Two Crows":

> A jay-bird sot on a hickory limb,
> He wink'd at me and I wink'd at him;
> I pick's up a stone and I hit his shin,
> Says he you better not do dat again.

Similarly, another verse may have been influenced by the British folk song "The Frog and the Mouse":

> A Bull-frog dress'd in sogers close,
> Went in a field to shoot some crows;
> De crows smell powder and fly away,
> De Bull-frog mighty mad dat day.[26]

Two verses, however, were undoubtedly created or adapted by Rice, referring as they did to theatrical representations of race:

> I went to de creek, I cou'dn't get a cross,
> I'd nobody wid me but an old blind horse;
> But old Jim Crow come riding by,
> Says he, old fellow your horse will die.

> *Chorus:*
> So Clare de Kitchen old folks young folks
> Clare de Kitchen old folks young folks
> Old Virginny never tire

> Dis love is a ticklish ting you know,
> It makes a body feel all over so;
> I put de question to Coal black Rose,
> She as black as ten of spades and got a lubly flat nose.

As the newspaper advertisements indicated, Rice's January 1833 performances in Washington, D.C., covered a variety of topics, including what appear to have been matters of topical concern like "The New Road" and "The Burning of the Rail-road baggage car." Rice's theme was frequently patriotic, too, as in "The Evacuation of New York by the British" (a reference to the final departure of British troops from the United States after the Revolutionary War) and the "Description of Boston" (which may have celebrated American heroism at the battle of Bunker Hill). More complex in terms of their social implications were the songs entitled the "Philadelphia Nigges" and "Dandy Ball." Both titles suggest that Rice may have appropriated his themes from the Philadelphia caricaturist Edward C. Clay, a future Whig, who produced print art for wealthy patrons in the United States and Britain. In a series of cartoons drawn in the late 1820s (and later published in Philadelphia and London), Clay depicted "Life in Philadelphia" in a manner that ridiculed the pretentious dress, manner, and language of black dandies. In one courtship scene, "Cesar" asked "Chloe" "How you find yourself dis hot weader . . . ?" Chloe replied "Pretty well I tank you . . . only I aspire too much!"[27] Clay's message was clear: blacks were ridiculous when they sought to rise above their subservient station, to cross or blur the racial border.

Precisely what Rice did with this possibly appropriated material is not certain, although his "Jim Crow" material and his "Ethiopian Operas" suggest that, while Clay's cartoons made a virtue of class (and race) distinction, Rice used rustic blackface characters to foil aristocratic pretension. After all, the centerpiece of Rice's performances in Washington and everywhere else was "Jim Crow," and Jim Crow was a "cornfield Negro" who went everywhere, saw everything, and commented on every topic of the day. Jim Crow came from the West and he roared with the bravado of Mike Fink and the legendary Davy Crockett:

> I come from ole Kentucky
> A long time a go
> Where I first learn to wheel about
> And jump Jim Crow
>
> I wip my weight in Wild-cats
> I eat an Alligator
> And tear up more ground
> Dan kiver fifty load of Tater
>
> I sit upon a Hornet's nest
> I dance upon my head
> I tie a wiper round my neck
> And den I goes to bed[28]

The verses of published "Jim Crow" sheet music vary considerably and the lyrics were probably changed frequently in Rice's performances to suit particular situations and audiences. But the published lyrics all repeat the same chorus after each verse and it was the chorus that seems to have been the occasion for Rice to offer his version of patting juba:

> Wheel a-bout, and turn a-bout
> And do jis so
> Ebry time I wheel a-bout,
> I jump Jim Crow

The lyrics for songs like "Jim Crow's Return to Washington" and "Jim Crow's Trip to the Capitol" do not survive in published form. But sheet music versions of topical pieces performed by Rice during his 1836 London engagement suggest the way in which "Jim Crow" commented on current events and interests. "Jim Crow's Trip to Greenwich" described, among other things, the workings of a steamboat. "Jim Crow's Peep at the Balloon" explained why he was not permitted to ascend, commenting lightheartedly on Britain's color line in the process:

> In joke I say dat I'll ascend,
> White man gave me a shove,
> Said he we want fine weder,
> And·it shant look black above.[29]

This tendency of "Jim Crow" to comment on current events suggests that Rice's performances of "The Jim Crow of all the States" and "Jim Crow's Trip to the Capitol" mixed a patriotic defense of the Union with burlesque commentary about politics. Some of the published lyrics of "Jim Crow" referred directly to the Nullification Crisis and, less directly, to an uncertain fidelity to "Union." They, or verses very much like them, were undoubtedly part of Rice's Washington performances:

> I am for Freedom
> An' for Union altogether
> Although I'm a Black Man
> De White is call'd my Broder
>
> I'm for Union to a Gal
> An' dis is a stubborn fact
> But if I marry an' don't like it
> I'll nullify de Act.
> . . .
> It's berry common 'mong de white,
> To marry and get Divorced,
> But dat I'll nebber do,
> Unless I'm really forced.

Rice's "Jim Crow" was neither a grotesque portrait of a black man nor a vehicle for ridiculing African Americans or their culture. But Rice's act was not an innocent exercise in cultural exchange: violence and cruelty always lay just beneath the surface. In fact, Rice's popularity may have derived from the capacity of his blackface act to mix burlesque parody with a hard-bitten humor that veered from reassurance toward a tough uncertainty. The verses of one of Rice's early "Negro Songs," "Long Time Ago," tell an outlandish but ominous story. The singer meets "Clem the weaver" in a rough section of town called "shinbone alley." Clem "shoots a nigger" and skins him for his hide and tallow. The singer gets Clem "corned" on whiskey. Clem falls into the river and loses the hide and tallow and returns to call the singer a thief.[30]

The humor of the piece—the lithographic cover of the published sheet music version depicts a ragged Negro dancing with a stick and a pan for a drum, suggesting frivolity—lies in its cynicism: Clem literally transformed the "nigger" into a commodity, lost that commodity when he was plied with whiskey, and completed the cycle of cynicism by calling the blackface singer-narrator a thief. Like Rice's "Jim Crow" songs, "Long Time Ago" had more than one version. In this instance the lyrics for a second version, "De Oder Song," were printed with the original sheet music. Again the focus is on the casual shooting of a "nigger," but this time the violence and cruelty are utterly pointless:

> As I was gwoin down shinbone alley
> Long time ago
> Dare I met ole Johnny Glatty
> Long time ago
>
> He had a musket on his shoulder
> Long time ago
> He look as bold as sheep and bolder
> Long time ago
>
> I ax him where he was a gwoin to
> Long time ago
> Long time afore he tell me
> Long time ago
>
> He gwoin down to shoot a nigger
> Long time ago

He cok a gun and pull a trigger
Long time ago

He shot a nigger throu' de collar
Long time ago
Der poo cuffe kick and holler
Long time ago

I ax him what he do dat dere for
Long time ago
De nigger no say why nor wherefore
Long time ago

Ole Johnny Glatty pull de trigger
Long time ago
And dats de last o' dat dere nigger
Long time ago

Rice played at Baltimore's Front Street Theatre in the fall of 1832 before beginning his January 1833 Washington performance.[31] "Long Time Ago" was published in Baltimore and it may have had a specific local appeal—it may have borrowed from a local African American song with topical references. In any case, the hard-bitten humor of the piece—its toughness—stands in sharp contrast to the reassuring sentimentality characteristic of Stephen C. Foster's style of minstrel music of the 1840s and to the morally instructive songs inspired by Harriet Beecher Stowe's *Uncle Tom's Cabin* in the 1850s.[32] "Johnny Glatty's" boldness is that of a cowardly sheep; his cruelty is senseless. This distinction—between a sentimental blackface tradition that extended the cultural domain of bourgeois propriety and a Jim Crow tradition that defied such limits—is central to an evaluation of the role of blackface in American popular culture.

MEANINGS

Spectators described early blackface performances as "authentic" representations of the American Negro. When Thomas D. Rice opened his Jim Crow act at New York's Bowery Theatre in 1832 it was the authenticity of the racial masquerade, as one spectator described the phenomenon, that seemed to account for its enormous popularity:

> Entering the theatre, we found it crammed from pit to dome, and the best representative of our American Negro that we ever saw was stretching every mouth in the house to its utmost tension. Such a natural gait!—such a laugh!—and such a twitching-up of the arm and shoulder! It was the Negro, par excellence.[33]

But what, exactly, did authenticity mean? Clearly it did not require performances of African American folk music and dance. Neither did it require African American performers. Instead, blackface gave theatrical representation to a process of cultural exchange that permeated the scientifically constructed racial border. Perhaps it would be more accurate to say that blackface theatricality simply ignored the racial border. Certainly most spectators never read Agassiz, Gray, or Darwin. It was in blackface explorations of cultural exchange between black and white that audiences found the authenticity they sought in the representation of race in America. To be sure, it was typically whites in blackface who staged these representations, but it is critical to an understanding of the genre to realize that this was not necessarily so. From the outset, black performers participated in the staged representations of cultural exchange. Over time, the presence and influence of black performers increased and the representation of cultural exchange became the wellspring of American popular culture.

The most celebrated black performer in the antebellum era was William Henry Lane, known on stage as "Boz's Juba." As Lane's stage name suggested, his dancing style incorporated elements of African American dance. Just how closely staged representations of cultural exchange followed the actual experience of financial exchange is suggested in an account of Juba's rivalry in New York in the late 1830s with a white jig dancer, John Diamond. Still young enough to be apprenticed to his manager, P. T. Barnum, "Master" Diamond danced regularly at Barnum's Museum. Juba danced at Pete Williams's dance house; he, too, was very young, a teenager at the time and not yet thirty when he died in 1852. The theatrical proximity of Juba and Diamond prompted some of "the boys" to get up a challenge dance between the two. The match took place at Pete Williams's dance house about eleven o'clock one night after Diamond's show at

Barnum's Museum had closed. Diamond's supporters came over from Barnum's place to support their favorite. Juba had his supporters, too, including a good many "negroes" who "had bet all their coppers on their champion." The musicians consisted of five fiddlers and a tambourine player. Juba went first: "One of the fiddlers played a reel for him, and he shuffled, and twisted, and walked around, and danced on for one hour and fifteen minutes by the watch." He ended with a loud tap with his left foot and, amid cheers from the spectators, went to the bar for a drink. Diamond followed, appearing nonchalant but determined to uphold his reputation and beat Juba's time. The result of the match would unavoidably "get wind among the boys"; moreover, if Juba won, Barnum would not be pleased. But there was more at stake for Diamond (and for Juba):

> There was another thing about this match-dance that made Diamond want to win. You see it was not only a case of Barnum's Museum against Pete Williams's dance-house, but it was a case of white against black. So Jack Diamond went at his dancin' with double energy—first, for his place, next, for his color.

When Diamond beat Juba's time he "gave a hop, skip and a jump, a yell and a bow." One of the "colored boys" was said to have yelled out: "He's a white man, sure . . . but he's got a nigger in his heel."[34]

Racial rivalry combined with cultural exchange as Juba danced a British reel in the distinctive African American manner that he had appropriated in his stage name. And Diamond responded with flourishes intended to meet and better Juba's challenge. Both dancers would soon leave New York for wider fields abroad. Barnum, who made a virtue of "humbugs," took Diamond to New Orleans and then sent him on a tour of Southern theaters in an act that featured dances with challengers from the audience: "Challenge: MASTER DIAMOND, who delineates the Ethiopian character superior to any other *white* person, hereby challenges any person in the world to a trial of skill at Negro Dancing, in all its varieties, for a wager of from $200 to $1000."[35] Juba went on, in 1846, to become a major draw at Charles White's Melodeon in the Bowery, where he performed with White's Serenaders, a blackface group. In 1848, Gilbert Ward Pell engaged Juba and sailed with him to England, where they joined Gilbert's brother, Richard Pell. Richard Pell, known as Dick Pelham on stage, had begun his blackface career in 1835 at the Bowery Theatre, where he appeared in an early Ethiopian Opera starring Thomas D. Rice. Pelham went to England in 1843 with the Virginia Minstrels and remained there to manage Pell's Serenaders. Now joined by Gilbert Pell and by Lane, the latter appearing as "Boz's Juba" on tambourine, the new group, calling itself "G. W. Pell's Serenaders," continued their blackface English tour.[36]

Authenticity in blackface referred not to African American folk culture but to the theatricality of blackface itself—to the manner in which blackface offered audiences experiences authentic to their perceptions of themselves and the world around them. Audiences went to theaters seeking entertainment, of course, but the entertainers knew that the comic and sentimental appeal of blackface, like other theatrical forms, was strongest when it approached (without confronting) the realm of experience. As Jean-Christophe Agnew has observed of English theater in the early seventeenth century, playwrights seized "upon the problem of social representation and misrepresentation as the theme and touchstone of their drama." Their audiences, "equally perplexed by the fluidity of social relations used the idiom of the theater to frame the problem for themselves."[37] In the American crisis of social representation, authenticity in blackface performances referred to what might be termed emotional verisimilitude, whereby a performance elicited a response from a spectator that seemed to be appropriate to its subject. Viewing the same phenomenon from the perspective of popular culture and cultural hegemony, Eric Lott recently described blackface as "a realm neither of populist desire nor of commercially imposed distraction, but a stage on which appropriated goods and manufactured daydreams are transformed into culture."[38] From either perspective, what is presented for observation (by black and white performers) necessarily assumed the tenor and tone that the spectator's imagined social identity made available to it. The fact that African Americans were also among the spectators whose responses shaped the blackface genre becomes critically important to any effort to subject blackface theater to historical analysis.

During the first half of the nineteenth century, American theater audiences resembled those of Elizabethan England.[39] It was not until the late 1840s that elite audiences in New York were large enough to form a separate theater market; and it was not until the Astor Place Riot (1849) that New York's elite felt itself to be secure enough socially to break away from the popular theater and begin to define and defend an elite theatrical culture.[40] Before midcentury, and long after in most of the country, theater managers and performers, together with the ladies and gentlemen who occupied the theater boxes, placated, indulged, or simply suffered the rowdy, insolent, and often insulting demeanor of the pit and gallery. The cultural meanings originally inscribed in blackface performances can be recovered only with reference to the polyglot assemblages to whom the performances were directed. Three examples of audience composition from antebellum playbills will underscore a basic point alluded to in earlier histories of American theater but neglected in recent studies of blackface: the audiences whose sense of authenticity shaped blackface performances were a diverse and racially mixed lot.[41]

In June and August of 1840, T. D. Rice appeared as "Jim Crow" and other blackface characters at New York's Bowery Theatre. Playbills for Rice's performances did not list the prices or categories of admission, but an undated playbill that followed his June 18, 1840, performance listed private boxes at $3.00 and $5.00, the dress circle and upper boxes at $.25, the pit at $.12, the gallery at $.10, and "Colored Boxes" at $.25.[42]

On April 23, 1860, the American tragedian Edwin Booth appeared at the St. Louis Theatre in Shakespeare's *Hamlet*. The evening's entertainment concluded with a musical farce called *Jenny Lind!* in which Miss Laura Honey (who had played Ophelia in *Hamlet*) played "Jenny Leatherlungs" and sang the minstrel spiritual "Jordan Am a Hard Road to Travel," followed by a duet and dance called "Old King Crow" performed in the manner of the "Minstrel d'Ethiope." The price of admission to the dress circle and orchestra seats was $.50. Tickets to the pit and gallery cost $.25. Private boxes sold for $5.00. Admission to the "Colored Boxes" cost $.50.[43]

In Mobile, Master Jack Diamond appeared in a performance called *Masquerade; or, Negro Doorkeeper* in February 1841. On January 19, 1841, the Mobile Theatre had announced its prices for the season. Private boxes sold for $1.25. Entry to boxes and the pit cost $1.00. Patrons were admitted to the gallery for $.50. The managers reserved seating for "Free colored People on the right hand third tier" for $1.00. "Colored Servants" would not be admitted "without a pass from their owner expressing their approbation." Admission for servants (that is, slaves) was $.50.[44]

The presence of blacks, mulattoes, and a cross section of social classes in antebellum theater audiences during blackface performances helps to account for the tendency of black as well as white observers of popular culture to find these representations of cultural exchange authentic. In

April 1860, for example, the prominent Massachusetts black abolitionist William C. Nell received a letter from a black abolitionist colleague, William Anderson, of New London, Connecticut, concerning the role of African Americans in the looming national crisis. "When in Boston last August," wrote Anderson, "I laughed to hear a colored woman say that she was one of the onions in the wheat of the country; that could not be separated." Anderson found the remark "rather significant!" but he went further:

> Permit me to say that the black man, free or enslaved, pure or mix[ed], is the great National Character of the United States. I have mentioned that he is the producer of all the great staples. Another feature of his character is prominent nationally, I allude to the music of the United States. The world is familiar with it, the plaintive cadence of "Oh Susannah!," the mournful song of "Way down in Tennessee" or the lively strains of "Jim Along a Josey," "Dandy Jim of Caroline," with hundreds of others of the same tenor, constitute the National Music of the United States.[45]

Like onions growing in the wheat, the process of cultural exchange in the formation of American popular culture could not be negated by acts of cultural appropriation or by visions of ethnic autonomy or cultural hegemony. Thomas Wentworth Higginson, an abolitionist commander of South Carolina black troops during the Civil War, found aspects of his antebellum sympathy for Southern slaves challenged by his wartime experiences. Christian patience and forbearance, the virtues of Uncle Tom in the novel and play, also figured prominently in Higginson's imaginative identification with the suffering slaves, and he recorded with satisfaction the spirituals he heard his soldiers sing. But the soldiers knew that their Yankee commander admired their spirituals, and they sensed that he did not admire their frivolous songs. Higginson noted that his soldiers stopped singing such songs (and stopped the dancing that went with them) when he approached their camp fires. But Higginson saw enough of this type of singing and dancing to note that "A few youths from Savannah, who were comparatively men of the world, had learned some of the 'Ethiopian Minstrel' ditties, imported from the North."[46] Higginson's observation takes us to the heart of the matter. Blacks, whether one liked it or not, participated in blackface representations of cultural exchange. Blackface, whether one approved of it or not, provided a theatrical forum within which blacks could, to a degree and never free of the scientific construction of race, talk back and participate in the social representation of an African American self.

Chapter Five

Who Freed the Slaves?
Emancipation and Its Meaning

Ira Berlin

O N January 1, 1863, Abraham Lincoln promulgated his Emancipation
Proclamation.[1] A document whose grand title promised so much
but whose bland words seemed to deliver so little, the Emancipation Proclamation was an enigma from the first. Contemporaries were unsure
whether to condemn it as a failure of idealism or applaud it as a triumph
of *realpolitik*, and the American people have remained similarly divided
ever since. Few officially sponsored commemorations currently mark the
day slaves once called "The Great Jubilee," and, of late, black Americans
have taken to celebrating their liberation on Juneteenth, a previously little-
known marker of the arrival of the Union army in Texas and the announce-
ment of emancipation in the most distant corner of the Confederacy. Unlike
other American icons—the Declaration of Independence and the Constitution, for example—the Emancipation Proclamation is not on regular
display at the National Archives.

For this reason, the public exhibition of the Emancipation Proclamation in January 1993 on the occasion of the 130th anniversary of its issu-
ance was a moment of some note. The exhibit sent thousands of Americans into the streets, where they waited in long lines on frigid January
days to see Lincoln's handiwork. At the end of the five-day exhibit, some
thirty thousand people had filed passed the Proclamation. As visitors left

the Archives' great rotunda, reporters waited with microphones in hand. Before national television audiences, visitors declared themselves deeply moved by the great document. One told a reporter from the *Washington Post* that it had changed his life forever.[2]

Such interest in a document whose faded words cannot be easily seen, let alone deciphered, and whose intricate logic cannot be easily unraveled, let alone comprehended, raises important questions about the role of history in the way Americans think about their racial past and present. It appears that the very inaccessibility of the Emancipation Proclamation makes Lincoln's pronouncement a focal point for conflicting notions about America's racial destiny. For many Americans, both black and white, the Proclamation signifies the distance the American people have traveled from the nightmarish reality of slavery—what one visitor called a "humiliation too painful to speak of." For others, it suggested the distance that had yet to be traversed: "we have to build on the changes that started with our ancestors 130 years ago."[3]

However they viewed the Proclamation, visitors used Lincoln's edict as the occasion to call for rapprochement between black and white in a racially divided nation. Dismissing the notion that Lincoln embodied—rather than transcended—American racism (the greatest "honky" of them all, Julius Lester once declared[4]), the men and women who paraded before the Proclamation saw the document as a balm. It was as if Lincoln, or his words, could reach out across the ages and heal the wound. Mrs. Loretta Carter Hanes, a suburban Washington schoolteacher whose insistent requests for a public presentation of the Proclamation had initiated the exhibit, told reporters of her hope that the display would inaugurate another new birth of freedom.[5]

The exhibit of the Proclamation also brought historians out in force. Meeting in Washington in December 1992, the American Historical Association convened a panel entitled "Black, White, and Lincoln." Professor James M. McPherson of Princeton University delivered the lead paper entitled "Who Freed the Slaves?"[6]

For historians, the issues involved in McPherson's question—and, by implication, Lincoln's proclamation—took on even greater significance because they reflected a larger debate between those who look to the top of the social order for cues in understanding the past and those who look to the bottom. It was an old controversy that had previously appeared in the guise of a contest between social history and political history. Although the categories themselves had lost some of their relevance in the poststructuralist age, the politically charged argument over the very essence of the historical process retained much of its bite.[7]

The question of who freed the slaves thus not only addressed the specific issue of responsibility for emancipation in the American South; it also encompassed contemporary controversies over "Great Men" in the history books and "Great Literature" in the curricular canon. McPherson's paper and the discussion that followed reverberated with sharp condemnations and stout defenses of "white males." Lines between scholars who purportedly gave "workers, immigrants, [and] women" their due and those who refused to acknowledge the "so-called 'non-elite'" were drawn taut. While some celebrated history-from-the-bottom-up and condemned elitism, others called for a recognition of the realities of power and belittled a romanticization of the masses.

The public presentation of the Emancipation Proclamation at the National Archives and the debate among historians at the American Historical Association's meeting marked a rare but salutary confluence of the interests of citizens and scholars alike. Both events addressed conflicting notions about the role of high authority, on the one hand, and the actions of ordinary men and women, on the other, in shaping American society. Both the citizens who queued up outside the National Archives and the scholars who debated the issue within the confines of the historical association's meeting rooms found deep resonance in the exhibition of the Emancipation Proclamation. It gave reason to consider the struggle for a politics (and a history) that is appreciative of ordinary people and respectful of rightful authority in a democratic society. For that reason, it is worth probing the current debate about the largest emancipation of modern times.

The debate over the origins of Civil War emancipation in the American South can be parsed in such a way as to divide historians into two camps: those who understand emancipation primarily as the product of the slaves' struggle to free themselves, and those who see the Great Emancipator's hand at work. James McPherson made precisely such a division. While acknowledging the role of the slaves in their own liberation, he came down heavily on the side of Lincoln's authorship of emancipation, a fact he maintained most ordinary Americans grasped intuitively but one that eluded some scholars whose taste for the complex, the nuanced, and the ironic had blinded them to the obvious. McPherson characterized the critics of Lincoln's preeminence—advocates of what he called the "self-emancipation thesis"—as scholarly populists whose stock in trade was a celebration of the "so-called 'non-elite.'" Such scholars, McPherson implied, denied the historical role of "white males," and perhaps all regularly constituted authority, in a misguided celebration of the masses.

McPherson singled out Vincent Harding as the high priest of the self-emancipationists, declaring Harding's *There Is A River: The Black Struggle for Freedom in America* "almost a Bible" for the revisionists.[8] But there were other culprits, among them Robert F. Engs and myself and my colleagues on the Freedmen and Southern Society Project at the University of Maryland, whose multivolume documentary history, *Freedom,* he termed "the largest scholarly enterprise on the history of emancipation."[9] He gave special attention to Barbara Jeanne Fields, a member of the project who had articulated many of *Freedom's* themes on Ken Burns's TV documentary "The Civil War."[10] Together, these historians were responsible for elevating the "self-emancipation thesis" into what McPherson called "a new orthodoxy."

McPherson discussed corollaries to the new orthodoxy that had important political implications. In portraying Lincoln as more a hindrance than a help to the cause of freedom, the revisionists, McPherson believed, purveyed the pernicious view that white historians had distorted the history of emancipation "to deprive blacks of credit for achieving their own freedom." McPherson cited Robert Engs's contention that the glorification of Lincoln as the Great Emancipator was an attempt to convince black people that "white America" had given them "their freedom [rather] than allow them to realize the *empowerment* that taking it implied."[11] If history was politics carried on by other means, the history of emancipation had deep meaning in contemporary racial politics.

McPherson's concerns were echoed in the protests of other scholars. Mark E. Neely, Jr., editor of the *Lincoln Encyclopedia* and a Pulitzer prize–winning study of Lincoln and civil rights, was angered by those who would "rob Lincoln of the credit for taking a leadership role in emancipation." Like McPherson, Neely believed the proponents of self-emancipation distorted historical understanding by characterizing emancipation as the product of "white men sitting behind desks in Washington, D.C., writing legalistic documents [that] did not really free any particular person." But unlike McPherson, who saw Vincent Harding as the source of the problem, Neely targeted Leon F. Litwack and his *Been in the Storm So Long: The Aftermath of Slavery*. By Neely's count, Litwack mentioned the Emancipation Proclamation "only ten times" in his 625-page book and then "usually in unflattering passages." But Neely also found Litwack to be a willing co-conspirator with the editors of the Freedmen and Southern Society Project. In the most bizarre of charges, Neely claimed to have uncovered the project's agenda in the sequence in which its volumes had been published, finding ideological significance in the fact that series 2 of *Freedom, The Black Military Experience,* was published before the first volume in series 1, *The Destruction of Slavery.* To Neely, the purpose of this bit of historiographic chicanery was the promotion of the new orthodoxy. "The focus, again, was taken off Lincoln's proclamation itself." "After the military volume, in reverse chronological order, the editors dealt with emancipation."[12]

Lincoln's proclamation of January 1, 1863, as its critics have noted, freed not a single slave who was not already entitled to freedom under legislation passed by Congress the previous year. It applied only to the slaves in territories then beyond the reach of Federal authority. It specifically exempted Tennessee and Union-occupied portions of Louisiana and Virginia, and it left slavery in the loyal border states—Delaware, Maryland, Kentucky, and Missouri—untouched. Indeed, in a strict sense, the Proclamation went no further than the Second Confiscation Act of July 1862, which freed all slaves who entered Union lines professing that their owners were disloyal, as well as those slaves who fell under Federal control as Union troops occupied Confederate territory. Moreover, at its fullest, the Emancipation Proclamation rested upon the President's wartime power as commander in chief and was subject to constitutional challenge. Lincoln recognized the limitations of his ill-defined wartime authority, and, as his commitment to emancipation grew firmer in 1863 and 1864, he pressed for passage of a constitutional amendment to affirm slavery's destruction.

What then was the point of the Proclamation? It spoke in muffled tones that heralded not the dawn of universal liberty but the compromised and piecemeal arrival of an undefined freedom. Indeed, the Proclamation's flat prose, ridiculed by the late Richard Hofstadter as having "all the moral grandeur of a bill of lading," suggests that the true authorship of African American freedom lies elsewhere—not at the top of American society but at its base.[13] McPherson, Neely, and others are correct in noting that the editors of the Freedmen and Southern Society Project and other revisionists built upon this insight.

From the first guns at Fort Sumter, the strongest advocates of emancipation were the slaves themselves. Lacking political standing or a public voice, forbidden access to the weapons of war, slaves nevertheless tossed aside the grand pronouncements of Lincoln and other Union leaders that the sectional conflict was only a war for national unity. Instead, they moved directly to put their own freedom—and that of their posterity—atop the national agenda. Steadily, as opportunities arose, slaves risked their all for freedom. By abandoning their owners, coming uninvited into Union lines, and offering their lives and labor in the Federal cause, slaves forced Federal soldiers at the lowest level to recognize their importance to the Union's success. That understanding traveled quickly up the chain of command. In time, it became evident to even the most obtuse Federal commanders that every slave who crossed into Union lines was a double gain: one subtracted from the Confederacy and one added to the Union. The slaves' resolute determination to secure their liberty converted many white Northern Americans—soldiers and civilians alike—to the view that the security of the Union depended upon the destruction of slavery. Eventually, this belief tipped the balance in favor of freedom, even among Yankees who displayed little interest in the question of slavery and no affection for black people.

Slaves were not without allies. Abolitionists, black and white, dismissed the Republican doctrine that slavery should be respected and given constitutional protection where it existed. Instead, abolitionists, like the slaves, saw the war as an opportunity to assault a system they believed was immoral and pressed for its extradition. Rather than condemn slavery from the comfort of their drawing rooms, some radical opponents of slavery volunteered to fight slavery on its own terrain, strapped on their haversacks, and marched south as part of the Union army. But soldiering was young men's work, and sex, age, condition, and circumstance barred many radicals from the Federal army. Most abolitionists could only fume against slavery in petitions, editorials, and sermons. Although their campaign on behalf of emancipation laid the foundation for congressional and then presidential action against slavery, the majority of abolitionists had but slender means to attack slavery directly. Only slaves had both the commitment and the opportunity to initiate the assault on slavery.

Some slaves did not even wait for the war to begin. In March 1861, before the first shots at Fort Sumter, eight runaways presented themselves at Fort Pickens, a federal installation in Florida, "entertaining the idea"— in the words of the fort's commander—that Federal forces "were placed here to protect them and grant them their freedom." The commander believed otherwise and delivered the slaves to the local sheriff, who returned them to their owner.[14] Although their mission failed, these eight runaways were only the first to evince publicly a conviction that eventually became widespread throughout the slave community.

In making the connection between the war and freedom, slaves also understood that a Union victory was imperative. They did what they could to secure it, throwing their full weight behind the Federal cause, volunteering their services as teamsters, stable hands, and boatmen; butchers, bakers, and cooks; nurses, orderlies, and laundresses; blacksmiths, coopers, and carpenters; and, by the tens of thousands, as common laborers. Slaves "tabooed" those few in their ranks who shunned the effort.[15] Hundreds of thousands of black men and women would work for the Union army, and more than 135,000 slave men became Union soldiers. Even deep within the Confederacy, where escape to Federal lines was impossible, slaves did what they could to undermine the Confederacy and strengthen the Union—from aiding escaped Northern prisoners of war to praying for Northern military success. With their loyalty, their labor, and their lives, slaves provided crucial muscle and blood in support of the Federal war effort. No one was more responsible for smashing the shackles of slavery than the slaves.

Still, slaves could not free themselves. Nowhere in the four volumes of *Freedom* do the editors of the Freedmen and Southern Society Project claim they did. Nowhere in the four volumes of *Freedom* is the term *self-emancipation* employed. As far as I can discern, Harding, Litwack, and Engs do not use the term *self-emancipation.* Slaves could—and they did— put the issue of freedom on the wartime agenda; they could—and they did—make certain that the question of their liberation did not disappear in the complex welter of the war; they could—and they did—ensure that there was no retreat from the commitment to emancipation once the issue was drawn. In short, they did what was in their power to do with the weapons they had. They could not vote, pass laws, issue field orders, or promulgate great proclamations. That was the realm of citizens, legislators, military officers, and the president. However, the actions of the slaves made it possible and necessary for citizens, legislators, military officers, and the president to act. Slaves were the prime movers in the emancipation drama, not the sole movers. Slaves set others in motion, including many who would never have moved if left to their own devices. How they did so is nothing less than the story of emancipation.[16]

Among the slaves' first students were Union soldiers of the lowest rank. Arriving in the South with little direct knowledge of slavery and often contemptuous of black people, Federal soldiers encountered slaves who were eager to test their owners' fulminations against Yankee abolitionists and black Republicans. Union soldiers soon found their camps inundated with slaves, often breathless, tattered, and bearing marks of abuse who were seeking sanctuary and offering to assist them in any way possible. In so doing, slaves took a considerable risk. They not only faced sure punishment if captured, but Union soldiers often turned upon them violently.

Still, some gained entry into Federal lines, where they found work aplenty. Sometimes the slaves' labor cut to the heart of the soldiers' military mission, as slaves understood that the enemy of their enemy was their friend and were pleased to impart information about Confederate troop movements, assist in the construction of Federal fortifications, and guide Union troops through a strange countryside. But just as often, slaves ingratiated themselves with Federal troops in ways that had no particular military significance. They foraged for firewood, cooked food, cleaned camps, and did dozens of onerous jobs that otherwise would have fallen to the soldiers themselves.

Northern soldiers did not have to be Free-Soilers, abolitionists, or even radical egalitarians to appreciate these valuable services. Thus, soldiers were dismayed to discover that they had violated orders by harboring the fugitives. They were more upset when the men and women who cleaned their camps and cooked their food were dragged off to certain punishment by angry masters or mistresses. Indeed, even those soldiers who stoutly maintained that they fought only for Union bitterly resented being implicated in the punishment of men and women who had done nothing more than do them a good turn in exchange for a blanket and a few morsels of food. "I don't care a damn for the darkies," declared one midwestern volunteer in March 1862, "but I couldn't help to send a run-

away nigger back. I'm blamed if I could."[17] The "blame" many Union soldiers felt at being implicated in slavery was compounded by their outrage
when they discovered that the very same men and women they had returned to bondage were being mobilized by the Confederate enemy against
them. To Union soldiers, the folly of denying themselves the resources
that their enemy used freely—indeed, assisting their enemy in maintaining those resources—seemed senseless to the point of absurdity.

These same lessons were also learned by Federal officers. The protection and employment offered to fugitive slaves by individual Northern
soldiers created numerous conflicts between slaveholders and the Union
army, embroiling officers in disagreeable contests whose resolution required
considerable time and effort. Slaveholders, many of them brandishing
Unionist credentials, demanded that Northern troops return fugitives who
had taken refuge within their encampments. If regimental officers could
not or would not comply, they blustered about connections that reached
the highest level in Washington. Generally, the bluster was just that. But
often enough, the officers soon felt the weight of high authority upon
them. Officers of the middle ranks not only bore the brunt of the soldier's
frustrations with Federal policy but also the sting of official rebuke. Made
apologists for policies that they too believed contradicted experience and
good sense, many field officers found themselves in the uncomfortable
position of having to enforce that which they disdained. They objected
particularly to being compelled to do the slave master's dirty work, and
they intensely disliked being demeaned before their men. The high-handed
demands of slave owners turned many Federal officers into the slaves' champion. When Federal policy toward fugitive slaves finally changed in the
summer of 1862, one could hear an almost-audible sigh of relief from the
Union officer corps. "This thing of guarding rebels property has about
'played out.' . . . We have guarded their homes and property long enough.
. . . The only way to put down this rebellion is to hurt the instigators and
abettors of it. Slavery must be cleaned out."[18]

Faced with conflicting demands—the need for labor versus the require-
ments of Federal policy, the desire to protect hapless fugitives versus the
demands of Unionist owners—many Union soldiers and officers searched
for ways to stand clear of the entire business, to be, in the idiom of the
day, neither slave catcher nor slave stealer. Union policy toward slaves
beginning in the fall of 1861 through the spring of 1862 was designed to
eliminate the "devilish nigger question," as one Maryland official called it,

by excluding fugitive slaves from Union lines. But slaves refused to surrender their belief that the Federal army was a refuge from slavery; they would not allow Federal soldiers to evade the central reality of the war.

Slaves continued to press themselves on soldiers, bringing gifts of food, information, and of course labor. There always seemed to be a few Yankee soldiers who, for whatever reason, sheltered runaways, and a handful who encouraged slave flight. But even when the fugitives were denied entry to Federal lines, they camped outside, just far enough away to avoid expulsion by Union commanders, just close enough to avoid capture by Confederate soldiers. Meanwhile, alert for ways to turn the military conflict to their own advantage, slaves continued to search the seams of Federal policy looking for an opening: the ascent of a sympathetic commander or a crisis that might inflate the value of their knowledge or their muscle. Many learned the letter of the law so that they could seemingly recite from memory passages from the House Resolution of 1861, the additional Article of War of March 1862, the First Confiscation Act of August 1861, or the Second Confiscation Act of July 1862. Time and time again, slaves forced Federal soldiers and officers to make the choice, a choice that became easier as the Union army's need for labor grew. Change did not come at once, but it came.

The lessons slaves taught soldiers and soldiers taught officers slowly ascended the Union chain of command and in November 1861 reached Lincoln's cabinet for the first time. Secretary of War Simon Cameron publicly endorsed a proposal to arm slaves to fight for the Union and freedom.[19] Lincoln quieted Cameron and packed him off to Russia as minister, but the slaves continued undeterred to press their case.

The slow shift in Federal policy gained momentum as the Union army penetrated deeper into the Confederacy, where slaveholders were not reluctant Unionists but outright rebels. In these circumstances, some field commanders became quick learners. Their respect for the old order yielded to a willingness to challenge the rights of the master and finally to a firm determination to extirpate slavery. Others learned slowly, imperfectly, or not at all. However, before long, the most obdurate generals began to disappear from places of high command, and the quick studies rose to the top.

The broad outline of the story was always the same. Slaves forced the issue: what should be done with them? Deciding the matter was always difficult, for it required a choice between the contradictory interests of the master and of the slave. At first slaveholders held the upper hand, but in time the advantage slipped to the slaves. When the slaves' loyalty became more valuable than the masters' in the eyes of Federal authorities, the Federal army became the slaves' willing partner rather than its reluctant enemy. The process by which the Union army became an army of liberation was in its essence political and reveals how black people had been incorporated into American politics long before they had the vote, the right to petition, or independent standing at law.

But if the story was always the same, it was also always different. Individuals made a difference. A few generals—John C. Frémont, David Hunter, John W. Phelps—openly advertised their Free-Soil and abolitionist convictions; some generals, especially in the border states, were themselves slaveholders or sympathizers, and others were tied to the Democratic party; many, like William Tecumseh Sherman, would have preferred to avoid the "negro problem," although Sherman had his own understanding of the relationship of slavery to the war.

But the beliefs of individual field commanders and their willingness to act on them only partially accounted for differences in the evolution of Federal policy; the story also differed from place to place and changed over time. Acceptance of the slaves' truth generally came quickest in the Confederate heartland. Marching through Alabama in May 1862, Gen. Ormsby M. Mitchel considered that the "negroes are our only friends," an insight he quickly shared with Secretary of War Edwin M. Stanton, whose own evolution to an advocate of emancipation was proceeding apace in the spring and summer of 1862.[20] Doubtless the greatest change came with the enlistment of black soldiers and later news of their battlefield valor at Fort Wagner, Port Hudson, and Milliken's Bend.

The slaves' lesson, moreover, did not travel merely within the military chain of command. As news of the war filtered northward, it moved outside of military lines entirely. In their letters home, citizen-soldiers not only informed the Northern public; they formed Northern opinion. At a time when rumor competed with gossip and hopes with wishes, perhaps nothing carried as much weight as the opinion of a husband, father, or son battling the enemy. Thus, the lesson slaves had taught soldiers reverberated in general-store gossip, newspaper editorials, and sermons throughout the North. It seemed particularly compelling to wives who wanted their husbands home and to parents who were fearful for their sons. It appealed to Northerners who were tired of the war and fearful of the

Federal government's seemingly insatiable appetite for young men. Many white Northerners enlisted in the slaves' cause even though they feared and despised black people. In August 1862, Governor Samuel J. Kirkwood of Iowa, no friend of abolition, put the matter bluntly in commenting on the possible employment of slave laborers. "When this war is over & we have summed up the entire loss of life it has imposed on the country I shall not have regrets if it is found that a part of the dead are *niggers* and *all* are not white men."[21]

The lesson that slaves taught common soldiers, that common soldiers taught officers, that officers taught field commanders, that field commanders taught their desk-bound superiors in Washington, and that resonated in the North was not wasted on Abraham Lincoln. In many ways, Lincoln was a slow learner, but he learned.

Lincoln was no friend of slavery. He believed, as he said many times, that "if slavery is not wrong, nothing is wrong." But, as president, Lincoln also believed he had a constitutional obligation not to interfere with slavery where it existed. Shortly before his inauguration, he offered to support a proposed constitutional amendment that would have prohibited any subsequent amendment authorizing Congress "to abolish or interfere . . . with the domestic institutions" of any state, including slavery."[22] As wartime leader, he feared the disaffection of the loyal slave states, which he understood to be critical to the success of the Union. He crafted much of his wartime policy respecting slavery to avoid alienating loyal slaveholders, especially in Kentucky, Missouri, and Maryland. "I think to lose Kentucky is nearly the same as to lose the whole game," Lincoln wrote to Orville H. Browning, the senator from Illinois, in the fall of 1861. "Kentucky gone, we can not hold Missouri, nor, as I think, Maryland. These all against us, and the job on our hands is too large for us." Lincoln needed the border states, and even courted slaveholders in tiny Delaware, where fewer than two thousand black people remained in slavery.[23]

But Lincoln's solicitude for the concerns of slaveholders, particularly Whiggish ones, went beyond the strategic importance of the border states and the fear that if they opted for secession, or refused to furnish soldiers to the Federal cause, the Union would be indefensible. Throughout the war, Lincoln held tight to the notion that Whiggish slaveholders retained a residual loyalty to the Union and could be weaned away from the Confederacy. Much of his policy in wartime Louisiana was crafted precisely toward this end, and this premise would shape his plans for postwar Reconstruction.[24]

Lincoln also doubted whether white and black could live as equals in American society and thought it best for black people to remove themselves physically from the United States.[25] Like many white Americans from Thomas Jefferson to Henry Clay, Lincoln favored the colonization of former slaves in Africa or elsewhere. At his insistence, the congressional legislation providing for the emancipation of slaves in the District of Columbia in April 1862 included a $100,000 appropriation to aid the removal of liberated slaves who wished to leave the United States. The Second Confiscation Act added another half million dollars to the funds for the same purpose. Through the end of 1862, Lincoln continually connected emancipation in the border states to the idea of colonizing slaves somewhere beyond the boundaries of the United States. Lincoln clung to the policy of expatriating black people long after most had abandoned it as a reasonable strategy to gain acceptance for emancipation or as a practical policy to address the consequences of emancipation.[26]

Where others led on emancipation, Lincoln followed. Lincoln responded slowly to demands for emancipation as they rose through the military chain of command and as they echoed on the Northern home front. Even as pressure for emancipation grew in the spring of 1862, Lincoln continued to urge gradual, compensated emancipation. The compensation would be to slaveholders for property lost, not to slaves for labor stolen. In late September 1862, even while announcing that he would proclaim emancipation on January 1 if the rebellious states did not return to the Union, he again called for gradual, compensated emancipation in the border states and compensation for loyal slaveholders elsewhere. The preliminary emancipation proclamation also reiterated his support for colonizing freed slaves "upon this continent or elsewhere."[27] While some pressed for the enlistment of black soldiers, Lincoln doubted the capacity of black men for military service, fearing that former slaves would simply turn their guns over to their old masters.

As black laborers became essential to the Union war effort and as demands to enlist black men in the Federal army mounted, the pressure for emancipation became inexorable. By the summer of 1862, Lincoln understood the importance of the sable arm as well as any. On July 12, making yet another plea for gradual, compensated emancipation in the Union's own slave states, Lincoln bluntly warned border-state congressmen that slavery was doomed "by mere friction and abrasion—by the mere incidents of the war," and that it would be impossible to restore the Union with slavery in place.[28] Ignored once again, Lincoln acted on his own advice. In late July 1862, five days after signing the Second Confiscation and the Militia acts, he issued an executive order translating the new legislation into instructions for the Union army and navy. He authorized military commanders operating in the seceded states to "seize and use any property, real or personal, which may be necessary or convenient for . . . military purposes," and he instructed them to "employ as laborers . . . so many persons of African descent as can be advantageously used for military and naval purposes." Although he also reiterated the customary injunctions against wanton or malicious destruction of private property, there was no mistaking the import of Lincoln's order.[29]

Lincoln had decided to act. On July 22, he informed the cabinet of his intention to issue a proclamation of general emancipation. The slaves' determination had indeed made every policy short of emancipation untenable.[30] To those who might raise a voice in opposition, Lincoln declared that he could not fight "with elder-stalk squirts, charged with rose water. . . ." "This government," he added on the last of July 1862, "cannot much longer play a game in which it stakes all, and its enemies stake nothing."[31]

On January 1, 1863, Lincoln fulfilled his promise to free all slaves in the states still in rebellion. Had another Republican been in Lincoln's place, that person doubtless would have done the same. Without question, some would have acted more expeditiously and with greater bravado. Without question, some would have acted more cautiously and with lesser resolve. In the end, Lincoln did what needed to be done. Others might be left behind; Lincoln would not. It does no disservice to Lincoln—or to anyone else—to say that his claim to greatness rests upon his willingness to act when the moment was right.

When Lincoln finally acted, he moved with confidence and determination. He stripped the final Emancipation Proclamation of any reference to compensation for former slaveholders or colonization for former slaves.[32] He added provisions that allowed for the service of black men in the Union army and navy. The Proclamation opened the door to the eventual enlistment of more than 179,000 black men, most of them former slaves. More than anything else, the enlistment of black men, slave as well as free, transformed the Federal army into an army of liberation. At war's end, the number of black men in Federal uniform was larger than the number of soldiers in Lee's Army of Northern Virginia. Military enlistment became the surest solvent of slavery, extending to places the Emancipation Proclamation did not reach, especially the loyal slave states. Once slave men entered the Union army, they were free and they made it clear that they expected their families to be free as well. In March 1865, Congress confirmed this understanding and provided for the freedom of the immediate families of all black soldiers. Lincoln's actions, however tardy, gave force to all that the slaves had risked. The Emancipation Proclamation transformed the war in ways only the president could. After January 1, 1863, the Union army marched for freedom, and Lincoln was its commander.[33]

Lincoln understood the importance of his role, both politically and morally—just as the slaves had understood theirs.[34] Having determined to free the slaves, Lincoln declared he would not take back the Emancipation Proclamation even when military failure and political reversals threatened that policy. He repudiated his misgivings about the military abilities of black soldiers and became one of their great supporters. Lincoln praised the role of black soldiers in preserving the Union and ending chattel bondage and vowed not to "betray" them. The growing presence of black men in the Union army deepened Lincoln's commitment to emancipation. "There have been men who proposed to me to return to slavery the black warriors of Port Hudson & Olustee to . . . conciliate the South," Lincoln reflected in August 1864. "I should be damned in time & in eternity for doing so."[35] Lincoln later suggested that black soldiers might have the vote, perhaps his greatest concession to racial equality.[36] To secure the freedom that his proclamation had promised, Lincoln pressed for the final liquidation of slavery in the Union's own slave states where diehards obstructed and delayed. To that end and to write freedom into the nation's highest charter, Lincoln promoted passage of the Thirteenth Amendment, although he did not live to see its ratification.

The Emancipation Proclamation's place in the drama of emancipation is thus secure—as is Lincoln's. To deny it is to ignore the intense struggle by which freedom arrived. It is to ignore the Union soldiers who sheltered slaves, the abolitionists who stumped for emancipation, and the thousands of men and women who, like Lincoln, changed their minds as slaves made the case for universal liberty. Reducing the Emancipation Proclamation to a nullity and Lincoln to a cipher denies human agency just as personifying emancipation in a larger-than-life Great Emancipator denies the agency of the slaves and many others, and trivializes the process by which the slaves were freed. And, as in many other cases, process is critical.

Both Lincoln and the slaves played their parts in the drama of emancipation. Denying their complementary roles limits understanding of the complex interaction of human agency and events that resulted in slavery's demise. The editors of *Freedom*, who have sought to make the slaves central to the study of emancipation, have tried to expand the terrain of historical understanding, documenting the *process* by which freedom arrived. They have maintained that the slaves were the prime movers of emancipation; they do not believe they were the only movers, and nowhere do they deny Lincoln's importance to the events that culminated in universal freedom. In fact, rather than single out slaves or exclude Lincoln (as the term *self-emancipation* implies), the editors argue for the significance of others as well: white Union soldiers—few of them racial egalitarians—who saw firsthand how slavery weakened the Union cause; their families and friends in the North, eager for Federal victory, who learned from these soldiers the strength the Confederate regime drew from bonded labor; the Northern men and women, most of whom had no connection with the abolition movement, who acted upon such news to petition Congress; and the congressmen and senators who eventually moved in favor of freedom. This roster, of course, does not include all those involved in the social and political process that ended slavery in the American South. It omits the slaveholders, no bit players in the drama. Taken as a whole, however, the new understanding of emancipation does suggest something of the complexity of the process by which freedom arrived and the limitation of seeing slavery's end as the product of any one individual—or element—in the social order.

Emphasizing that emancipation was not the work of one hand underscores the force of contingency, the crooked course by which universal freedom arrived. It captures the ebb and flow of events which, at times, placed Lincoln among the opponents of emancipation and then propelled him to the forefront of freedom's friends. It emphasizes the clash of wills that is the essence of politics, whether it involves enfranchised legislators or voteless slaves. Politics, perforce, necessitates an on-the-ground struggle among different interests, not the unfolding of a single idea or perspective, whether that of an individual or an age. Lincoln, no less than the meanest slave, acted upon changing possibilities as he understood them. The very same events—secession and war—that gave the slaves' actions new meaning also gave Lincoln's actions new meaning. To think that Lincoln could have anticipated these changes—or, more strangely still, somehow embodied them—imbues him with a power over the course of events that no human being has ever enjoyed. Lincoln was part of history, not above it. Whatever he believed about slavery in 1861, Lincoln did not see the war as an instrument of emancipation.[37] The slaves did. Lincoln's commitment to emancipation changed with time because it had to. The slaves' commitment to universal freedom never wavered because it could not.

Complexity—contrary to McPherson—is not ambivalence or ambiguity. To tell the whole story, to follow that crooked course, does not diminish the clarity of an argument or mystify it into a maze of "nuance, paradox, or irony." Telling the entire tale is not a form of obfuscation. If done right, it clarifies precisely because it consolidates the mass of competing claims under a single head. Elegance or simplicity of argument is useful only when it encompasses all of the evidence, not when it excludes or narrows it.

In the perennial tests in which constituted authority searches for the voice of the people and when the people are testing the measure of their leaders, it is well to recall the relationship of both to securing freedom's greatest victory. In this sense, slaves were right in celebrating January 1, 1863, as the Day of Jubilee. As Loretta Hanes noted 130 years later, "It meant so much to people because it was a ray of light, the hope of a new day coming. And it gave them courage."[38] Indeed, the Emancipation Proclamation reminds all—both those viewing its faded pages and those studying it—that real change derives both from the actions of the people and from the imprimatur of constituted authority. It teaches that "social" history is no less political than "political" history, for it too rests upon the bending of wills, which is the essence of politics, and that no political process is determined by a single individual. If the Emancipation Proclamation speaks to the central role of constituted authority—in the person of Abraham Lincoln—in making history, it speaks no less loudly to the role of ordinary men and women, seizing the moment to make the world according to their own understanding of justice and human decency. The connection between the two should not be forgotten.

Chapter Six

ॐ

Quandaries of Command:
Ulysses S. Grant and Black Soldiers

BROOKS D. SIMPSON

M OST historians of the American Civil War once either ignored or
minimized the role that black soldiers and sailors played in preserving the Union. In characterizing the struggle as a war between brothers, they overlooked the fact that some of the "brothers" were black. Recent studies, building upon the foundations provided by the work of
George W. Williams and Dudley Cornish, have examined the experience
of blacks in uniform and the relationship between black soldiers and white
officers. The initial volume of the highly acclaimed documentary history
of emancipation, *Freedom,* concerned African Americans in uniform; the
movie *Glory* shared the story of the 54th Massachusetts and the battle of
Fort Wagner with an eager audience. Americans today, white and black,
are far more aware than they were a generation ago of the role taken by
African Americans in fighting for their freedom during the Civil War.[1]

In their eagerness to rediscover the black military experience, historians have concentrated on the consequences of military service for blacks
and for the whites who commanded them. Scholars view the enlistment
of blacks as a laboratory for social change, a microcosm of the shifting
racial relationships caused by the impact of war and emancipation. Yet
there were other dimensions to the role of black soldiers in the war. Generals had to answer questions involving their use as combat soldiers, as

support personnel working behind the lines, and as an occupation force. These specific issues in turn place the issue of employing black troops in the wider context of civil and military policy during and after the war. The use of black soldiers in occupation duty in the postwar South, for example, remains mostly an untold story, although their employment in such duties caused much controversy. By examining the issues surrounding the deployment of black regiments within the context of larger policies and problems of command, we gain a better sense of the conflicting pressures upon white commanders as they sought to grapple with the implications of arming African Americans.

One general who dealt with many of the issues surrounding the employment of black troops was Ulysses S. Grant. As his divisions moved south along the Mississippi valley, Grant confronted the fact that the army of national reunification was also an army of emancipation. By the end of 1862 he embraced this mission; the following year his command played a major role not only in liberating blacks but also in enlisting them in the Union army. He grappled with issues of how best to use black soldiers, whether to use them in combat, and how to respond to reports of Confederate mistreatment of black prisoners. As general in chief, Grant grasped the importance of black soldiers to winning the war, for their swelling numbers would go far to compensate for the decline in Union manpower caused by heavy casualties, expiring enlistments, and the inferior quality of many conscripts and bounty hunters who comprised more and more of his army. After Appomattox, he confronted the problem of trying to balance a policy of reconciliation toward Southern whites with the fact that a large part of his occupation force would be black. His responses to these challenges suggested both the possibilities and the boundaries for blacks not just in military service but also in Reconstruction America, a dilemma shaped in part by the priorities of white policy makers.[2]

Grant was no early convert to the notion of enlisting blacks in the Union army. When the subject was first discussed in 1862, he recalled, he "was bitterly, very bitterly, opposed."[3] Arming blacks, he reasoned, would embitter Southern whites, further complicating the difficulties of reconciliation inherent in a war for reunion. Convinced of the staunchness of Southern recalcitrance as he struggled with the problems of occupation in western Tennessee in 1862, Grant dropped his earlier reservations about emancipation and its consequences, for he came to believe that the only way to overcome the intensity of Southern resistance was to escalate the Union war effort and broaden the scope of the conflict. By the end of 1862, with an eye toward the future, he had provided for the establishment of refugee camps. Explaining his plan to Chaplain John Eaton of the 27th Ohio, Grant remarked that once the black dispelled the notion that he would not work except under coercion, "it would be very easy to put a musket in his hands and make a soldier of him, and if he fought well, eventually to put the ballot in his hand and make him a citizen."[4]

During the next several months, whatever thoughts Grant had of enlisting blacks took a back seat to his efforts to capture Vicksburg. Reports that several of his officers were hostile to blacks and opposed to their emancipation made their way back to Washington; at a time when Grant found himself under fire for his failure to take Vicksburg, these reports did little to lessen the precarious nature of his position. At the end of March, General in Chief Henry W. Halleck decided to offer Grant some advice. Over the past year, Halleck noted, the administration had dropped the notion of fighting a limited war, one that did not affect slavery except when necessary, in an effort to forge a reconciliationist peace. Now, Confederate resources and citizens could be considered just as legitimate military targets as were the Confederate soldiers themselves: one way or another, the Confederacy must be defeated, and if that involved a direct attack on slavery, so be it. The Emancipation Proclamation and other policies adopted by the Lincoln administration and Congress marked this change in thinking. One of these new measures called for the raising of black regiments. Lincoln, Halleck wrote, wanted "to use the negroes of the South so far as practicable as a military force for the defense of forts, depots, &c." The general added that "those who have examined the question without passion or prejudice" believed that blacks would fight well. Officers who opposed such measures would be deprived of their commands—and there had been rumors that some of Grant's generals might be among that number. To assist Grant in the raising of black regiments, Secretary of War Edwin M. Stanton dispatched Adjutant General Lorenzo Thomas to the Mississippi valley in the spring of 1863. The war secretary directed Thomas to inform Grant of "the importance attached by the Government to the use of the colored population emancipated by the president's proclamation, and particularly for the organization of their labor and military strength."[5]

Grant responded to these messages by ordering his commanders to gather black refugees with an eye toward recruiting them for military service. He welcomed Thomas at headquarters, arranged for his soldiers to hear Thomas publicly promulgate the new policy, and quelled whatever concerns Thomas and others had had about his support of the new policy. The adjutant general reported that Grant and his generals "are perfectly willing and ready to afford every aid in carrying it out to a successful issue," although some, including Sherman, did so quite reluctantly. Grant made it clear, however, "that all Commanders will especially exert themselves in carrying out the policy of the Administration, not only in organizing colored regiments and rendering them efficient, but also in removing prejudice against them."[6]

"At least three of my Army Corps Commanders take hold of the new policy of arming the negroes and using them against the rebels with a will," Grant told Halleck. "They at least are so much of soldiers as to feel themselves under obligations to carry out a policy (which they would not inaugurate) in the same good faith and with the same zeal as if it was of their own choosing." Not all the officers and men in Grant's command proved as ready as he to adapt to the new situation; by the end of the month several officers had resigned, and Grant recommended instead that they be dismissed from the service. He supported Col. Isaac F. Shepard's decision to whip a white soldier in retaliation for his having abused black soldiers. He also took steps to make sure that the authorities in Washington were informed of his support for enlisting blacks. "I have given the subject of the arming of the negro my hearty support," he assured Lincoln. "This, with the emancipation of the negro, is the heaviest blow yet given to the Confederacy. . . . By arming the negro we have added a powerful ally. They will make good soldiers and taking them from the enemy weakens him in the same proportion they strengthen us." In fact, he wanted to enlist as many as he could, especially after the fall of Vicksburg on July 4, 1863 gave him new territory to guard. "I am anxious to get as many of these negro regiments as possible and to have them full and completely equipped," he told Thomas; the adjutant general wired Washington that Grant gave him "every assistance in my work."[7]

Grant chose to use the new black regiments to guard posts and build fortifications. During the hot summer months of 1863 he wanted to spare his white soldiers from such endeavors. Such a decision seemed wise in light of the black recruits' lack of training; yet it also betrayed notions that

blacks were somehow better equipped than whites were to withstand ill-
ness in hot areas (although they might well possess immunities to local
diseases that white farmers and clerks from the Old Northwest lacked). It
would keep the new regiments apart from their white counterparts, thus
avoiding possible friction. Finally, Grant's decision was in accordance with
the preferences expressed by Lorenzo Thomas, and it addressed President
Lincoln's concern about the treatment of black prisoners of war by removing black units from frontline duty, thus minimizing their chances for
combat.[8]

Black regiments, regardless of their mission to guard rear areas and
garrison captured areas, were soon thrust into combat situations. One of
the first engagements involving black troops took place on June 7, 1863, at
Milliken's Bend, Louisiana, where two recently raised black regiments
and a white regiment came under attack. In fierce hand-to-hand combat
they battled the Confederates until the arrival of Union gunboats forced
the rebels to retreat. "Their conduct is said . . . to have been most gallant,"
Grant reported, "and I doubt not but with good officers they will make
good troops." Events bore out his prediction. In engagements near Vicksburg, he remarked, "the negro troops whipped the rebels wherever they
met."[9]

After Milliken's Bend, Grant learned of reports that some black soldiers taken prisoner at that clash, along with a white officer and a ser-
geant, had been executed. "I feel no inclination to retaliate for the offenses
of irresponsible persons," he informed Confederate commander Richard
Taylor, "but if it is the policy of any General entrusted with the command
of troops to show 'no quarter,' or to punish with death prisoners taken in
battle, I will accept the issue." If Confederate authorities proposed "a different line of policy towards Black troops and Officers commanding them to
that practiced towards White troops," he stated that all Union authorities
"are bound to give the same protection to these troops that they do to any
other troops." Taylor denied the allegations, but added that Confederate
policy required that black prisoners be turned over to civil authorities.
Grant, accepting Taylor's denial at face value, nevertheless could not "see
the justice of permitting one treatment for [black soldiers], and another
for the white soldiers. This however is a subject I am not aware of any
action having been taken upon." For the moment he let the matter rest.[10]

By the fall of 1863 Grant had become a full-fledged convert to the raising of black regiments. He told one young officer that blacks "would make

the best class of soldiers." Although "some prejudices still existed" against enlisting blacks, Grant believed that "they were rapidly passing away." In fact, he believed that they were "easier to preserve discipline among than our White troops and I doubt not will prove equally good for garrison duty." He assured Halleck that "All that have been tried have fought bravely."[11] Such findings were reassuring to a man who would need all the men he could get when he was named general in chief in March 1864.

After achieving that rank, Grant continued to encourage the raising of black regiments. But he was not happy with the efforts of some Northern governors, especially John A. Andrew of Massachusetts, to use black enlistments to fill their own manpower quotas—and thus reduce their state's obligations. "The negroes brought within our lines are rightfully recruits to the United States Service and should not go to benefit any particular state," he protested. Once more he viewed their primary responsibility as garrison duty, which would free white soldiers for the front. He urged deploying black units along the west bank of the Mississippi River to guard that river and adjoining plantations. Similar orders went out to Nathaniel Banks regarding garrisons along the Rio Grande. Whenever possible, Grant sought to place black soldiers under commanders who "will take an active interest in this work."[12]

When it came to employing black soldiers in combat, however, Grant hesitated. Although they had proved themselves in the Mississippi valley, he first refrained from using them versus the Army of Northern Virginia in 1864. One division of Ambrose E. Burnside's Ninth Corps, commanded by Brig. Gen. Edward Ferrero, was composed of newly raised black regiments; it guarded the extensive supply trains of the Army of the Potomac. Grant thought so highly of Ferrero's services that he urged his reappointment as a brigadier when the Senate failed to confirm his nomination. Not only had Ferrero "protected our immense wagon train with a Division of undisciplined Colored troops" and detachments of dismounted cavalry, he had also "disciplined his troops at the same time so that they come through to the James River better prepared to go into battle than if they had been at a quiet school of instruction at the same time." By the time he believed Ferrero's men were ready for combat, however, the siege of Petersburg was under way. He wanted to transfer the division to Benjamin F. Butler's Army of the James, where it would join other black units that had participated in the opening attacks on Petersburg. As siege operations commenced in June, Grant ordered the transfer of the Nineteenth Corps, which included both black and white troops, to the Virginia front.[13]

The heavy casualties of the Wilderness campaign made Grant reconsider his stance on committing black units in combat. Black regiments from Butler's Army of the James participated in the initial battles around Petersburg, acquitting themselves well. Their performance encouraged Grant to consider a larger role for them. Before long an opportunity presented itself. During the last week of June, Lt. Col. Henry Pleasants of the 48th Pennsylvania Infantry proposed digging a mine under the Confederate position south of Petersburg's Blandford Church, packing it with powder, and exploding a hole in the enemy defenses. Burnside, whose Ninth Corps included Pleasants's regiment, decided that the ensuing assault should be conducted by Ferrero's well-rested black division. In preparation, Ferrero rehearsed his men in the plan of assault, which called for the lead elements to exploit the hoped-for hole in the Confederate lines by rolling up the Confederate flanks and pushing through to the rebel rear. The black soldiers eagerly awaited their opportunity to spearhead an offensive which, if successful, might result in the fall of Petersburg. For his part, Grant instructed George G. Meade to make sure that Burnside "should have all the material at hand in readiness to load his mines in the shortest time." The commanding general hoped to coordinate Burnside's assault with another blow at Lee's lines east of Richmond.[14]

On the eve of the assault, however, Meade had a change of heart about Burnside's plans. Meade, who had never displayed much confidence in the mine, decided that the black division could not lead the assault. Whether this decision stemmed from reservations about the fighting abilities of the black soldier is unclear; Meade justified it by claiming that if the assault ended in disaster, the Union high command would be accused of throwing blacks away in a fruitless slaughter. Grant backed Meade. Burnside, frustrated, left it to the commanders of his three white divisions to decide who would lead that assault. James H. Ledlie was chosen by lot. A poorer choice could not have been made, for Ledlie was not only incompetent but liked to fortify himself with alcohol before battle. Grant knew of this decision but inexplicably failed to intervene, although he judged Ledlie the worst of Burnside's divisional commanders.[15] What followed is well known. The explosion created a gap in the Confederate entrenchments, but Ledlie's men failed to exploit the breach, and Burnside's other divisions, including Ferrero's men, piled into the crater. Once the Confederates recovered from the initial shock, they surrounded the crater, making the position untenable, and Burnside's men withdrew after sustaining terrible losses.

"So fair an opportunity will probably never occur again for carrying fortifications," Grant told Meade. To Halleck he made clear his frustration: "It was the saddest affair I have witnessed in this war." He was so disappointed that he actually fell ill. But the commanding general had no one but himself to blame. Aware of the friction between Burnside and Meade, he failed to intervene, allowing others to bungle a chance to break the stalemate in front of Petersburg. In retrospect he judged that the assault would have been successful had Ferrero's men been employed in the first wave. But, like Meade, he believed "that if we put the colored troops in front . . . and it should prove a failure, it would then be said, and very properly, that we were shoving those people ahead to get killed because we did not care anything about them."[16]

Butler, angry at Meade's dismissal of the fighting qualities of black soldiers, urged Grant to give his black units a chance. The chance came at the end of September when Butler's men launched an assault against Forts Gilmer and Harrison, making inroads against the Confederate position but failing to crack the defenses. During the battle Grant visited a black brigade belonging to the Tenth Corps. "As soon as Grant was known to be approaching," recalled one officer, "every man was on his feet & quiet, breathless quiet, prevailed. A cheer could never express what we felt."[17] They were simply returning the trust Grant had placed in them by featuring black units in the assault.

Before long Grant had an opportunity to repay the tribute. He had always been adamant about the treatment of Union prisoners of war, regardless of their skin color. When in April 1864 he heard reports that Confederates had butchered surrendered black soldiers at Ft. Pillow, Tennessee, he responded, "If our men have been murdered after capture retaliation must be resorted to promptly." In this instance he was overruled; he would not be so again. He had refused to engage in prisoner exchanges so long as the Confederates refused to consider captured black soldiers as subject to exchange; in the aftermath of the clashes at Forts Harrison and Gilmer he received yet another opportunity to state his position when Confederate commander Robert E. Lee proposed an exchange of prisoners "with a view of alleviating the sufferings of our soldiers." Grant responded by inquiring whether Lee was prepared to include black prisoners in the exchange. When Lee replied that he could not include "negroes belonging to our Citizens," Grant, pointing out that the United States "is bound to secure to all persons received into her Armies the rights due to soldiers," declined the offer.[18]

Several weeks later, Grant learned that Lee was using black prisoners to work on his fortifications around Fort Gilmer, where they might fall under fire. In retaliation, he approved Butler's decision to put Confederate prisoners of war to work on the Dutch Gap Canal within range of Confederate fire. Lee defended Confederate policy regarding the employment of black prisoners of war on the front lines, although he distinguished between free blacks, who were treated just like other prisoners of war, and former slaves, who were to be returned to their masters. The latter, he insisted, could be used by the Confederate army until their owners came to claim them. In reply, Grant demanded equal treatment for all United States prisoners, white and black, free and freed. Although he found recourse to retaliatory measures regrettable, he insisted that it was his duty "to protect all persons received into the United States, regardless of color or Nationality."[19]

Grant often struggled with his subordinates about recruiting and employing black soldiers. Perhaps William T. Sherman, Grant's closest colleague, posed the biggest problem. Sherman had grumbled about the policy when Lorenzo Thomas visited the Mississippi valley; to those who pointed out that a black man could stop a bullet as well as a white man, he retorted that a cotton bale was better than either. No black regiments accompanied him on his advance against Atlanta, and he ignored Grant's advice as to drawing upon the freedmen as he moved southward. When he heard of the Fort Pillow massacre, he expressed shock not at the murder of black prisoners but at the fact that the fort was occupied in the first place. He refused to use black soldiers to garrison Savannah after its capture in December 1864, telling Grant that the city's residents would be "dreadfully alarmed. . . . Now no matter what the Negro soldiers are, you know that people have prejudices which must be regarded. Prejudice like Religion cannot be discussed." Edwin M. Stanton, who visited Sherman in Savannah, reported that the general "does not seem to appreciate the importance of this measure and appears indifferent if not hostile." Grant sought to placate both Sherman and Stanton by asking Sherman to organize black units for coastal duty, leaving a white unit to occupy Savannah.[20] George G. Meade and Edward O. C. Ord, in command of Grant's two field armies at the beginning of the Appomattox campaign, cared little for black soldiers and preferred not to use them; in contrast, some of Grant's most incompetent subordinates—most notably Butler and Nathaniel P. Banks—proved most enthusiastic about and committed to the use of black soldiers.

Grant remained enthusiastic about black soldiers. Before long he was looking to establish a corps composed entirely of black regiments. His previous effort to establish a black corps out of the regiments organized in Tennessee, Alabama, and Georgia had been thwarted by Washington, but as general in chief he could now accomplish this goal. In November he ordered the transfer of Ferrero's division to the Tenth Corps and elevated Godfrey Weitzel to command it. Soon after, he acceded to Butler's request to reorganize his army, uniting all black regiments in one corps, numbered the Twenty-fifth Corps. Although many proponents of black enlistment (including Butler) had pushed for this step for some time, it also made it easier to assign black units to specified tasks. Black units participated in the offensive operations of the Appomattox campaign, but once again they were soon relegated to holding positions already taken, owing in large part to the prejudices of the new commander of the Army of the James, Edward O. C. Ord, who replaced Butler in January 1865.[21]

The formation and fate of the Twenty-fifth Corps suggested that while Grant no longer worried about committing blacks to combat, white soldiers continued to get the nod. Nevertheless, he believed that blacks made good soldiers if they were trained well. His more extended responses to the question of black military performance contain traces of old stereotypes about the submissiveness of African Americans to whites: "I believe the colored man will make a good soldier," he had told a friend in January 1864. "He has been accustomed all his life to lean on the white man, and if a good officer is placed over him, he will learn readily and make an efficient soldier." This opinion did not change much during the campaign in Virginia. He told Lincoln's private secretary, John Hay, that blacks "are admirable soldiers in many respects; quick and docile in instruction and very subordinate; good in a charge; excellent in fatigue duty." However, he doubted "that an army of them could have stood the week's pounding at the Wilderness and Spotsylvania as our men did," but neither could any other troops. Other remarks reveal that his sentiments were not shaped solely by racial beliefs. Speaking to an English visitor, Grant remarked of his black soldiers: "In battle they displayed extraordinary courage but as their officers were picked off they could not stand a charge, no more [than] could their Southern masters. The power of standing firm after the loss of leaders is possessed only by regiments where every private is as good as his captain and colonel, such as the North-Western and New England volunteers." Of course, by war's end many of these volunteers were no longer in the army; in light of the conscripts and bounty hunters who were now mixed in the ranks, the distance between the fighting abilities of white and black Union soldiers must have narrowed and perhaps disappeared altogether.[22]

By war's end Grant valued his black regiments. They had played an important role in bolstering his army at a time of heavy casualties and expiring enlistments among white veterans. After some reluctance, he had even used them in combat, and praised their performance under fire. His insistence on equal treatment for black and white prisoners of war suggests the importance of military service to the black quest for equality. Such actions also suggest that his own racial prejudices were but lightly held and not the result of deep conviction or thought: they eroded, although they were not completely eradicated, in the face of wartime experiences, an indication that white racial attitudes could change. If Grant often made concessions to the racism of his able subordinates, he did not give in to it, and, when possible, sought to place black soldiers under the command of capable generals who would be interested in their welfare. Most of all, he realized their value as a symbol of what the war had come to mean. It was no accident that on April 16 he ordered the transfer of one of his best black regiments to Washington, D.C. He wanted to make sure that black soldiers would participate in the funeral ceremonies for Abraham Lincoln.[23]

Historians have long noted that aside from a few pioneers from Sherman's army, no black regiments marched down Washington's Pennsylvania Avenue in the Grand Review of May 23–24, 1865. In part, this was owing to the identity of the units that did participate: neither Meade's Army of the Potomac nor the armies under Sherman in the Carolinas contained black units by the end of the war. As noted, Grant had shifted the black regiments in the Army of the Potomac to the Army of the James; Sherman had no use for black regiments and left them with George H. Thomas in Tennessee, where they performed well at Nashville. But the absence of black units was also readily explainable by another fact: their work was not yet done. The Twenty-fifth Corps of the Army of the James remained on occupation duty in Richmond and Petersburg; as the white volunteers paraded, their black counterparts were making preparations to transfer to the Texas-Mexico border. Other black regiments were scattered throughout the South, and there they would stay for some time to come.

For the story of black Union soldiers did not end with Appomattox. Instead, they found themselves the most visible symbol of federal authority in the defeated Confederacy—a role that became ever more visible as white volunteers returned north to be mustered out and white regulars went west to the frontier. In our preoccupation with the war, we often overlook or treat summarily their role in the postwar world. But their presence presented Grant with new questions about their deployment and the effect of their use as occupation troops on postwar Reconstruction.

In the aftermath of Appomattox, Grant was eager to exercise leniency toward the defeated. For most white Southerners, however, military occupation was rendered even more distasteful when the occupiers were black. Many claimed that to station black soldiers in the South was to rub salt into their wounds at a time when Grant wanted to heal those wounds. Yet for the moment, at least, black soldiers were the main manpower source on which Grant could draw. At the end of the Civil War white volunteers clamored to be mustered out and to go home; Grant could not very well resist this sentiment. Officially, the terms of service of many white volunteers terminated whenever the war was declared officially to be over—which did not happen until 1866—or at the end of a specified period of time (usually three years), whichever came first. However, in practice it proved difficult to retain many white volunteers in service long after the end of hostilities. Thus Grant turned to two other sources of manpower to construct an occupation force: white regulars and black volunteers. Many regulars had spent the war on frontier duty, however, and it would take some time to transfer them south. As many black regiments, especially those raised in the South, were Federal volunteers with some time—usually at least a year—left on their terms of service, Grant could retain them for a longer period of time. Nor could politicians overlook the fact that while white volunteers could vote, most black volunteers could not. White volunteers thus possessed a leverage that was unavailable to their black counterparts, which helped to expedite their discharge from service. And few politicians could overlook the importance of the soldier vote after they had witnessed its impact in 1864. By keeping black soldiers in the army, Grant also kept employed a certain proportion of the black population and ensured that they remained under direct Federal control at a time when other freed blacks were beyond such control, and perhaps protection.

Nor were white Southerners the only people angered by the use of black soldiers as occupiers. Equally important were the prejudices of some Union generals and white volunteers. Nowhere were the sentiments of some of Grant's subordinates more evident than in the first major debate over the use of black soldiers in the postwar South. Members of the Twenty-fifth Corps of the Army of the James had been among the first to enter the Confederate capital of Richmond and Petersburg. One of its divisions was left behind to occupy these cities as Grant's men, including another of the Twenty-fifth's divisions, pursued Lee's columns to Appomattox Court House. The surrender of Lee's army and Grant's return to Washington sparked a reshuffling of responsibilities. In an effort to find Chief of Staff Henry W. Halleck a job, Grant assigned him to command the newly created Military Division of the James; Halleck made his way down to Richmond, where he found Edward O. C. Ord in charge.[24]

Unlike the previous commander of the Army of the James, Benjamin F. Butler, Ord had never shown much sympathy for black soldiers. Grant's appointment of him to head the army reflected the general in chief's appreciation of his skills as a combat commander, but it led to difficulties for the Twenty-fifth Corps. Division commander William Birney remarked that during the Appomattox campaign Ord had kept his black units "back from the front whenever he could"; some twenty-four hours before Lee's surrender, Ord had actually broken up Birney's division and sent its commander to the rear. No sooner had Ord returned to Richmond after Lee's surrender than he ordered the black regiments out of Richmond, directing them to camps south of Petersburg. The commander of the Twenty-fifth Corps, Godfrey Weitzel, grumbled that "you know the niggers had to leave there. The smell was offensive to the F.F.V.s." Black newspaper correspondent Thomas M. Chester agreed. "There is no remedy so effectual in chilling the warm blood of the South as to put arms in the hands of the negroes. The influence of this element upon the F.F.V.'s—*Fleet-Footed Virginians*—has ever been of a demoralizing tendency . . . which may in part explain why it is they are kept so far from these large towns."[25]

Removing the Twenty-fifth Corps from Richmond and Petersburg proved only a prelude to Ord's decision to remove the corps from Virginia. Eager to placate Southern whites and ill-disposed toward black soldiers, Ord, supported by Halleck and Gen. George Hartsuff, commanding occupation forces at Petersburg, worked to persuade Grant to order the Twenty-fifth Corps elsewhere. What soon became a familiar litany of charges filled the trio's reports. Black soldiers were disorderly, ill-disciplined, and poorly commanded, and they encouraged other blacks to stop working; Halleck cited cases of "atrocious rape." The burden of occupation duty, he claimed, "requires officers and men of more intelligence and character than we have in the 25th Corps."[26]

Accepting Halleck's complaints at face value, Grant ordered him to send the Twenty-fifth Corps to Bermuda Hundred or City Point "until some disposition is made for them for defense on the seacoast." Corps commander Weitzel countered that Halleck, Ord, and Hartsuff had misattributed the behavior of other soldiers, both white and black, to his command. Such protests, while they may have blunted the force of the original charges, did not change Grant's mind or his priorities. He was at this point far more concerned about wooing whites than about protecting blacks, even if they were United States soldiers. Whether or not the charges made about their behavior were grounded in fact mattered little; the fact that Southern whites made such charges in itself was a sign of the disruptive impact of black occupation forces on the process of reconciliation. Other considerations also shaped Grant's decision. Sheridan needed men on the frontier; the Twenty-fifth was available and could be made ready to go in a short period of time. Grant also believed that once in the West, black soldiers might well decide to stay, or even journey to Mexico, where, as his close friend, Mexican representative Matías Romero, noted, "the Negro race is not the victim of prejudice." Some of the soldiers did not see it the same way. Angry to be sent away from their families in Maryland and Virginia, many protested the transfer, and some mutinied.[27]

Halleck and Ord continued to place such emphasis on reconciliation that by early June one black correspondent noted that in Richmond "military rule . . . has been squared, as far as possible, in accordance with the feelings of the rebels." A delegation of Richmond blacks headed north to present President Andrew Johnson with a protest, observing that their "present condition is, in many respects, worse than when we were slaves, and living under slave law."[28] Other complaints reached Washington about

Ord's behavior; something had to be done. In the end the men of the Twenty-fifth Corps were not the only Yankees to leave Richmond: in mid-June, Ord himself headed to a command north of the Ohio River.

Grant's decision to transfer the Twenty-fifth Corps to the Rio Grande, however, ended only the first of a series of debates over the deployment of black regiments in postwar America. Over the next several months differing policy priorities pulled Grant in opposite directions. His attempts to reconcile these increasingly divergent goals resulted in contradictory and sometimes confusing directives. Grant wanted to transfer black units westward because he believed that their continued presence in the occupied South created more opportunities for interracial friction, thus hampering efforts at sectional reconciliation. At the same time, he believed that the army needed to retain a presence in the South until former Confederates acquiesced in the results of the war and could be entrusted to govern themselves. With the rapid demobilization of white volunteers, however, Grant had no choice but to use black soldiers as part of his occupation force so long as he believed that such a force was necessary—and his sentiments on this issue changed in response to reports about the behavior of former Confederates toward loyal whites and blacks, whether soldiers or civilians. This shift replicated his own hardening toward white Southerners during the war; once more the behavior of Southern whites caused him to take a tougher stand, superseding his earlier sentiments in favor of reconciliation. Nor was he the only person on whom these contrasting themes played in war and peace. In a recent study, Robert Zalimas highlighted continuities in the experiences of black soldiers during the war and its aftermath. "For black soldiers, the postwar [period] mirrored their wartime experience," he argues. "They constituted the primary force that garrisoned southern towns and secured southern property. They continued to fight Union military leaders for equal treatment in the enlisted ranks and retaliated aggressively against civilians to quell southern white misconduct and abuse."[29]

Nevertheless, the use of black soldiers as an occupation force carried with it serious implications for Reconstruction. It reminded white Southerners that the old order of slavery no longer existed, although many Southern whites tried to resurrect as much of it as they could in the year after Appomattox. Many white Southerners rebelled against the presence of black soldiers precisely because it served as a blunt reminder of shattering change. It was an insult, one white Alabamian protested, "an unnecessary aggravation which will tend greatly to imbitter the feelings of those whom it should be our principal aim to conciliate." South Carolina planter Henry W. Ravenel characterized black soldiers as a "gang of diabolical savages sent here with arms in their hands to insult and degrade us." Some Southern whites started rumors of a possible insurrection to justify a crackdown on blacks, civilians and soldiers alike; other Southern whites readily accepted these stories as true. Andrew Johnson's mail was filled with reports of rape, robbery, murder, and disorderly conduct by black soldiers; Southern whites charged them with making former slaves "lazy idling thievish & impudent" and spreading rumors of land redistribution and a possible insurrection. Protests about these and other problems sounded the same theme: if the Federal government truly sought reconciliation, then the black regiments would have to go.[30]

It was true that civilian blacks crowded around the encampments of black soldiers; some whites complained that the soldiers encouraged laziness, made blacks more assertive, and made it more difficult for whites to manage the former slaves. Such charges reflected long-held notions of black behavior shaped by racial prejudice. Blacks were not lazy; rather, they simply refused to work as hard or as long as they had under the coercion of slavery. Secure in the belief that they now need not fear standing up to whites, many blacks did so. Empowered by the presence of black soldiers, they no longer needed to don the mask of submissiveness once so essential to survival. For those Southern whites who maintained that freed blacks would not work unless they were compelled to do so, it was frustrating to find that blacks now had the ability to resist coercion. Gang labor reminded too many blacks of slavery. In many black families, women no longer worked nearly as long in the fields, if they did so at all, preferring to attend to other family responsibilities. Beneath many whites' protests about their former bondsmen's behavior was the refusal to accept the fact that slavery was over, that they would never again exercise the kind of control they once possessed over the lives of slaves. As one Mississippian put it, "Their general behavior in other respects is as good as could be expected from negroes who are taught to believe they are the white mans equal."[31]

Reports concerning the behavior of black soldiers had multiple layers of meaning and implications. Soldiers, white and black, misbehaved on occupation duty; few relished it. That black as well as white soldiers committed transgressions is undoubtedly true. It is equally true that Southern whites could also be abrasive or violent toward white soldiers. But the vast majority of Southern whites singled out black soldiers for their special attention. They repeatedly insisted that what they found most troublesome was not the presence of an occupation force—although, to be sure, there were protests about this as well—but that the occupiers were black. They used the same terms to describe these soldiers that they applied to other blacks: they were at once lazy and defiant, ill-disciplined and violent, a threat to the very order they were supposed to preserve.

Yet a careful reading of these protests suggests that the black soldier's greatest offense was not in failing to preserve order but in representing a new one. Blacks wanted equal treatment and black soldiers had the weapons to enforce this. Soldiers could protect black families (including, no doubt, the families of their comrades on duty elsewhere) and demand respect. There was more friction between Southern whites and black soldiers than between the defeated and their white occupiers. The added element of race made every confrontation a contest between different social orders, as both black soldiers and white Southerners sought to define the rules of their new world. It was also more likely that black soldiers would protect the freedmen than would their white counterparts, who often shared in varying degrees the prejudices of the conquered.[32]

Thus the presence of black soldiers was more disruptive than the presence of white soldiers as a force of occupation would have been. Emancipation transformed the process of reunion in ways that promised the forging of a new order rather than the simple restoration of an old one. However, given Grant's initial emphasis on sectional reconciliation, it was understandable that he would want to reduce the presence and lower the profile of black soldiers. But to Grant reconciliation did not mean letting white Southerners have everything their own way. Gradually he became convinced that the majority of Southern whites did not accept the new order; reports of violence, the failure to preserve law and order, and continued challenges to Federal authority led him to reassess his priorities and to advocate continued occupation. In time, he would also come to accept black enfranchisement as an immediate necessity as opposed to a privilege to be gained gradually. Yet he never gave up the hope that white Southerners would accept emancipation and its consequences as a fact; to encourage this, he was willing to satisfy some of their concerns about black soldiers, accommodating the very prejudices he believed would erode only over time.

Grant also had to obey the directives of a president whose attitudes toward black soldiers stood in stark contrast to those of his predecessor. Andrew Johnson had little but contempt for black soldiers. His sentiments were symptomatic of a racism so deep-seated and virulent that observers remarked on his "morbid distress and feeling against the negroes."[33] If Grant's perspective was sometimes colored by racial prejudice, Johnson's view of the world was dominated by it. Nothing made this clearer than his reaction to a rumor that his old house in Greenville, Tennessee, had been taken over by black soldiers for use as a brothel. No story could more clearly confirm his belief that blacks were lazy and licentious: "It was bad enough to be taken by traitors and converted into a rebel hospital, but a negro whore house is infinitely worse," he complained. Elsewhere he had heard that black soldiers were "domineering over and in fact running the white people out of the neighborhood." He instructed George H. Thomas to look into the matter and, if necessary, strip east Tennessee of black soldiers. Taken aback, Thomas pointed out that he lacked sufficient white soldiers for occupation duty; that a white family occupied Johnson's old home; and that the black soldiers on the whole were well-behaved.[34]

Opponents of black soldiers knew how to play on the president's beliefs in part because they shared them. They repeatedly pointed out how the continued presence of black soldiers served to obstruct his policy. From North Carolina, Harvey M. Watterson, on a tour of inspection for Johnson, reported that whites in New Bern "are deeply impressed with the belief that they deserve no such punishment as Gen. [Charles J.] Paine and his negro troops." Wilmington, North Carolina whites also petitioned the president that "the presence of *colored troops* in our midst is not calculated to allay public anxiety and produce the harmony and cheerful submission to the laws" that Johnson desired. The black bluecoats were "a fruitful source of discontent, and demoralization to the civilians of their own race in our midst, and of irritation, and dissatisfaction to the whites." When black regiments were removed from Columbia, South Carolina, one white resident reported to Johnson that it "seems to please all here," adding that such measures encouraged Southern whites to support the chief executive. "You can readily understand why the white troops will be the best for Southern garrisons," one Tennessean told the president.[35]

Other observers offered different perspectives. Secretary of War Edwin M. Stanton pointed out that "wherever there is any loyal sentiment, there appears to be no difficulty in regard to the presence of colored troops—

complaint being confined chiefly to the most rebellious States—South Carolina and Mississippi." Another Mississippi white claimed that much of what Johnson had heard was fiction: "Nine tenths of the outrages as published committed by Negro troops are either false, or greatly exaggerated." But Johnson had made up his mind. He wanted Grant to remove black regiments from the South as soon as possible.[36]

Generals in charge of the military divisions that were stationed in much of the South vigorously disagreed with the reports of misbehavior among black soldiers. In September 1865, George G. Meade, in charge of the Military Division of the Atlantic, was ordered by Stanton to report on the status of black soldiers under his command. Meade traveled through Virginia and the Carolinas; he returned convinced that the charges against black soldiers were "groundless." He admitted that "colored troops fraternize more with the laboring population than white soldiers," and that blacks tended to cluster around army posts, but he dismissed the impact of such behavior as "trifling." White Southerners' prejudice against black soldiers was clear, however, and this caused Meade to direct the removal of the black regiments to the coast, where they could man fortifications and "will be measurably removed from contact with whites." George H. Thomas, who headed the Military Division of the Tennessee (Alabama, Georgia, Tennessee, Kentucky, and eventually Mississippi), was more blunt. "As a general rule the negro soldiers are under good discipline," he told Johnson. "I believe that in the majority of cases of collision between whites and negro soldiers that the white man has attempted to bully the negro, for it is exceedingly repugnant to southerners to have negro soldiers in their midst & some are so foolish as to vent their anger upon the negro because he is a soldier."[37]

Nevertheless, as demobilization began, Grant paid special attention to black soldiers. His decisions weighed the impact on racial friction of mustering out the black regiments. At the end of May, Grant recommended that recruiting for black units cease. Two months later he specifically asked Stanton to muster out the 54th and 55th Massachusetts Infantry. Before long he drew distinctions between regiments raised in the North (to which the black soldiers, upon leaving the service, would presumably return) and those raised in the South (where the discharged black soldiers might well add to racial friction and be beyond military control). Gen. Quincy A. Gillmore, who headed the Department of South Carolina, observed that to discharge all black units would be a mistake, for "the discharged men might not be a desirable addition to the community at this time." He felt that it would be better to exercise some control over their behavior by keeping them in uniform. Grant agreed, reasoning that it was better when possible to transfer these men elsewhere, away from both white and black civilians. On July 31, he ordered Gillmore to commence mustering out those black regiments under his command that were raised in the North. The general in chief also took steps to minimize conflict, although the measures he took were adverse to black interests. Traditionally, soldiers were allowed to purchase their weapons upon discharge. But the idea of armed blacks alarmed Philip Sheridan, who telegraphed headquarters that to sell arms to black veterans "will create some uneasiness in this section of the country." Back came instructions to prohibit such purchases.[38]

Along with demobilization came orders to redistribute the black regiments that remained on duty. In early November, Grant instructed Thomas to use black soldiers to garrison coastal posts, away from cities and the countryside, as well as from whites and blacks. Similar orders went out to Meade; Grant cited in support what he judged as "the peaceful condition of the South." At the same time other black units were dispatched to the western plains, although harsh weather sometimes forestalled these plans. Grant told Sherman that blacks would prove better soldiers "than dissatisfied Volunteers," and in the future they "may furnish labor . . . for our railroad and mining interests." One other possible station of duty was Panama, where, he told Secretary of State William H. Seward, they could "guard the surveying party against hostile Indians and . . . do all the labor upon land."[39]

These measures did little to halt white Southerners from complaining about the presence and impact of black soldiers. Provisional governors appointed by the president forwarded their protests to the White House; so did the governors of Louisiana and Tennessee. Southern whites also wrote directly to Grant. Residents of St. Augustine, Florida, petitioned for the removal of the black units, pointing out that Northern vacationers would stay away from their city. Blacks would crowd into St. Augustine, leading to increased crime and vice, for "negroes will be negroes."[40]

At the end of November, Grant decided to see things for himself. Over the course of ten days he traveled through Virginia, the Carolinas, and Georgia. At Hilton Head, South Carolina, on December 3, he reviewed one black regiment; elsewhere, however, he met with many more white than black Southerners. Returning to Washington, he cautiously expressed hopes for the eventual success of reconciliation. He reported to Johnson that "the mass of thinking men of the south accept the present situation of affairs in good faith"; however, he added, "Four years of war . . . have left the people possibly in a condition not to yield that ready obedience to civil authority" necessary for civil government to prosper. He advocated the retention of occupation forces, adding that Southern whites concurred in this conclusion: "The white and black mutually require the protection of the general government." Nevertheless, he added that white units should garrison the interior, while black regiments should be removed to the coast. "The presence of black troops, lately slaves, demoralizes labor, both by their advice and by furnishing in their camps a resort for the freedmen for long distances around"; in contrast, white soldiers "generally excite no opposition, and therefore a small number of them can maintain order in a given district."[41]

Grant seemed most concerned about questions of order when it came to the problems posed by emancipation, for he also expressed concern about the operations of the Freedmen's Bureau and the problems of establishing free labor contracts in the South. Although most of his criticisms concerned the impact of rumors about confiscation and the presence of black soldiers on the freedpeople, he added, "It cannot be expected that the opinions held by men at the south for years can be changed in a day, and therefore the freedmen require, for a few years, not only laws to protect them, but the fostering care of those who will give them good counsel, and on whom they rely." This reflected his awareness of the persistence of racism and the need for a transition period. That many blacks relied on black soldiers for protection from violence seems not to have crossed his mind, which suggests that he still paid insufficient heed to the problem of interracial violence.[42]

Within weeks, however, Grant became more attuned to the problem of antiblack violence. Essential in alerting him to its prevalence was another report on conditions in the South, filed by Carl Schurz. The former Union general and Radical Republican had toured the South at the president's behest in the summer of 1865; however, Johnson ignored his accounts of interracial conflict and his efforts to ensure protection for the freedpeople. Most interesting were Schurz's comments about the behavior of black soldiers. It was true that some soldiers had "put queer notions into the heads of negroes" and that their quarters "are apt to be a point of attraction for colored women"; but tighter discipline rather than removal was the answer. Besides, white soldiers were also not always on their best behavior, and they wanted to go home. Finally, to garrison the South with black regiments would "produce one important moral result"—it would remind whites that blacks were free: "And there is nothing that will make it more evident than the bodily presence of a negro with a musket on his shoulder."[43]

When Schurz took part in a debate between Mississippi governor William Sharkey and Gen. Henry W. Slocum over the need for a white militia, the president disavowed Schurz's mission; nevertheless, Schurz submitted a lengthy final report, aware that once Congress convened in December, Senator Charles Sumner would call on the president to share the document with the country. In fact, Johnson had sought Grant's letter with the intent of using it to offset Schurz's criticisms, and had responded to Sumner's request by releasing both documents. While both senators and the press debated the relative merits of the two reports, Grant read Schurz's detailed and documented account; within days he requested his subordinates to forward information on interracial violence and crime. The results, documenting numerous cases of white violence against blacks, suggested that his earlier remarks were wide of the truth. On January 12, 1866, Grant issued General Orders No. 3, directing his subordinates to intervene to stop legal proceedings instituted by Southern civil courts against military personnel for acts done under orders, against loyalists for acts against the Confederacy or its supporters, against people who occupied confiscated land, or against blacks "charged with offenses for which white persons are not prosecuted or punished in the same manner and degree"—thus effectively nullifying the Black Codes.[44]

General Orders No. 3 marked a shift in Grant's thinking from an emphasis on reconciliation to one favoring the continuation of military occupation. He maintained that a military presence in the South remained necessary so long as civil authorities failed to enforce the laws in all cases, and he opposed efforts to reorganize Southern state militias. He accumulated information about interracial violence and submitted the results to Johnson. Southern blacks also took their case to the general; as a petition from Florida freedmen said, "We hope Sir, that the unitted states Will give us Protection, and Not allow us to be Stript of Every Defence in the World, if We are Not allowd to have Something to Defend ourselves under Certain Circumstances, We are Werst than When We Were Slaves, yes, ten to one." Reports from members of his staff reinforced Grant's concern. Ely S. Parker recommended the continuance of military occupation. Noting that a smaller number of white troops might well perform the duty "as efficiently and more satisfactorily to the resident population than the black troops can," Parker nevertheless wondered "whether . . . this should be conceded to the refractory and rebellious element of the South," adding that this was "a question that I cannot pretend to determine."[45]

Meanwhile, Johnson continued to receive letters protesting the continued presence of black soldiers. Correspondents described incidents of violence and insolence; governors sought the soldiers' transfer. Grant repeatedly forwarded evidence of the still-unsettled condition of the South to Johnson, although such reports made little impression on the president.[46] The president seemed determined to end military occupation as soon as possible. That this would result in the reassertion of a white supremacist order grounded in violence and coercion, far from disturbing him, would signify the restoration of civil society as he understood it.

Although Grant had become far more aware of white violence against blacks, his belief that the presence of black soldiers on occupation duty led to "unnecessary irritation and the demoralization of labor" persisted. He continued to look for ways to remove them from the South, pressing for the passage of a bill to organize the postwar army in part so that he could station white regulars in the South. However, such legislation would not become law for months; in the meantime the general in chief had to accept the fact that as white volunteers went home, black soldiers, even in reduced numbers, remained the most visible sign of Federal authority in the South. At winter's end he suggested that only twenty-one black regiments remain in service, with the vast majority to be stationed in the South. He hoped to dispatch several black regiments to the frontier, and retained those regiments on duty along the Rio Grande. Meanwhile he pushed for mustering out all remaining white regiments as he impatiently awaited the passage of the army reorganization bill.[47]

When reports reached Grant of continued friction between black soldiers and white civilians in Georgia, he angrily wired George H. Thomas. Hadn't Thomas obeyed his orders about posting black regiments along the coast? Yet, on the same day, Grant also told Thomas that all remaining white volunteer regiments should be mustered out unless it was absolutely necessary to retain them. Thomas replied that if he complied with

Grant's instructions, "the State Authorities will administer the laws directly or indirectly to the prejudice" of loyalists, white and black, whereupon Grant directed Thomas to use his discretion. At the same time, however, Grant expressed concern over possible attacks against black soldiers. "It is our duty to avoid giving unnecessary annoyance but it is a greater duty to protect troops acting under Military Authority, and also all loyally disposed persons in the Southern states," he told Thomas. Such instructions revealed the tensions, even contradictions, in what Grant was trying to do. It was proving difficult indeed to protect black soldiers, placate white prejudices, and solve the problems of demobilization.[48]

Just over a month later, riots in Memphis, Tennessee, offered evidence both of the continued friction between black soldiers and white civilians and of the willingness of whites to resort to violence. A black artillery regiment had been stationed in town for some time: its members "were not under the best of discipline," and at times this fact complicated their use as "the instruments to execute the orders of Government agents," including those of the provost marshal, to enforce the law. Local law enforcement officials frequently arrested black soldiers, just as black soldiers had arrested local whites (including an occasional police officer), and, remarked the area commander, "in both cases those arrested have not infrequently been treated with a harshness altogether unnecessary." At the same time, the city became a gathering place for the soldiers' families and other blacks seeking protection: these people crowded into the southern portion of town. The discharge of the black artillerymen at the end of March gave local whites an opportunity for revenge, and before long fighting broke out when police officers began arresting blacks. What occupation forces remained could do little more than try to separate the contending parties with only intermittent success. Only the belated arrival of more United States soldiers brought an end to the riot.[49] Grant characterized the riot as a "massacre," presenting "a scene of murder, arson, rape & robery in which the victims were all helpless and unresisting negroes stamping lasting disgrace upon the civil authorities that permitted them."[50]

In light of these signs of continued white intransigence, Grant in May 1866 recommended the continuance of military occupation, acknowledging that "it cannot be forseen [*sic*] that this force will not be required for some time to come." But it was obvious to him that volunteers—white or black—would no longer suffice as an occupation force. What few white volunteers remained on duty were becoming restless more than a year after Appomattox: "By reason of dissatisfaction they are no longer of use and might as well be discharged at once." Moreover, "the colored Volunteer has equal right to claim his discharge but as yet he has not done so. How long will existing laws authorize the retention of this force even if they are content to remain?" In fact, of course, black regiments had been discharged for some time; however, it would not be until year's end that Grant would direct the mustering out of all remaining black volunteers.[51]

Although he preferred the discharge of black volunteer regiments, Grant advocated making black regiments an integral part of the postwar army, countering the notion that their earlier use was merely a wartime expedient. In October 1865 he not only suggested that a postwar army of 80,000 soldiers be authorized, but he also proposed that the president be permitted to raise some 20,000 additional black soldiers. In 1866, as Congress debated a bill to reorganize the army, Grant told Senator Henry Wilson, head of the Senate Military Affairs Committee and a proponent of black enlistment, that he had "no objection to the use of colored troops and think they can be obtained more readily than white ones." He also endorsed the commissioning of black officers, although he added that officers should command only soldiers of their own race—which maintained segregated units and promised to introduce confusion in the chain of command should black officers ever have cause to issue orders to white enlisted men.[52] These units would be posted on the frontier and on the coast; white regulars would take over the responsibility of maintaining order in the South—and Grant continued to hold out hope that this force could be removed as soon as possible.

Only with the passage of an army reorganization bill in July 1866 could Grant begin to implement his policy. The legislation provided for four regiments of black infantry and two of cavalry. Black volunteers were mustered out; black regulars were sent to the frontier. From now on white soldiers would, where possible, patrol the South. In recommending the organization of additional black regiments for frontier duty, Grant kept in mind Senator Wilson's desire to have them commanded by white officers who were strong supporters of black rights, although Grant did not follow the senator's recommendations for officers.[53]

With the passage of the army reorganization bill Grant's dilemma regarding the deployment of black regiments on occupation duty in the South came to an end. The bill provided him with a way to reconcile the need to maintain a military presence with the need for not relying on black regiments in the occupation. Nevertheless, his road toward this end bears examination, for Grant's attitude toward these units embodied the tensions inherent in an effort to reconcile the various goals of Reconstruction. He had come to realize that blacks and their white allies needed protection; however, he acknowledged that the continued presence of black units would erode chances for reconciliation. He desired the restoration of peace, unwilling to admit that the just peace he had in mind was impossible without the cooperation of Southern whites. The same racism that led to violence led also to protests against black soldiers; Grant's efforts to counter the former while placating the latter proved impossible to reconcile. At the same time, Grant's remarks about the impact of black regiments on the surrounding freedmen suggest the limits of his vision as to what emancipation meant for the former slave.

Yet to dismiss Grant's behavior as racist or indifferent is to miss the point. A blanket charge of racism obscures the wide spectrum of attitudes and behaviors encompassed by that term, lumping together people with quite different perspectives and policies. Grant's attitudes were not deeply held ones, and they proved malleable in response to experience—a characteristic not shared by all his contemporaries. If he failed to meet the criteria for enlightenment favored by today's historians, it must be noted that blacks such as Frederick Douglass and John Mercer Langston were inclined to be far more charitable. Moreover, it would be a serious mistake to conclude that Grant's approach to the problem of black soldiers in the South primarily reflected his racial attitudes. It is far more accurate to conclude that he was continually struggling to reconcile different preferences, desires, and perceptions as he sought reconciliation and justice. Whether it was possible to satisfy both goals remains a compelling question. Other considerations also played a role in his decisions, including his understanding of the racial attitudes of others: much, after all, depended on the attitude of the chief executive from whom Grant took his orders. Although Grant's racial attitudes undoubtedly contributed to his decisions, they formed but a part of a larger matrix of concerns, most of which played a far larger role in determining how he viewed the use of black soldiers in war and peace.[54]

Ulysses S. Grant always meant to do well. His ability to comprehend all aspects of a problem, a quality that served him well as a warrior, often led him to hesitate in peace. His pragmatic acceptance of the possible too often resulted in his honoring the boundaries of his world rather than

pressing against them; in marked contrast, as a general he often transcended traditional notions of strategy. Despite the lingering residue of
racism and paternalism in his mind, he tried to do right by black and
white alike. His use of black soldiers during the war reflected a man coming to terms with a new world at an uneven rate; his stance on the use of
black regiments as an occupation force in the postwar South exemplified
the complexity of Reconstruction. Both need to be understood before they
can be judged, for if the study of the Civil War and Reconstruction tells us
anything, it is that it is much easier to judge than to understand.

Chapter Seven

☙

Quarrel Forgotten or a Revolution Remembered?

Reunion and Race in the Memory

of the Civil War, 1875–1913

David W. Blight

It's gonna hurt now, anything dead coming back to life hurts.
—Amy Denver to Sethe, while helping deliver Sethe's baby, some-
where along the Ohio River during the 1850s, in Toni Morrison's
Beloved, 1987

I believe that the struggle for life is the order of the world . . . if it is
our business to fight, the book for the army is a war-song, not a
hospital sketch.
                    —Oliver Wendell Holmes, Jr., "A Soldier's Faith," 1895

Americans . . . have the most remarkable ability to alchemize all
bitter truths into an innocuous but piquant confection and to trans-
form their moral contradictions, or public discussion of such contradictions into a proud decoration, such as are given for heroism on
the field of battle.—James Baldwin, "Many Thousands Gone," 1951

THE historical memory of a people, a nation, or any aggregate evolves
over time in relation to present needs and ever-changing contexts.
Societies and the groups within them remember and use history as a source
of coherence and identity, as a means of contending for power or place,

and as a means of controlling access to whatever becomes normative in society. For better and worse, social memories—ceaselessly constructed versions of a group past—are the roots of identity formation. In spite of all we would like to think we have learned about how *culture* is invented, and how *heritage* is a social construct that ultimately defies fixed definition, people jealously seek to own their pasts. The post-1989 world has demonstrated this dilemma with tragic consequences. As historian John Gillis has aptly put it, "identities and memories are not things we think *about,* but things we think *with.*"[1] As such, the historical, in the form of social memory, becomes political.

The study of historical memory might be defined, therefore, as the study of cultural struggle, of contested truths, interpretations, moments, events, epochs, rituals, or even texts in history that thresh out rival versions of the past which are in turn put to the service of the present. As recent events in world politics, curriculum debates, national and international commemorations and anniversaries have shown, historical memories can be severely controlled, can undergo explosive liberation or redefinition from one generation, or even one year, to the next. The social, political, and psychological *stakes* of historical memory can be high. The "public" that consumes history is vast, and the marketplace turbulent. Like it or not, we live in an era in which the impulse to teach the young to have an open *sense* of history is not enough; that sensibility will be challenged. The pragmatic, questioning sense of history will encounter social memory—in the classroom, at the international negotiating table, at the movies, and in the streets. This dilemma desperately calls for trained historians seeking evidence, demanding verification, offering reasoned explanations of events. But the truth is that historians, and their cousins in related disciplines, are only playing one part in this drama. As Natalie Zemon Davis and Randolph Starn, among others, have cautioned, "whenever memory is invoked we should be asking: by whom, where, in which context, against what?"[2]

As the 1990 PBS film series "The Civil War," by Ken Burns, demonstrated once again, one of the most vexing questions in the formation of American historical memory has been to understand the meaning and memory of the Civil War. The Civil War itself has long been the object of widespread nostalgia and the subject of durable mythmaking in both North and South. In the final episode of the film series scant attention is paid to the complicated story of Reconstruction. The consequences of this American *Iliad* are only briefly assessed as viewers (likely quite taken by an artistically brilliant and haunting film) are ushered from the surrender at Appomattox through some fleeting discussion of Reconstruction politics, past Ulysses S. Grant's final prophecy of an "era of great harmony," to Joseph E. Johnston's bareheaded encounter with pneumonia and quick death after attending the funeral in 1891 of his former battlefield rival, William Tecumseh Sherman, and finally to that irresistible footage of the old veterans at the 1913 and 1938 Gettysburg Blue-Gray reunions. Along the way, the narrative is punctuated by the Mississippi writer Shelby Foote informing us that the war "made *us* an *is*" (a reference to how the United States "is" rather than "are" became a common expression) and by historian Barbara Fields reminding us of William Faulkner's claim that history is "not a *was* but an *is*." The film does leave one with a sense that the Civil War was an event with lasting significance for the entire world, that the past and the present inform, even flow into, one another, and that legacies have power over us. But it is a point made as much with feeling, with music and sentiment, as it is with historical analysis. The "Blue" and the "Gray"— men out of a distant past, who were once such familiar images at American train stations and on town greens—became television images for the first time. They charmed millions of late-twentieth-century viewers, their very presence at those picturesque reunions declaring that the nation had survived all the carnage in the previous episodes. They looked at *us* reassuringly as narrator David McCullough announces: "the war was over."[3]

"The Civil War" is epic history converted into superb television. The series always moves and instructs its varied audiences; it leaves indelible sounds and images in the hearts and minds of viewers, and it teaches that the Civil War was a terrible passage through which Americans emerged forever changed. Among the broad populace of history enthusiasts, and in American and international classrooms, that film series is now the base of popular memory about the Civil War. I have used this film series with many American students, as well as with German students at the University of Munich. The reactions of German students were especially interesting. They typically asked questions like: why are there so many sunsets and moonrises in this film? Why is it so "sentimental"? Some actually brought in their own personal collections of Civil War ballad music or Negro spirituals. One student said "The Battle Hymn of the Republic" had always been one of his favorite songs along with those of Elvis Presley and Jimi Hendrix. But another German student asked me whether Americans had ever considered comparing the devastation and sense of loss in their Civil War with that of the Thirty Years' War in Europe? To the latter question, a stretched analogy, I had to answer that most Americans have never heard of the Thirty Years' War. Sometimes, perspective is all. Burns touched many heartstrings, and left some puzzlement among European viewers of his film as well.

But some of these questions go to the heart of another problem: the American tendency toward claims of exceptionalism and consensus in our historical consciousness. At the annual meeting of the Association for the Study of Negro Life and History, in Durham, North Carolina, in October 1961, John Hope Franklin reflected at length on the meaning of Civil War memory. He worried about the persistent American tendency to dissolve the conflict at the base of the war, and to constantly drum it into a "common unifying experience." Franklin characterized the semicentennial commemoration of the war (1911–15) as a time when the nation collectively found it "convenient to remember that slavery had been abolished and to forget that the doctrine of the superiority of the white race was as virulent as ever." Moreover, he characterized the centennial under way in 1961 as a "national circus," and a public cultural outpouring with a "studied lack of appreciation for the implications of the victory at Appomattox."[4] An ever troubled past flowed, indeed, into an ever sovereign present.

On one level, the ending of Burns's remarkable film series offers a vivid reminder of just how much interpretations of the Civil War provide an index of our political culture, of how much the central issues of the war— union and slavery, reunion and racial equality, diversity as the definition of America or as the source of its unraveling—remain for each succeeding generation of Americans to grapple with. However, on another level, the ending of the film offers many Americans the legacy they find most appealing: the rapid transition from the veteran just returned to his farm, standing on a corn wagon in 1865 (almost an image of a horn of plenty), to the 1913 Gettysburg reunion is the stuff of earnest nostalgia, and it makes good fast-forward history. As Richard Slotkin has written, "Burns evokes as well as anyone the paradoxical and complex emotion of Civil War nostalgia, in which one recognizes the awful tragedy of the war, yet somehow *misses* it." In American collective memory, sectional reconciliation virtually required that some of the deeper tragedies of that conflict be "missed."

Such an ending (in Burns's film) becomes transhistorical in American social memory: the time between the real battle of Gettysburg and its fiftieth
anniversary reunion is at once a great distance and no distance at all. Time
itself can be transcended; and in those mystical exchanges between gra-
cious old veterans on what seem ancient battlefields, one can entertain the
notion that American history endures all traumas in its troubled but inexorable path of progress, and that the day may arrive when there will no
longer be any need to think historically about long-term consequences.
Abraham Lincoln's haunting passage about the "mystic chords of memory,
stretching from every battlefield and patriot grave . . ." had, indeed, swelled
"the chorus of the Union," and conquered time itself. The pleading poetry
in Lincoln's First Inaugural Address in 1861 (from which Burns takes his
title for the final episode, "The Better Angels of Our Nature") was delivered, of course, in the midst of crisis and on the brink of war. But the
deeper conflicts and contradictions buried in the new "patriot graves" (after the Civil War) could be finely displaced, comfortably forgotten, and
truly "mystic" as Joshua Lawrence Chamberlain, the hero of Little Round
Top at the battle of Gettysburg (and one of Burns's principal "characters"), describes the 1913 reunion as a "transcendental experience" and a
"radiant fellowship of the fallen." American history had "progressed"
through Reconstruction, the Gilded Age, the myriad crises of the 1890s,
vicious racial violence, unprecedented labor strife, a short foreign war with
Spain, massive urbanization and industrialization to be a society divided
by a racial apartheid and seething with ethnic pluralism on the eve of World
War I. Rarely was there a more confirming context for William Dean
Howells's turn-of-the-century assertion that "what the American public
always wants is a tragedy with a happy ending."[5]

Explanations of the meaning and memory of the Civil War—whether
expressed in fiction, monuments, historiography, the movies, politics, jour-
nalism, public schooling, veterans' organizations, the strongly gendered
attractions of war-gaming, tourism, or reenactments—have, intentionally
or not, provided a means of assessing the elusive question of national self-
definition in America. Such constructions of the memory of our most
divisive event have also reflected the persistent dilemma of race in public
policy, as well as our ongoing challenge to build one political structure
that can encompass the interests of the many. By and large, the legions of
Americans who transmit a fascination for the Civil War across generations still prefer the drama of the immediate event to discussions of causes

and consequences; they continue to be enthralled with the fight as much as, if not more than, with its meanings. This is, of course, partly a measure of human nature, of audiences, and of public tastes for history generally. Burns effectively mixed the broad military struggle with the voices of ordinary people and the perspectives of local communities. The influence of the new social history is altogether apparent in the film. We learn that the Civil War was a ruthless and all-encompassing experience in places like Clarksville, Tennessee, and Deer Isle, Maine. We hear the common soldier's syntax and the war's meaning interpreted from the diaries of ordinary women. Burns put slavery and emancipation at the center of the wartime story; Frederick Douglass's compelling voice commands attention at several turning points in the narrative. Emancipated slaves are real people, and they too help to tell the story. But in the end, the film series is still a narrative about the making and consequences of war (and the horror and destruction are unmistakable), told from headquarters and the perspectives of larger-than-life individuals. The legends of such figures as Robert E. Lee, Stonewall Jackson, Nathan Bedford Forrest, William Tecumseh Sherman, and Lincoln himself are well preserved in Burns's self-conscious attempt at documentary epic. For Burns, as a filmmaker/historian, all of these were, of course, artistic as well as historical choices; at times he simply created what works best on film, with a clear artifice in mind.[6]

For Americans broadly, the Civil War has been a defining event upon which we have often imposed unity and continuity; as a culture, we have preferred its music and pathos to its enduring challenges, the theme of reconciled conflict to resurgent, unresolved legacies. We have displaced complicated consequences by endlessly focusing on the contest itself. We have sometimes lifted ourselves out of historical time, above the details, and rendered the war safe in a kind of Passover offering as we watch the Blue and the Gray veterans shake hands across the little stone walls at Gettysburg. Like stone monuments, monumental films, as well as some monumental books, are sometimes as much about forgetting as they are about remembering. Deeply embedded in an American mythology of mission, and serving as a mother lode of nostalgia for antimodernists and military history buffs, the Civil War remains very difficult to shuck from its shell of sentimentalism. Historian Nina Silber has demonstrated how "a sentimental rubric took hold of the reunion process" during the three decades after the war. Indeed, Silber shows how gender (conceptions of manliness and femininity, and the popular literary ritual of intersectional marriage) provided a principal source of metaphor and imagery through which sectional reconciliation was achieved.[7]

Through scholarship and schooling, much has changed in recent decades regarding the place of the black experience in the era of the Civil War. But in the half century after the conflict, as the sections reconciled, the races increasingly divided. The intersectional wedding that became such a staple of mainstream popular culture had no interracial counterpart in the popular imagination. Quite the opposite was the case. So deeply at the root of the war's causes and consequences, and so powerful a source of division in American social psychology, "race"—and its myriad manipulations in American culture—served as the antithesis of a culture of reconciliation. The memory of slavery, emancipation, and the Fifteenth Amendment never fit well into a culture in which the Old and New South were romanticized and welcomed back to a new nationalism. Persistent discussion of the "Race Problem" (or the "Negro Question"), across the political and ideological spectrum at the turn of the century, meant that American society could not also remember a "Civil War problem," or a "Blue-Gray problem." Interpretations of the Civil War in the broad American culture continue to illustrate what Daniel Aaron meant when he said that, among American writers, the conflict "has not been so much unfelt, as it is unfaced." And, if W. E. B. Du Bois was at all correct in his famous 1903 declaration that "the problem of the twentieth century is the problem of the color line," then we can begin to see how the problem of "reunion" and the problem of "race" were trapped in a tragic, mutual dependence.[8]

The aim of this essay is to suggest in the broadest terms how American culture processed the meaning and memory of the Civil War and Reconstruction down to World War I, with special emphasis on these overlapping themes of reunion and race. In this process, black and white voices spoke both to and completely around each other. In the introduction to the 1991 edition of *Imagined Communities,* Benedict Anderson warns us about the delusion of "shedding" ourselves of the problem of nationalism in the modern world. "The 'end of an era of nationalism,' so long prophesied," writes Anderson, "is not remotely in sight. Indeed, nation-ness is the most universally legitimate value in the political life of our time." Moreover, in his discussion of the function of "memory and forgetting" in the shaping of nationalism, Anderson left this telling comment about the American Civil War: "A vast pedagogical industry works ceaselessly to oblige young Americans to remember/forget the hostilities of 1861–65 as a great 'civil' war between 'brothers' rather than between—as they briefly were—two sovereign nation-states. (We can be sure, however, that if the Confederacy had succeeded in maintaining its independence, this 'civil war' would have been replaced in memory by something quite unbrotherly."[9] There may never be an end to nationalism as we know it, just as there is no end to history. But there are manifest breaks in the process of history, events and commemorations of those events that expose how we use history.

In "The New Negro" (1925), philosopher Alain Locke believed he discerned one of those turning points, both in black self-consciousness and in the nation's race "problem." And the change had everything to do with memory and forgetting. "While the minds of most of us, black and white, have thus burrowed in the *trenches* of the Civil War and Reconstruction," wrote Locke, "the actual march of development has simply *flanked* these positions, necessitating a sudden reorientation of view. We have not been watching in the right direction; set North and South on a sectional axis, we have not noticed the East till the sun has us blinking" (emphasis added). Preoccupied in remembering/forgetting the war as a North-South fight, mired in the increasingly nostalgic details of a heroic war in a lost past, American culture had lost sight of what the fight had been all about. Time would tell whether Locke's optimism about a new generation of blacks' "spiritual coming of age" would be a solution to or an evasion of these problems in American historical memory, whether the blinking of a new era would turn to collective insight.[10] For more than two decades before Locke wrote, the reform fervor of the Progressive era, with its quests for order, honesty, and efficiency, and its impulse against monopolism, compelled Americans to look inward and forward, but they did so in a culture full of sentimentalized remembrance. Moreover, for at least the same twenty years, black thinkers had been fashioning definitions of the "New Negro" for the new century. But what would be the place of "New Negroes" at Blue-Gray reunions in the land of Jim Crow? In a society inexorably looking ahead, the culture of sectional reconciliation would force millions, consciously or not, to avert their eyes.

The chronological reach of this essay is long, and large aspects of the topic will, therefore, have to be left to later explorations. Such aspects include the impact of popular literature (the "plantation school") on Northern readers and editors in the late nineteenth century, the post-Reconstruction generation of black and white writers who wrote directly and indirectly about the legacies of the Civil War and emancipation, the myriad ways sectional politics and the emergence of Jim Crow (in law and life) melded into an uneasy national consensus from the 1880s to World War I, and the cultural nostalgia rooted in the alienation born of rapid industrialization.[11] I have selected two ways to demonstrate the dialectic between race and reunion as the memory of the Civil War evolved in American culture: first, an encounter between two major African American leaders, Alexander Crummell and Frederick Douglass, over how blacks should best remember slavery and the Civil War; and second, the 1913 fiftieth anniversary Blue-Gray reunion at Gettysburg as a ritual of national reconciliation, an event in which race, black participation in the war, indeed the very idea of slavery as cause and emancipation as result of the war might be said to be thunderously conspicuous by their absence.

In 1875, as the march away from radicalism and protection of African American rights threatened to become a full retreat, Frederick Douglass gave a Fourth of July speech in Washington, D.C., entitled "The Color Question." Events, both personal and national, had cast a pall over the normally sanguine Douglass, forcing him to reflect in racialized terms on the American Centennial, which was to be celebrated the following year. The nation, Douglass feared, would "lift to the sky its million voices in one grand Centennial hosanna of peace and good will to all the white race . . . from gulf to lakes and from sea to sea." As a black citizen, he dreaded the day when "this great white race has renewed its vows of patriotism and flowed back into its accustomed channels." Douglass looked back upon fifteen years of unparalleled change for his people, worried about the hold of white supremacy on America's historical consciousness, and asked the core question in the nation's struggle over the memory of the Civil War: "If war among the whites brought peace and liberty to the blacks, *what will peace among the whites bring?*"[12] (emphasis added). For more than a century, through cycles of great advancement and periods of cynical reaction in American race relations, Douglass's question in various forms has echoed through our political culture. Answers to Douglass's question have depended, of course, on context—on time, place, one's positioning along the color line, the available sources for scholars, access to power, the medium through which the history is transmitted, and differing revisionist questions and agendas. But always, the answers have emerged from the struggle over the content, meaning, and uses of the past. John Hope Franklin recognized this in a 1979 essay on what he describes as the "enormous influence" of the combination of Thomas Dixon's novel *The Clansman* (1903), D. W. Griffith's film *Birth of a Nation* (1915), and Claude Bowers's popular history *The Tragic Era* (1928), all produced within the first three decades of the twentieth century. Franklin's analysis of how history can be used as "propaganda" in the shaping of a nation's memory of itself echoed Ralph Ellison's poignant comment during the same year (1979). Nothing in our past, said Ellison, like the question of race in the story of the Civil War and Reconstruction had ever caused Americans to be so "notoriously selective in the exercise of historical memory."[13] All practice of historical memory formation is, of course, selective. How some selections become or remain dominant, taking on mythic dimensions, and others do not is the tale to be told.

The 1880s were a pivotal decade in the development of traditions and social memories of the Civil War. The "Lost Cause" in the South, as well as a growing willingness among Northerners to embrace sectional reconciliation, underwent cultural transformation. The situation among black intellectuals was similar; an index of their struggle over how and if to remember slavery and the Civil War era can be found in a debate between Alexander Crummell and Frederick Douglass. Then as now, no single persuasion controlled African American thought; black social memories were often as diverse as were debates within the Grand Army of the Republic (G.A.R.) or among advocates of the Lost Cause tradition. As editors, ministers, community leaders, or writers, black intellectuals in the late nineteenth century were as compelled as anyone else to engage in what became an intraracial debate over the meaning and best uses of the age of emancipation. The contours of such debates were established well before Booker T. Washington and W. E. B. Du Bois came to embody the classic division in black thought over historical consciousness and political strategies.[14]

At Storer College, in Harpers Ferry, West Virginia, on May 30, 1885 (Memorial Day), Alexander Crummell, one of the most accomplished and well-traveled black intellectuals of the nineteenth century, gave a commencement address to the graduates of that black college, which had been founded for freedmen at the end of the Civil War. Crummell, an Episcopal priest, educated at the abolitionist Oneida Institute in Upstate New York and at Cambridge University in England in the 1840s, had spent nearly twenty years as a missionary and an advocate of African nationalism in Liberia (1853–71). Crummell later considered the Storer address, entitled "The Need of New Ideas and New Aims for a New Era," to be the most important he ever gave. Although Crummell could not resist acknowledging that Harpers Ferry was a setting "full of the most thrilling memories in the history of our race," his aim was to turn the new generation of blacks, most of whom would have been born during the Civil War, away from dwelling "morbidly and absorbingly upon the servile past," and toward an embrace of the urgent economic and moral "needs of the present." As a minister and theologian, and as a social conservative, Crummell was concerned not only with racial uplift—his ultimate themes were family, labor, industrial education, and moral values—but with the unburdening of blacks from what he believed was the debilitating, painful memory of slavery. Crummell made a careful distinction between memory and recollection. Memory, he contended, was a passive, unavoidable, often essential part of group consciousness; recollection, on the other hand, was active, a matter of choice and selection, and dangerous in excess. "What I would fain have you guard against," he told the graduates, "is not the memory of slavery, but the constant *recollection* of it." Such recollection, Crummell maintained, would only degrade racial progress in the Gilded Age; for him, unmistakably, "duty lies in the future."[15]

Prominent in the audience that day at Harpers Ferry (probably in the front row or on the stage) was Frederick Douglass, whom Crummell described as his "neighbor" from Washington, D.C. According to Crummell's own account, his call to reorient African American consciousness from the past to the future met with Douglass's "emphatic and most earnest protest." Douglass rose to the occasion, as he did so many times in the 1880s on one anniversary or Memorial Day after another, to assert an African-American/abolitionist memory of the Civil War era, which almost always included an abiding reminder of the nature and significance of slavery.[16] No verbatim account of what Douglass said at Harpers Ferry survives; but several other speeches from the 1880s offer a clear picture of what the former abolitionist may have said. Douglass and Crummell shared a sense of the dangers and limitations of social memory, especially for a group that had experienced centuries of slavery. A healthy level of forgetting, said Douglass, was "Nature's plan of relief." But in season and out, Douglass insisted that whatever the psychological need for avoiding the woeful legacy of slavery, it would resist all human effort to suppress it. The history of black Americans, he said many times in the 1880s, could "be traced like that of a wounded man through a crowd by the blood."[17] Better to confront such a history, he believed, than to wait for its resurgence.

Douglass's many postwar speeches about the memory of the conflict typically began with an acknowledgment of the need for healing and living. But then he would forcefully call his audiences to remembrance of the origins and consequences, as well as the sacrifices, of the Civil War. He would often admit that his own personal memory of slavery was best kept sleeping like a "half-forgotten dream." But he despised the politics of forgetting that American culture seemed to necessitate in the 1880s. "We are not here to visit upon the children the sins of the fathers," Douglass told a Memorial Day audience in Rochester, New York, in 1883, "but we are here to remember the causes, the incidents, and the results of the late rebellion." Most of all, Douglass objected to the historical construction that portrayed emancipation as a great national "failure" or "blunder." The argument that slavery had protected and nurtured blacks and that freedom had gradually sent them "falling into a state of barbarism" forced Douglass to argue for an aggressive use of memory. The problem was not merely the rise of the Lost Cause myth of Southern virtue and victimization. The problem was "not confined to the South," declared Douglass in 1888. "It [the theory of black degeneration coupled with historical misrepresentations of emancipation and Reconstruction] has gone forth to the North. It has crossed the ocean. It has gone to Europe, and it has gone as far as the wings of the press, and the power of speech can carry it. There is no measuring the injury inflicted upon the negro by it."[18] Such, Douglass understood, were the stakes of conflicts over rival versions of the past, when combined with sociobiological theories of racial inferiority, and put to the service of the present. Douglass died the year before the *Plessy v. Ferguson* Supreme Court decision. But he had lived long enough to peer across the horizon and see the society America was becoming in the age of Jim Crow. In all discussion of the "race question" in America, Douglass had long understood that the historical was always political.

Even before the most violent outbreaks of lynching and an increasingly radical racism took hold in the South, there was good reason to be worried about the uses of the theory of black degeneration. The theory would eventually be spread widely in popular literature, emerge full-blown in minstrelsy, film, and cartoons, and, most tellingly, it gained many spokesmen in academic high places. Produced by historians, statisticians in the service of insurance companies, and scientists of all manner, a hereditarian and social Darwinist theory of black capacity fueled racial policies of evasion and repression. By the turn of the century, the negrophobia practiced in daily conversations among many ordinary whites was now buttressed by highly developed, academic notions of blacks as a "vanishing race," destined to lose the struggle of natural selection.[19]

In 1900, Dr. Paul B. Barringer, chairman of the medical faculty at the University of Virginia, gave the keynote address at a major symposium (on heredity and the Southern "Negro problem") of the Tri-State Medical Society, in Charleston, South Carolina. Barringer began with a discussion of dog species and habits, and the dangers of "indiscriminate breeding." He then found his central theme, the "habits of a race." Barringer's clinical analysis of his topic demonstrates the structure of thought Douglass and others had good reason to fear. "Let us apply this biological axiom to the human race, taking as our example . . . the Southern Negro," declared the doctor:

> I will show from the study of his racial history (phylogeny) that his late tendency to return to barbarism is as natural as the return of the sow that is washed to her wallowing in the mire. I will show that the degradation under which he was formed and the fifty centuries of historically recorded savagery with which he came to us cannot be permanently influenced by one or two centuries of enforced correction if the correcting force be withdrawn . . . when the correcting force of discipline was removed he, like the released planet, began to fall . . . a motion as certain in its results as the law of gravitation. Fortunately for us experience (history) shows that these savage traits can be held down, and we have seen that if held down long enough, they will be bred out. In this one fact lies the hope of the South.

With these words and more, Barringer demonstrated that for the sheer virulence of white supremacy and racial demagoguery, some academics took no back seat to politicians. Throughout, his speech mixed social with biological prescriptions. He predicted the worst: "unless a brake is placed upon the natural ontogeny of this savage, the South will be uninhabitable for the white." But Barringer preferred to place his hope in "education of trade or industrial type" for blacks. "Then and not till then," he concluded, "will the franchise become for him [blacks] a reality and the Jim Crow car a memory."[20]

Although black intellectuals were by no means immune to notions of "race" as the source of group characteristics and traits—such a conception was pervasive in turn-of-the-century Western thought—they would, as a whole, denounce the Barringers and their ideas. Against such racism, whether in this vicious, biological form or in a calmer, paternalistic mode, older memories of emancipation had to contend with newer memories of segregation and lynch mobs in black communities. Indeed, what African American historical memory faced in the new century was not only a pedagogical and historiographical consensus about the "failure" of Reconstruction that seemed to render further discussion of the Fourteenth and Fifteenth Amendments moot; most bluntly, what the racial equalitarian legacy of the Civil War faced was, as George Fredrickson has shown, the sense of permanence and determinism in white supremacist theory and practice.[21] "Race" theory, whether held passively or advanced aggressively, had everything to do with the way white Americans chose to remember emancipation, or whether they chose to remember it at all. From such spokesmen as Barringer, Douglass's question—what will peace among the whites bring?—received some loud and terrible answers.

Although Douglass and Crummell had great respect for each other, they spoke during their Storer confrontation with different agendas, informed by different experiences and representing different traditions. Crummell had never been a slave; he achieved a classical education, was a missionary of evangelical Christianity, a thinker of conservative instincts, and had spent almost the entire Civil War era in West Africa. He returned to the United States twice during the war to recruit black Americans for possible emigration from America to Liberia, while Douglass worked aggressively as an advocate of the Union cause, demanded emancipation, and recruited approximately one hundred members of the Fifty-fourth Massachusetts black regiment (two of whom were his sons Charles and Lewis). Crummell represented a paradoxical brand of black nationalism, which survived through Marcus Garvey and beyond: a combination of Western, European Christian civilizationism and race pride and purity. Crummell contended that the principal problems faced by American blacks were moral weakness, self-hatred, and industrial primitiveness. In the 1870s, Crummell became the founding pastor of St. Luke's Episcopal

Church in Washington, D.C., while Douglass became a regular speaker at the middle-class Metropolitan A.M.E. Church in the same city.[22]

Douglass, the former slave, had established his fame by writing and speaking about the meaning of slavery; his life's work and his very identity were inextricably linked to the transformations of the Civil War. The past made and inspired Douglass; there was no meaning for him without memory, whatever the consequences of "recollection." He believed he had remade himself from slavery to freedom, and he believed that blacks generally had been regenerated in the Second American Revolution of emancipation and the Civil War. The past had also made Crummell; but his connection to many of the benchmarks of African American social memory had been largely distant, and informed by African nationalism and Christian mission. For Douglass, emancipation and the Civil War were truly *felt* history, a moral and legal foundation upon which to demand citizenship and equality. For Crummell, they were the potentially paralyzing memories to be resisted; they were not the epic to be retold, merely the source of future needs. Crummell sought to redeem Africa, and to inspire moral values in the freedpeople by the example of an elite black leadership. Douglass was devoted to the same values and essentially the same model of leadership; he sought, preeminently, however, to redeem the civil and political rights promised by the verdicts of Fort Wagner and Appomattox. Both men believed that the talented had to uplift the ordinary, although they, certainly in Douglass's case, had fallen out of touch with much of the material plight of Southern freedmen. Crummell had tried to be a founding father of Liberia; Douglass dearly wished to see himself as a founding father of a reinvented American republic. Both were from the same generation, had traveled far, seen great changes, and, at Storer College, were speaking to the postfreedom generation. With different reasons and aims, Crummell and Douglass both sought to teach this new generation how to understand and use the legacy of slavery and the Civil War era, how to preserve yet destroy the past.

The contrast between them could be overdrawn in the pursuit of dualities in African American thought. But such a comparison is suggestive of the recurring dilemma of black intellectuals in American history. Is the black experience in America a racial memory, or is it thoroughly intertwined with a collective, national memory? Is the core image of the black experience in America represented by black institutions, cultural forms, and aesthetics that have flourished by rejecting American nationalism or

European cultural forms, or by the black Civil War soldier and the Fourteenth Amendment? By Booker T. Washington's image of the "hand and the fingers," or by Thurgood Marshall standing on the steps of the Supreme Court after winning *Brown v. Board of Education*? In a Garvey-UNIA parade, or in the Selma march? In Malcolm X at a Harlem street rally, or Martin Luther King at the Lincoln Memorial? Can there be a single, core image at all? When does it matter how benchmark African American memories are directly linked to the changing master narratives of American history, and when does it not? Are there not multiple core images of African American historical memory—jagged, diverse, regional, rural, and urban? These kinds of questions are, in part, what keeps African American history at the center of research agendas in the new histories. Dichotomies have sometimes blurred more truth than they have revealed. All such comparisons—among scholars or in larger public uses of memory and history—must, of course, be historicized. However politicized, romanticized, regionalized, or class-based these questions have become in each succeeding generation, the answers have always been contested and complex. Rival memories among black thinkers should be treated as equally dynamic as similar struggles in the larger culture.[23]

As America underwent vast social changes in the late nineteenth century, and fought a foreign war in 1898, so too the memory of the Civil War changed as it was transmitted to new generations. This is a complex story, but one of the principal features of the increasingly sentimentalized road to reunion was the celebration of the veteran, especially at Blue-Gray reunions, which became important aspects of popular culture in an age that loved pageantry, became obsessed with building monuments, and experienced a widespread revival of the martial ideal.[24] A brief focus on the fiftieth anniversary reunion at Gettysburg in 1913 may help illuminate the relationship of race and reunion in Civil War memory.

As early as 1909 the state of Pennsylvania established a commission and began planning for the 1913 celebration. In the end, the states appropriated some $1,750,000 to provide free transportation for veterans from every corner of the country. Pennsylvania alone spent at least $450,000, and the federal government, through Congress and the War Department, appropriated approximately $450,000 to build the "Great Camp" for the "Great Reunion," as it became known. A total of 53,407 veterans attended the reunion, and again as many spectators were estimated to have de-scended upon the small town of Gettysburg for the July 1–4 festival of reconciliation.[25]

The railroad transportation of any Civil War veteran, living anywhere in the United States, was paid for by public monies. Some one hundred veterans arrived in Gettysburg from California, ten of them Confederates. Vermont sent 669 men, four of them listed as Confederates. Nevada and Wyoming were the only states not accounted for at the reunion, although New Mexico sent only one Union veteran. The whole event was an organizational, logistical, and financial triumph. Not only did a small army of souvenir salesmen flood the streets of the town of Gettysburg, but no fewer than forty-seven railroad companies operating in or through Pennsylvania alone were paid a total of $142,282 for the transportation of veterans. One hundred fifty-five reporters from the national and international press covered the event, which was headlined (along with stunning photographs) in most newspapers during the week of the reunion. Once the old men had arrived in their uniforms, decked out in ribbons, and graced with silver beards, the tent city on the old battlefield became one of the most photogenic spectacles Americans had ever seen. For most observers, the veterans were men out of another time, images from the history beyond memory, icons that stimulated deep feelings, a sense of pride, history, and idle amusement all at once. They were an irresistible medium through which Americans could see their inheritance, and be deflected from it at the same time.[26]

Many reunions had been held and a vast array of monuments constructed at Gettysburg long before 1913. But if social memory on the broadest scale is best forged and transmitted by performed, ritual commemorations, as many anthropologists have argued, then the memory of the Civil War as it stood in the general American culture in the early twentieth century never saw a more fully orchestrated expression than at Gettysburg on the battle's semicentennial. The Great Camp, covering 280 acres, serving 688,000 "cooked meals" prepared by 2,170 cooks, laborers, and bakers using 130,048 pounds of flour, must have warmed the hearts of even the most compulsive advocates of Taylorism. Frederick W. Taylor's *Principles of Scientific Management* had just been published in 1911, and the Taylor Society had been founded in the same year as the Civil War semicentennial began. The forty-seven miles of "avenues" on the battlefield, lighted by 500 electric arc lights, provided a perfect model of military mobilization and mass production. Those thirty-two automatic "bubbling ice water fountains" throughout the veterans' quarters offered a delightful, if hardly conscious, experience with "incorporation." Taylorite advocates of efficiency warmly approved the extraordinary "preparedness" of the Red Cross and the army medical corps in their efforts to provide first-class hospital care for the veterans during the encampment. The average age of veterans at the event was seventy-four, and the Pennsylvania Commission's report celebrated the fact that only nine of the old fellows died during the reunion, a statistic many times lower than the national average for such an age group. Moreover, efficiency enthusiasts could marvel at the ninety elaborate, modern latrines (men's and women's) constructed all over the encampment. The commission's report was careful to include notes on the successful functioning of all latrine mechanisms, cleaning procedures, and estimates of tonnage of waste material. The press was full of celebration of such efficiency. The *Philadelphia Inquirer* marveled at the "more painstaking care, more scientific preparation and a better discipline than has ever before been known on such an occasion." The camp was "policed in a way," observed the *Inquirer*, "that made it the healthiest place on earth . . . there never was anything better done in our history."[27]

As one would expect, the theme of the reunion from the earliest days of its conception was nationalism, patriotism, and harmony—the great "Peace Jubilee," as the planning commission had announced as early as 1910. Fifty years after Pickett's charge (and the Emancipation Proclamation, which was utterly ignored during the week's ceremonies), Douglass's question received a full-throated answer. I have found only limited reference to the attendance of black veterans at the 1913 reunion. In a book by Walter H. Blake, a New Jersey veteran who compiled a narrative of anecdotes and personal reminiscences of his journey to the event, one finds the claim that "there were colored men on both sides of the lines." The Pennsylvania Commission "had made arrangements only for negroes from the Union side," lamented the New Jersey veteran, "forgetful of the fact that there were many faithful slaves who fought against their own interests in their intense loyalty to their Southern masters." Numerous black men worked as camp laborers, building the tent city and distributing mess kits and blankets (they appear in photographs published by the commission and elsewhere). Nowhere in its detailed, 281-page published report does the Pennsylvania Commission indicate how many black veterans attended the reunion. The commission was explicitly concerned that *"only"* those determined to be "known veteran[s] of the Civil War" by their documented honorable discharges were to receive free transportation. Presumably this included black G.A.R. members; if so, further research will reveal how many, if any, attended as well as how black veterans may have responded to the reunion's tone and purpose. One of Walter Blake's anecdotes of the reunion is what he calls a "very pretty little incident" in which "a giant of an old negro, Samuel Thompson," was resting under a shade tree. Some Confederate veterans came up to shake hands with "the old darky" and exchange greetings. It is not made clear whether Thompson was a veteran or not. Blake declares this incident another triumph for kindness and concludes without the slightest sense of irony: "no color line here."[28]

The reunion was to be a source of lessons transmitted between generations, as several hundred Boy Scouts of America served the old veterans as aides-de-camp, causing scenes much celebrated in the press. Like any event fraught with so much symbolism, the reunion also became a "site" for contentious politics. Suffragists lobbied the veterans' camp, asking that they shout "votes for women" rather than the refurbished "rebel yell," a scene much derided by some of the press. Most of all, the reunion was a grand opportunity for America's political officialdom, as well as purveyors of popular opinion, to declare the meaning and memory of the Civil War in the present. One does have to wonder if there had ever been an assembly quite like this in the history of the modern world: can we imagine another event commemorated by so many actual participants in so grand a manner, involving such imagery of past, present, and future? Lafayette's tour of America in 1827, the United States Centennial in 1876, and the Columbian Exposition in Chicago in 1893, as well as other world's fairs, come to mind as possible comparisons. But for the transmission of a public, social memory of an epoch, such a platform had rarely existed as that given the state governors and the president of the United States on July 3 and 4, 1913.[29]

On the third day of the reunion the governors of the various states spoke. All, understandably, asserted the themes of sectional harmony and national cohesion. As one would expect, the soldiers' valor was the central idea of such reunion rhetoric. Perhaps William Hodges Mann, the governor of Virginia, struck the most meaningful chord of memory on that occasion: "We are not here to discuss the Genesis of the war," said Mann, "but men who have tried each other in the storm and smoke of battle are here to discuss this great fight, which if it didn't establish a new standard of manhood came up to the highest standard that was ever set. We came here, I say, *not to discuss what caused the war of 1861–65,* but to talk over the events of the battle here as man to man" (emphasis added). The following day, July 4, in the great finale of the reunion staged in a giant tent erected in the middle of the field where Pickett's charge had occurred, the Blue and the Gray gathered to hear what turned out to be a short address by Woodrow Wilson, just recently inaugurated, the first Southern president elected since the Civil War. "We are debtors to those fifty crowded years," announced Wilson, "they have made us all heirs to a mighty heritage." What have the fifty years meant? Wilson asked. The answer struck that mystic chord of memory that most white Americans, North and South, probably desired to hear:

> They have meant peace and union and vigor, and the maturity and might of a great nation. How wholesome and healing the peace has been. We have found one another again as brothers and comrades, in arms, enemies no longer, generous friends rather, our battles long past, the *quarrel forgotten*—except that we shall not forget the splen-did valor, the manly devotion of the men then arrayed against one another, now grasping hands and smiling into each other's eyes. How complete the Union has become and how dear to all of us, how un-questioned, how benign and majestic as state after state has been added to this, our great family of free men! (emphasis added)[30]

That great "hosanna" that Douglass had anticipated forty years before had certainly come to fruition. "Thank God for Gettysburg, hosanna!" declared the *Louisville Courier-Journal.* "God bless us everyone, alike the Blue and the Gray, the Gray and the Blue! The world ne'er witnessed such a sight as this. Beholding, can we say happy is the nation that hath no history?" In Ernest Renan's famous essay, "What is a Nation?" (1882), he aptly described a nation as "a large-scale solidarity . . . a daily plebi-scite" constantly negotiated between "memories" and "present-day con-sent," and requiring a great deal of "forgetting." In varieties of irony, the United States in 1913 fit Renan's definition.[31]

The deep causes and consequences of the Civil War—the role of sla-very and the challenge of racial equality—in those fifty "crowded years" had been actively suppressed and subtly displaced by the celebration of what Oliver Wendell Holmes, Jr., had termed the "soldier's faith," the celebration of the veterans' manly valor and devotion. Oh what a glorious fight they had come to commemorate; and in the end, everyone was right, no one was wrong, and something so transforming as the Civil War had been rendered a mutual victory of the Blue and the Gray by what Governor Mann called the "splendid movement of reconciliation." And Wilson's great gift for mixing idealism with ambiguity was in perfect form. He gave his own, preacherly, restrained endorsement of the valor of the past. Then, putting on his Progressive's hat, he spoke to the present. "The day of our country's life has but broadened into morning," he declared. "Do not put uniforms by. Put the harness of the present on." Wilson's speech offers a poignant illustration of the significance of presidential rhetoric in the creation of American nationalism.[32]

If, as Garry Wills has argued, Abraham Lincoln, in the brevity of the "Gettysburg Address" in 1863, "revolutionized the revolution," and offered the nation a "refounding" in the principle of *equality* forged out of the crucible of the war, then Woodrow Wilson, in his Gettysburg address fifty years later, offered a subtle and strikingly less revolutionary response. According to Wills, Lincoln had suggested a new constitution at Gettysburg, "giving people a new past to live with that would change their future indefinitely." So did Wilson in 1913. But the new past was one in which all sectional strife was gone, and in which all racial strife was ignored or covered over in claims for Wilson's own brand of Progressivism. He appealed to a social and moral equivalent of war directed not at the old veterans but at the younger generations who "must contend, not with armies, but with principalities and powers and wickedness in high places." He came with "orders," not for the old men in Blue and Gray but for the "host" of the American people, "the great and the small, without class or difference of race or origin . . . our constitutions are their articles of enlistment. The orders of day are the laws upon our statute books." Lincoln's "rebirth of freedom" had become in fifty years Wilson's forward-looking "righteous peace" (Wilson's "New Freedom" program in the 1912 election campaign). The potential in the Second American Revolution had become the "quarrel forgotten" on the statute books of Jim Crow America. Wilson, of course, did not believe he was speaking for or about the ravages of segregation, or other aspects of racial division in America, on his day at Gettysburg. He was acutely aware of his presence at the reunion as a Southerner, and was no doubt still negotiating the uneasy terrain of a minority president, elected by only 42 percent of the popular vote in the turbulent four-way election of 1912. Wilson's Progressivism was antimonopolist, antitariff, and concerned with banking reform and other largely middle-class causes. Although racial issues only rarely occupied him while president, he was instinctively a state rightist.[33] Educated by events, and rising beyond his own constraints, Lincoln had soared above the "honored dead" to try to imagine a new future in America. Wilson soared above the honored veterans and described a present and a future in which white patriotism and nationalism flourished, in which society seemed threatened by disorder, and in which the principle of equality might be said, by neglect and action, to have been living a social death.

The ceremonies at Gettysburg in 1913 represented a public avowal of the deeply laid mythology of the Civil War (some scholars prefer the term *tradition*) that had captured the popular imagination by the early twentieth century.[34] The war was remembered primarily as a tragedy that led to greater unity and national cohesion, and as a soldier's call to sacrifice in order to save a troubled, but essentially good, Union, not as the crisis of a nation deeply divided over slavery, race, competing definitions of labor, liberty, political economy, and the future of the West, issues hardly resolved in 1913.

Press reports and editorials demonstrate just how much this version of Civil War history had become what some theorists have called "structural amnesia" or social "habit memory."[35] The issues of slavery and secession, rejoiced the conservative *Washington Post*, were "no longer discussed argumentatively. They are scarcely mentioned at all, except in connection with the great war to which they led, and by which they were *disposed of for all time.*" To the extent that slavery involved a "moral principle," said the *Post*, "no particular part of the people was responsible unless, indeed, the burden of responsibility should be shouldered *by the North for its introduction*" (emphasis added). Echoing many of the governors (North and South) who spoke at the reunion, the "greater victory," declared the *Post*, was that won by the national crusade to reunite the veterans, and not that of the Army of the Potomac in 1863. The *New York Times* hired Helen D. Longstreet (widow of the Confederate general James Longstreet, who had been much maligned by the Lost Cause devotees for his caution at Gettysburg and his Republicanism after the war) to write daily columns about the reunion. She entertained *Times* readers with her dialogues with Southern veterans about the value of Confederate defeat and the beauty of "Old Glory." She also challenged readers to remember the sufferings of women during the Civil War and to consider an intersectional tribute to them as the theme of the next reunion. The nation's historical memory, concluded the *Times*, had become so "balanced" that it could never again be "disturbed" by sectional conflict. The editors of the liberal magazine *The Outlook* were overwhelmed by the spirit of nationalism at the reunion, and declared it a reconciliation of "two conceptions of human right and human freedom." The war, said the *Outlook*, had been fought over differing notions of "idealism": "sovereignty of the state" versus "sovereignty of the nation." Demonstrating to what degree slavery had vanished from understandings of Civil War causation in serious intellectual circles, the *Outlook* announced that "it was slavery that raised the question of State sovereignty; but it was not on behalf of slavery, but on behalf of State sovereignty and all that it implied, that these men fought." So normative was this viewpoint—not to be replaced by a new historiographical consensus for several decades—that the *Outlook's* special correspondent at the reunion, Herbert Francis Sherwood, could conclude that the veterans' "fraternity . . . showed that no longer need men preach a reunited land, for there were no separated people." Such was the state of historical consciousness in Jim Crow America. In the larger culture, slavery (and the whole black experience) was read out of the formulas by which Americans found meanings in the Civil War. As in all deep ironies, the *Outlook* was both accurate and oblivious in its interpretation of the reunion; and thus could it conclude without blinking that "both sides" had fought for "the same ideal—the ideal of civil liberty."[36]

The Gettysburg reunion was an event so full of symbolic meaning, and perhaps so photogenic, that it compelled editorial comment from far and wide. The *Times* (London) correspondent reported back to England that the reunion had sent a "great and memorable lesson . . . eradicating forever the scars of the civil war in a way that no amount of preaching or political maneuvering could have done." Reporters from every section of the country registered their sense of awe and wonderment at the Gettysburg celebration. "The Reunion fifty years after stands alone in the annals of the world," said the *Cincinnati Enquirer*, "for no similar event has ever taken place." The *San Francisco Examiner*, in an editorial that modeled Lincoln's "Gettysburg Address" in form, declared the "jubilee" to be the "supreme justification of war and battle." Now "we know that the great war had to be fought, that it is well that it was fought," announced the *Examiner*, "a necessary, useful, splendid sacrifice whereby the whole race of men has been unified." Such martial spirit and claims of ritual purging were answered (albeit by a minority voice) in the *Charleston (South Carolina) News and Courier.* The newspaper in the city where secession began urged readers not to glorify the "battle itself," for it was "a frightful and abominable thing." If war "thrills us," declared the *News and Courier,* "we lose a vitally important part of the lesson." But the *Brooklyn Daily Eagle* kept the discussion on a higher plane with a theme that allowed, simultaneously, for a recognition of Northern victory, Southern respect, and faith in American providential destiny:

> Two civilizations met at Gettysburg and fought out the issue between them under the broad, blue sky, in noble, honorable battle.... In one, as historians have pointed out, the family was the social unit—the family in the old Roman sense, possibly inclusive of hundreds of slaves. In the other, the individual was the only social unit. Within half a century those two civilizations have become one. Individualism has triumphed. Yet has that triumph been tempered with a fuller recognition than ever before the war, of the charm and dignity and cultivation of what has yielded to the hand of Fate.... The ways of Providence are inscrutable.

The Brooklyn editor had neatly wrapped the whole package in nostalgia for the masses. He offered mystic honor to the Lost Cause of patriarchal "family" structure, combined with an uneasy celebration of the triumph of individualism in the age of industrialization, all justified by God's design.[37]

Such homilies about nationalism and peace, though often well-meaning in their context, masked as much as they revealed. One should not diminish the genuine sentiment of the veterans in 1913; the Civil War had left ghastly scars to be healed in the psyches of individual men, as well as in the collective memories of Americans in both sections. The war's impact on the social psychology of Americans of both sections and races had been enormous. Understandably, monuments and reunions had always combined remembrance with healing and, therefore, with forgetting. But it is not stretching the evidence to suggest that white supremacy was a silent master of ceremonies at the Gettysburg reunion. No overt conspiracy need be implied, but commemorative rituals are not merely benign performances; their content and motivation must be explored along with their form. The reunion was a national ritual in which the ghost of slavery might, once and for all, be exorcised, and in which a conflict among whites might be transmogrified into national mythology.

Black newspapers of the era were, understandably, wary and resentful of the celebration of the great "Peace Jubilee." At a time when lynching had developed into a social ritual of its own horrifying kind in the South, and when the American apartheid had become almost fully entrenched, black opinion leaders found the sectional love feast at Gettysburg to be more irony than they could bear. "We are wondering," declared the *Baltimore Afro-American Ledger*, "whether Mr. Lincoln had the slightest idea in his mind that the time would ever come when the people of this country would come to the conclusion that by the 'People' he meant only white people." Black memory of the Civil War seemed at such variance with what had happened at the reunion. The *Afro-American* captured the stakes and the potential results of this test of America's social memory. "Today the South is in the saddle, and with the single exception of slavery, everything it fought for during the days of the Civil War, it has gained by repression of the Negro within its borders. And the North has quietly allowed it to have its own way." The *Afro-American* asserted the loyalty of black soldiers during the war and of black citizens since, and pointed to President Wilson's recent forced segregation of federal government workers. The "blood" of black soldiers and lynched citizens was "crying from the ground" in the South, unheard and strangely unknown at the Blue-Gray reunion. When the assembled at Gettysburg paused to hear Lincoln's lines about that "government of the people," suggested the *Afro-American*, it ought to "recall the fact that at least part of the people of this country are Negroes and at the same time human beings, and civilized human beings at that; struggling towards the light, as God has given them to see the light."[38]

These reactions in the black press are especially telling given one of the most striking ironies of all during that summer of 1913: the Wilson administration's increasingly aggressive program of racial segregation in federal government agencies, which were major employers of black Americans. On the day after Decoration Day the official segregation of black clerks in the Post Office Department began. And on July 12, only a week after Wilson spoke at Gettysburg, orders were issued to create separate lavatories for blacks and whites working at the Treasury Department. These and other segregation policies, stemming in part from the many new white Southerners who had come to Washington with the Wilson administration (some racial radicals and some moderates), caused deep resentment and protest among blacks, led largely by the National Association for the Advancement of Colored People (NAACP). Such policies, and the sense of betrayal they caused among blacks, prompted Booker T. Washington, no friend of the NAACP, to declare that he had "never seen the colored people so discouraged and bitter" as they were in the summer of 1913. That summer the NAACP launched a sometimes successful campaign against segregation practices in the federal government.[39]

The *Washington Bee* was even more forthright than other papers in its criticism of the planned reunion at Gettysburg:

> The occasion is to be called a Reunion! A Reunion of whom? Only the men who fought for the preservation of the Union and the extinction of human slavery? Is it to be an assemblage of those who fought to destroy the Union and perpetuate slavery, and who are now employing every artifice and argument known to deceit and sophistry to propagate a national sentiment in favor of their nefarious contention that emancipation, reconstruction and enfranchisement are a dismal failure?

The *Bee's* editor, W. Calvin Chase, asserted that the Blue-Gray ritual was not a "reunion" at all, but a "Reception" thrown by the victors for the vanquished. Most significantly, he argued that the event was a national declaration of a version of history and a conception of the legacy of the Civil War. The message of the reunion, wrote Chase, was "an insane and servile acknowledgment that the most precious results of the war are a prodigious, unmitigated failure."[40] Commemorative rituals can inspire decidedly different interpretations; sometimes it depends simply on whether one is on the creating or the receiving end of historical memory. Sometimes it depends simply on whether a construction of social memory is to be used to sustain or dislodge part of the social order.

As with the earlier generation in the 1880s, when Douglass and Crummell conducted their debate, the stakes of social memory in 1913 were roughly the same. An interpretation of national history had become wedded to racial theory; the sections had reconciled, nationalism flourished, some social wounds had healed, and Paul Buck could later confidently write, in his Pulitzer Prize-winning *The Road to Reunion* (1937, still the only major synthetic work written on this subject), of the "leaven of forgiveness" that grew in a generation into the "miracle" of reconciliation, and of a "revolution in sentiment" whereby "all people within the country felt the electrifying thrill of a common purpose." Such a reunion had been possible, Buck argued, because Americans had collectively admitted that the "race problem" was "basically insoluable," and had "taken the first step in learning how to live with it." Gone with the wind, indeed. Peace between North and South, Buck wrote, unwittingly answering Douglass's question, had given the South, and therefore the nation, a "stability of race relations" upon which the "new patriotism" and "new nationalism" could be built. A segregated society required a segregated historical memory and a national mythology that could blunt or contain the conflict at the root of that segregation. Buck sidestepped, or perhaps simply missed, the irony in favor of an unblinking celebration of the path to reunion. Just such a celebration is what one finds in the *Atlanta Constitution*'s coverage of the Gettysburg reunion in 1913. With mystic hyperbole and what may seem to us strange logic, the *Constitution* declared that "as never before in its history the nation is united in demanding that justice and equal rights be given all of its citizens." No doubt, these sentiments reflected genuinely held beliefs among some white Southerners that Jim Crow meant "progress." The *Constitution* gushed about the "drama" and "scale" of the symbolism at the Gettysburg reunion, even its "poetry and its fragrance." But most important was "the thing for which it stands—the world's mightiest republic purged of hate and unworthiness, *seared clean of dross* by the most fiery ordeal in any nation's history"[41] (emphasis added). Such were the fruits of America's segregated mind and its segregated historical consciousness.

Theorists and historians have long argued that myth as history often best serves the ends of social stability and conservatism. That is certainly the case with the development of Civil War mythology in America. But we also know that mythic conceptions or presentations of the past can be innovative as well as conservative, liberating instead of destructive, or the result of sheer romance. Whether we like it or not, history is used this way generation after generation. "Only a horizon ringed with myths," warned Friedrich Nietzsche in 1874, "can unify a culture." As professional historians, we would do well to keep in mind C. Vann Woodward's warning that "the twilight zone that lies between living memory and written history is one of the favorite breeding places of mythology." But great myths have their "resilience, not completely controllable," as Michael Kammen reminds us. This reality is precisely the one W. E. B. Du Bois recognized in the final chapter of his *Black Reconstruction in America* (1935), published just two years before Buck's *Road to Reunion*. Du Bois insisted that history should be an "art using the results of science," and not merely a means of "inflating our national ego." But by focusing on the subject of the Civil War and Reconstruction in the 1930s, he offered a tragic awareness, as well as a trenchant argument, that written history cannot be completely disengaged from social memory. Du Bois echoed the *Atlanta Constitution* editor, admitting that there had been a "searing of the memory" in America, but one of a very different kind. The "searing" Du Bois had in mind was not that of the Civil War itself but that of a white supremacist historiography and a popular memory of the period that had "obliterated" the black experience and the meaning of emancipation by "libel, innuendo, and silence."[42] The stakes in the development of America's historical memory of the Civil War have never been benign. The answers to Douglass's question have never been benign either. "Peace among the whites" brought segregation and the necessity of later reckonings. The Civil War has not yet been disengaged from a mythological social memory, and perhaps it never will be. But likewise, the American reunion cannot be disengaged from black experience and interpretations, nor from the question of race in the collective American memory.

As with other major touchstones of American history, Americans will continue to use the Civil War for ends that serve the present. There are many reasons for this, but one of the most compelling perhaps is the fact that emancipation in America (contrary to the experience of every other country in the century of emancipations) came as a result of total war and social revolution. Revolutions, as we have all learned, can go backward as well as revive again in new, reconstructed forms from one generation to the next. All such questions, of course, must be explained in their contexts. But the Civil War and emancipation may remain in the mythic realm precisely because, in the popular imagination anyway, they represent reconciled discord, a crucible of tragedy and massive change survived in a society that still demands a providential conception of its history. Facing the deepest causes and consequences of the Civil War has always forced us to face the kind of logic Nathan Huggins insisted upon in his final work. "The challenge of the paradox [of race in American history]," wrote Huggins, "is that there can be no white history or black history, nor can there be an integrated history that does not begin to comprehend that slavery and freedom, white and black, are joined at the hip."[43]

~~✿~~

NOTES

INTRODUCTION

1. Eric Foner, "The Meaning of Freedom in the Age of Emancipation," *Journal of American History* 81 (Sept. 1994): 436.

Chapter One
THE SLAVE POWER CONSPIRACY REVISITED:
UNITED STATES PRESIDENTS AND FILIBUSTERING, 1848–1861

The author would like to thank Professor Howard Jones of the University of Alabama for his perceptive critique of this essay. His suggestions helped me to reformulate some of my arguments as well as to avoid several errors.

1. Richard H. Sewell, *Ballots for Freedom: Antislavery Politics in the United States, 1837–1860* (New York: Norton, 1976), 46, 52, 59, 86–95, 102–3, 106, 166, 199–200, 255–56, 267, 286, 304, 355; Russel B. Nye, *Fettered Freedom: Civil Liberties and the Slavery Controversy, 1830–1860* (East Lansing: Michigan State Univ. Press, 1949), 217–49; James Brewer Stewart, *Holy Warriors: The Abolitionists and American Slavery* (New York: Hill and Wang, 1976); Merton L. Dillon, *The Abolitionists: The Growth of a Dissenting Minority* (DeKalb: Northern Illinois Univ. Press, 1974), 86, 102, 105, 142–43, 161, 194; Eric Foner, *Free Soil, Free Labor, Free Men: The Ideology of the Republican Party before the Civil War* (New York: Oxford Univ. Press, 1970), 92–102, 119–20, 192; Larry Gara, "Slavery and the Slave Power: A Crucial Distinction," *Civil War History* 15 (Mar. 1969): 5–18. Gara contends that Republican party strength derived far more from fears of slave power encroachments than from sympathy for the plight of slaves.

2. Robert E. May, *The Southern Dream of a Caribbean Empire, 1854–1861* (Baton Rouge: Louisiana State Univ. Press, 1973).

3. *Annals of Congress*, 15th Cong., 1st sess., pt. 2:2567–70; Robert E. May, *John A. Quitman: Old South Crusader* (Baton Rouge: Louisiana State Univ. Press, 1985), 270–95; Charles H. Brown, *Agents of Manifest Destiny: The Lives and Times of the Filibusters* (Chapel Hill: Univ. of North Carolina Press, 1980), 195, 351–55; Ronnie C. Tyler, "The Callahan Expedition of 1855: Indians or Negroes?" *Southwestern Historical Quarterly* 70 (Apr. 1967): 574–85; Kimberly Ann Lamp, "Empire for Slavery: Economic and Territorial Expansion in the American Gulf South, 1835–1860" (Ph.D. diss., Harvard University, 1991).

4. *New-York Daily Times*, Mar. 18, 1852; Theodore Parker, "The Present Aspect of American Slavery," *Boston Liberator*, Feb. 27, 1857; John Bigelow to William Cullen Bryant, Dec. 28, 1857, John Bigelow Papers, New York Public Library; *Congressional Globe*, 35th Cong., 1st sess., 257; Sarah P. Remond speech, Jan. 24, 1859, C. Peter Ripley, *The Black Abolitionist Papers*, 5 vols. (Chapel Hill: Univ. of North Carolina Press, 1985–92), 1:436; *Richmond (Indiana) Palladium*, Oct. 2, 1856; Thomas Drew, comp., *The Campaign of 1856: Fremont Songs for the People, Original and Selected* (Boston, 1856), 56–58. See also related postsecession charges by individuals formerly involved in abolitionism and antislavery politics, such as: Joshua R. Giddings, *History of the Rebellion: Its Authors and Causes* (New York, 1864), 414–15; Henry Wilson, *History of the Rise and Fall of the Slave Power in America*, 3 vols. (Boston, 1879), 2:612–13; John Smith Dye, *History of the Plots and Crimes of the Great Conspiracy to Overthrow Liberty in America* (New York, 1866), 88.

5. David Brion Davis, *The Slave Power Conspiracy and the Paranoid Style* (Baton Rouge: Louisiana State Univ. Press, 1969), 6.

6. Paul Finkelman, *An Imperfect Union: Slavery, Federalism, and Comity* (Chapel Hill: Univ. of North Carolina Press, 1981), 320–38; Eric T. Dean, Jr., "Reassessing *Dred Scott:* The Possibilities of Federal Power in the Antebellum Context," *University of Cincinnati Law Review* 60 (Winter 1992): 752–54; Sewell, *Ballots*, 299–304; William M. Wiecek, "Slavery and Abolition Before the United States Supreme Court, 1820–1860," *Journal of American History* 65 (June 1978): 34–59.

7. Andrew F. Rolle, *California: A History* (New York: Crowell, 1969), 257. Generally, scholars give the Whig administrations of Zachary Taylor and Millard Fillmore higher marks with respect to preventing filibustering than those of the expansionist Democrats Franklin Pierce and James Buchanan. See particularly Elbert B. Smith, *The Presidencies of Zachary Taylor & Millard Fillmore* (Lawrence: Univ. Press of Kansas, 1988), 86–89, 227–30. But no president of the period has escaped censure on this issue. See Philip Foner, *A History of Cuba and Its Relations with the United States*, 2 vols. (New York: International Publishers, 1962–63), 2:46, 56; Larry Gara, *The Presidency of Franklin Pierce* (Lawrence: Univ. Press of Kansas, 1991), 131, 142–44, 150–52; Harold M. Hyman and William M. Wiecek, *Equal Justice Under Law: Constitutional Development, 1835–1875* (New York: Harper and Row, 1982), 171; Basil Rauch, *American Interest in Cuba, 1848–1855* (New York: Columbia Univ. Press, 1948), 262, 267–70, 273; Philip S. Klein, *President James Buchanan: A Biography* (University Park: Pennsylvania State Univ. Press, 1962), 319–20; Elbert B. Smith, *The Presidency of James Buchanan* (Lawrence: Univ. Press of Kansas, 1975), 72–73.

8. James D. Richardson, comp., *A Compilation of the Messages and Papers of the Presidents, 1789–1908*, 11 vols. (New York: Bureau of National Literature and Art, 1908), 5:7, 111, 271, 468.

9. Ibid., 230. The Senate deleted the provision. See J. Fred Rippy, *The United States and Mexico* (New York: F. S. Crofts, 1931), 148, 154–55; James Morton Callahan, *American Foreign Policy in Mexican Relations* (New York: Macmillan, 1932), 226; Charles I. Bevans, comp.,

Treaties and Other International Agreements of the United States of America, 1776–1949, 12 vols. (Washington, D.C.: GPO, 1968–74), 9:807–11.

10. William L. Marcy to Luis Molina, Apr. 25, 1856, Lewis Cass to Mirabeau B. Lamar, July 25, 1858, in William R. Manning, ed., *Diplomatic Correspondence of the United States: Inter-American Affairs, 1831–1860*, 12 vols. (Washington, D.C.: GPO, 1921–39), 4:82, 118–19; John J. Crittenden to Count Eugène de Sartiges, Oct. 21, 1851, ibid., 6:460–64; James Buchanan to Romulus Saunders, June 17, 1848, ibid., 11:58–59; William L. Marcy to Juan N. Almonte, June 12, 1854, ibid., 9:164–65.

11. *Washington Daily National Intelligencer*, Aug. 28, Nov. 10, 1848; *Pittsburgh Daily Morning Post*, May 9, 1850; Robert Benson Leard, "Bonds of Destiny: The United States and Cuba, 1848–1861" (Ph.D. diss., University of California, 1953), 52n; William C. Rives to John M. Clayton, June 13, 1850, in Manning, ed., *Diplomatic Correspondence*, 6:609; *Charleston Mercury*, Aug. 30, 1851; "Ion" to the *Baltimore Sun*, quoted in *New Orleans Daily Picayune*, Sept. 4, 1851; Thomas Palmer to John Dowling, May 21, 1851, John Dowling Papers, Indiana State Historical Society, Indianapolis; *New-York Daily Times*, Mar. 18, 1852; *The Guardian* (London), Sept. 10, 1851.

12. James Gadsden to William L. Marcy, Nov. 19, 1853, in Manning, ed., *Diplomatic Correspondence*, 9:666; *Daily Cincinnati Gazette*, July 1, 1853; *Buffalo Express*, June 26, 1854, quoted in *New York Herald*, July 4, 1854; Caleb Cushing to John McKeon, Feb. 7, 1857, in C. C. Andrews, ed., *Official Opinions of the Attorneys General of the United States* (Washington, D.C.: GPO, 1856), 375–76; José de Marcoleta to John M. Clayton, Jan. 6, 1855, John M. Clayton Papers, Manuscript Division, Library of Congress, Washington, D.C. (hereafter cited as LC); Kenneth Bourne, *Britain and the Balance of Power in North America, 1815–1908* (Berkeley: Univ. of California Press, 1967), 187, 190–91; [John David Borthwick], "Nicaragua and the Filibusters," *Blackwood's Edinburgh Magazine* 79 (Mar. 1856): 314; Philip Griffith to Earl of Clarendon, July 6, 1856, Great Britain, Foreign Office, F.O. 55/122, General Correspondence, Colombia and New Granada, Public Records Office, Kew, England (hereafter cited as PRO); *Philadelphia Public Ledger*, May 17, 1856; Justin S. Morrill to James A. Pearce, May 16, 1856, James A. Pearce Papers, Maryland Historical Society, Baltimore.

13. *Richmond (Indiana) Palladium*, Oct. 2, 1856; John Bigelow to William Cullen Bryant, Dec. 28, 1857 (copy), Bigelow Papers; Charles Wyke to John Russell, Jan. 17, 1861, Great Britain, Foreign Office, F.O. 39/12, Consular Despatches from Honduras, PRO; *New-York Times*, Oct. 18, 25, 1859; George Washington Hazard to J. D. Howland, Jan. 25, 1858, George Washington Hazard Papers, United States Military Academy Library, West Point, N.Y.; *New York Albion*, Dec. 19, 1857.

14. James K. Polk Diary, June 2, 9, 17, Aug. 29, 1848, *The Diary of James K. Polk*, ed. Milo Milton Quaife, 4 vols. (1910; rpt. New York: Kraus, 1970), 3:476–77, 485–87, 493, 4:104–5; James Buchanan to Romulus Saunders, June 17, 1848, Buchanan to Robert Rantoul, June 23, 1848, Buchanan to the Venezuelan Minister of Foreign Affairs, Aug. 7, 1848, Buchanan to Thomas J. Durant and others, Aug. 30, 1848, John Bassett Moore, comp. and ed., *The Works of James Buchanan*, 12 vols. (New York: Antiquarian Press, 1960), 8:90–102, 105, 159–60, 192–95; *Washington Daily Union*, Aug. 26, 1848.

15. A. Delmas to J. J. Walker, Aug. 1, 1849, *Sen. Ex. Doc.*, 31st Cong., 1st sess., no. 57:4. López was a native Venezuelan.

16. John M. Clayton to Logan Hunton, Aug. 8, 1849, Clayton to the U.S. District Attorney, Mobile, Aug. 23, 1849, William Ballard Preston to Foxhall A. Parker, Aug. 29, 1849,

Clayton to J. Prescott Hall, Sept. 19, 1849, *Sen. Ex. Doc.*, 31st Cong., 1st sess., no. 57:6–7, 12, 117–18, 17; Zachary Taylor to Clayton, Aug. 11, 1849 (copy), Preston Family Papers, Virginia Historical Society, Richmond; Rose O'Neal Greenhow to John C. Calhoun, Aug. 29, 1849, J. Franklin Jameson, ed., "Correspondence of John C. Calhoun," *Annual Report of the American Historical Association for the Year 1899*, 2 vols. (Washington, D.C.: American Historical Association, 1900), 2:1203–4; Clayton to J. Prescott Hall with note to James E. Harvey, Sept. 6, 1849, RG 59, Dept. of State, General Records, Despatches from Special Agents, M37, roll 9, National Archives (hereafter cited as NA).

17. Eben Farrand to V. M. Randolph, Sept. 4, 1849, J. Prescott Hall to John M. Clayton, Sept. 8, 1849, *Sen. Ex. Doc.*, 31st Cong., 1st sess., no. 57:91. Several of López's agents, it should be noted, claimed federal endorsement in order to attract recruits. Years later, López's second-in-command interpreted Taylor's decision not to prosecute the filibusters as evidence of federal collusion. However, the decision not to prosecute was based on the presumption that most of the filibusters had been duped into participating and that they would not pose any problem in the future. V. M. Randolph to William Ballard Preston, with enclosures, Sept. 20, 1849, *Sen. Ex. Doc.*, 31st Cong., 1st sess., no. 57:101–4; Ambrosio José Gonzales, *Manifesto on Cuban Affairs Addressed to the People of the United States* (New Orleans, 1853), 7–8; John M. Clayton to J. Prescott Hall, Sept. 7, 1849, RG 59, roll 9, NA; Clayton to Sir Henry Bulwer, Apr. 24, 1850, Kenneth Bourne and D. Cameron Watt, eds., *British Documents on Foreign Affairs: Reports and Papers from the Foreign Office Confidential Print*, pt. 1, ser. C (Ann Arbor: Univ. of Michigan Press, 1986), 4:39.

18. John M. Clayton Circulars to Logan Hunton, J. Prescott Hall, and Philip R. Fendall, all dated Jan. 22, 1850, Clayton to Hall, May 17, 1850, Clayton to Don Calderón de la Barca, May 18, 1850, *Sen. Ex. Doc.*, 31st Cong., 1st sess., no. 57:21, 33–34, 29–31.

19. William Ballard Preston to Josiah Tattnall, Victor M. Randolph, separate letters dated May 15, 1850; John M. Clayton to J. Prescott Hall, May 26, 1850 (extract); W. M. Meredith to U.S. customs collectors at Boston and other cities, May 28, 1850; Clayton to Henry Williams, May 25, 1850; Clayton to Logan Hunton and Peter Hamilton, May 27, 1850, separate letters, *Sen. Ex. Doc.*, 31st Cong., 1st sess., no. 57:54–56, 46, 129, 44; Clayton to Hunton, June 9, 1850, in Manning, ed., *Diplomatic Correspondence*, 11:83; Thomas Ewing to Logan Hunton, June 10 (separate letter and telegram), June 17, 1850, D. C. Goddard to Hunton, July 26, 27, 1850, RG 60, Department of Justice, General Records, Letters Sent by the Department of Justice Concerning Judiciary Expenses, M700, roll 1, NA; Clayton to Zachary Taylor, June 9, 1850, Clayton Papers. Federal efforts to prosecute filibuster organizers in New York also came to unsuccessful conclusions. Leard, "Bonds of Destiny," 79–80.

20. Daniel Webster to J. Prescott Hall, Sept. 7, 1850, Webster to the Collector of Customs at New Orleans, Jan. 21, 1851, Webster to Don Calderón de la Barca, Jan. 22, 1851, "Order addressed by Millard Fillmore, President of the United States to certain Collectors of Customs and Marshals of the United States," Sept. 2, 1851, in Manning, ed., *Diplomatic Correspondence*, 11:96n, 98, 98n, 111n; Webster to Logan Hunton, Jan. 20, 1851, *Sen. Ex. Doc.*, 31st Cong., 2d sess., no. 41:87; Webster to the District Attorney for Mississippi, Mar. 1851 (rough draft, no exact date), Daniel Webster Papers, microfilm ed., roll 24; W. A. Graham to J. Prescott Hall, Aug. 26, 1851, RG 60, M700, roll 1, NA; Frederick S. Calhoun, *The Lawmen: United States Marshals and Their Deputies, 1789–1989* (Washington, D.C.: Smithsonian Institution Press, 1989), 68–69; *New Orleans Daily Picayune*, Oct. 1, 1851; William A. Graham to John W. Livingston, Sept. 3, 1851, K. Jack Bauer, ed., *The New American State Papers: Naval Affairs*, 10 vols. (Wilmington, Del.: Scholarly Resources, 1981), 2:138–39; Foxhall A. Parker to

William A. Graham, Oct. 27, 1851, RG 45, Letters Received by the Secretary of the Navy from Commanding Officers of Squadrons, M89, roll 92, NA; Logan Hunton to Daniel Webster, Feb. 14, 1851, Webster to Hunton, Feb. 28, 1851, J. Prescott Hall to Daniel Webster, Aug. 8, 1852, Webster to Hall, Aug. 16, 1852, in Kenneth E. Shewmaker and Kenneth R. Stevens, eds., *The Papers of Daniel Webster; Diplomatic Papers,* ser. 3, 2 vols. (Hanover, N.H.: Univ. Press of New England, 1987), 2:363–64, 426–28.

21. *House Ex. Doc.,* 32d Cong., 1st sess., no. 112:1–2; Millard Fillmore to Hugh Maxwell, Nov. 12, 1852, quoted in *Washington Daily National Intelligencer,* Nov. 27, 1852. Spanish authorities had prohibited one of Law's vessels, the *Crescent City,* from landing passengers and mail in Havana because the ship's purser, William Smith, had been quoted in a New York paper as being critical of Spanish rule in Cuba. Spanish officials feared that Smith would smuggle incendiary publications into the island. Brown, *Agents,* 101–2.

22. Richardson, comp., *Messages and Papers,* 6:2731–32. Davis in 1852 had given addresses comparing Cuba filibusters to European adventurers who had joined American forces during the American Revolution. He also criticized President Fillmore for his antifilibustering pronouncements, claiming that they had encouraged Spanish authorities in their decision to execute captured filibusters. López's former second-in-command thanked Davis for vindicating the filibusters. Furthermore, Pierce's attorney general, Caleb Cushing, attended a banquet in September 1853 at which speeches were given by Southerners lamenting the fate of filibuster "martyrs" who had been executed by Spain. *Jackson Mississippian,* Jan. 16, June 18, 1852; Ambrósio José González to Jefferson Davis, Dec. 18, 1853, Lynda Lasswell Crist, ed., *The Papers of Jefferson Davis,* 9 vols. (Baton Rouge: Louisiana State Univ. Press, 1971–), 5:54; *Washington Daily National Intelligencer,* Sept. 17, 1853. Some of the Cuba filibusters had campaigned actively for Pierce's election and expected the president's cooperation as a reward for loyalty. Rauch, *American Interest,* 229.

23. J. F. H. Claiborne, *Life and Correspondence of John A. Quitman,* 2 vols. (New York, 1860), 2:195; Mike Walsh to John A. Quitman, May 25, 1854, J. W. Lesesne to John A. Quitman, June 8, 1854, John A. Quitman Papers, Houghton Library, Harvard University (hereafter cited as HU); John J. McRae to J. F. H. Claiborne, June 14, 1854, J. F. H. Claiborne Papers, F. Jones to John A. Quitman, June 10, 1854, John A. Quitman Papers, Mississippi Department of Archives and History, Jackson (hereafter cited as MDAH); *Natchez (Mississippi) Daily Courier,* June 3, 1854; *Congressional Globe,* 34th Cong., 1st sess., appendix, 1295; *New York Herald,* June 3, 1854.

24. José de Marcoleta to William L. Marcy, May 4, Nov. 22, Dec. 11, 1854, Felipe Molina to Marcy, Dec. 13, 1854, Manning, ed., *Diplomatic Correspondence,* 4:404–9, 425–27, 429–32; *Washington Daily Union,* Dec. 8, 1854; José de Marcoleta to John M. Clayton, Jan. 6, 1855, Clayton Papers; "Peterson" to Mansfield Lovell, Jan. 9, 1855 (copy), Mike Walsh to John A. Quitman, Jan. 25, 1855, John A. Quitman Papers, MDAH; William Brantly to Quitman, Jan. 17, 1855, Quitman Papers, HU.

25. Samuel D. Hay to Jefferson Davis, Mar. 28, 1854, RG 139, Records of the Department of State, Miscellaneous Letters, M179, roll 139, NA; Harwood Perry Hinton, "The Military Career of John Ellis Wool, 1812–1863" (Ph.D. diss., University of Wisconsin, 1960), 265–75; Winfield Scott to Jefferson Davis, May 30, 1855, Scott to Samuel Cooper, May 31, 1855, RG 107, Records of the Office of the Secretary of War, Letters Received, M221, roll 175, NA; Winfield Scott to Charles Boarman, May 31, 1855 (copy), Charles Boarman Letterbooks, LC.

26. John Slidell to James Buchanan, June 17, 1854, Buchanan Papers, Historical Society of Pennsylvania, Philadelphia; F. Jones to John A. Quitman, June 10, 1854, Quitman Papers,

MDAH; Sidney Webster, "Mr. Marcy, The Cuban Question and the Ostend Manifesto," *Political Science Quarterly* 8 (Mar. 1893): 14 15; [*Washington*] *Daily Union*, July 4, 6, 22, 1854; May, *Quitman*, 194–95.

27. Ethan Allen Hitchcock Diary, Dec. 16, 1853, *Fifty Years in Camp and Field: Diary of Major-General Ethan Allen Hitchcock, U.S.A.*, ed. W. A. Croffut (New York: G. P. Putnam's Sons, 1909), 405; James C. Dobbin to Levi D. Slamm [Dec. 1853], Dobbin to Bladen Dulany, Jan. 3, 1854, Dobbin to Thomas A. Dornin, Mar. 31, 1854, in Bauer, ed., *New American State Papers: Naval Affairs*, 2:159, 160, 161–62; John E. Wool to Jefferson Davis, Jan. 10, Feb. 28, Mar. 1, 1854, John E. Wool to Samuel Cooper, Mar. 31, 1854, Davis to Wool, Jan. 12, Apr. 14, Aug. 18, 1854, *House Ex. Doc.*, 35th Cong., 1st sess., no. 88:6, 9, 10, 19, 20, 52, 99; Alejandro Bolaños-Geyer, *William Walker: The Gray-Eyed Man of Destiny*, 5 vols. (Lake St. Louis, Mo.: Privately published, 1988–91), 2:254–55, 262–67; John E. Wool to Samuel Cooper, and endorsement by Cooper, Apr. 27, 1854, RG 94, Records of the Adjutant General's Office, Letters Received, M567, roll 507, NA.

28. William L. Marcy to Henry L. Kinney, Feb. 4, 1855, Marcy to José de Marcoleta, June 4, 1855, Manning, ed., *Diplomatic Correspondence*, 4:447n–48n, 69; John McKeon to Caleb Cushing, Apr. 27, 28, June 5, 1855, RG 60, Department of Justice, Attorney General's Papers, Letters Received, New York, NA; Franklin Pierce to Charles Boarman, May 25, 1855, Boarman to James C. Dobbin, May 27, 29, 1855, Charles Boarman Letterbooks, LC; *Galveston* (Weekly) *News*, May 22, 1855; James T. Wall, *Manifest Destiny Denied: America's First Intervention in Nicaragua* (Washington, D.C.: Univ. Press of America, 1981), 54–69; Brown, *Agents*, 271–73, 286–87; William S. Thayer to A. O. P. Nicholson, Oct. 8, [1855], Alfred Osborne Pope Nicholson Papers, Manuscript Department, New-York Historical Society. Later, Attorney General Cushing vehemently denied reports of Pierce's vested interest in the expedition, and instructed McKeon to proceed with the prosecution of Fabens without fear that evidence would surface incriminating the president. Caleb Cushing to John McKeon, Feb. 7, 1857, Andrews, ed., *Official Opinions of the Attorneys General*, 8:375–76.

29. Randall O. Hudson, "The Filibuster Minister: The Career of John Hill Wheeler as United States Minister to Nicaragua, 1854–1856," *North Carolina Historical Review* 49 (Summer 1972): 288–89; May, *Southern Dream*, 97–98; Tom S. M. Clay to Caleb Cushing, Apr. 9, 1856, Letters Received, Louisiana, John McKeon to Cushing, Feb. 4, 1856, McKeon to Thomas Lord, Jan. 4, 1856, Letters Received, New York, George S. Owens to Cushing, Jan. 3, 1856, Letters Received, Georgia, William R. Hackley to Cushing, Dec. 21, 1855, Letters Received, Florida, S. W. Inge to Cushing, Feb. 4, Apr. 1, 1856, Letters Received, California, all in RG 60, NA; Brown, *Agents*, 316–18; James C. Dobbin to Hiram Paulding, Nov. 16, 1855, in Bauer, ed., *New American State Papers: Naval Affairs*, 2:242–44; Caleb Cushing to John McKeon, Dec. 24, 1855, in *Philadelphia Public Ledger*, Dec. 27, 1855. Delays in the securing of witnesses by McKeon led to dismissal of charges against the *Northern Light* filibusters. *Frank Leslie's Illustrated Newspaper*, Apr. 19, June 7, 1856; *New-York Daily Times*, Apr. 28, 1856.

30. John McKeon to Caleb Cushing, Feb. 4, 1856, Letters Received, New York, S. W. Inge to Caleb Cushing, Feb. 4, 1856, Letters Received, California, both in RG 60, NA; *Washington National Era*, Jan. 10, 1856; Brown, *Agents*, 318; J. Egbert Farnum to G. B. Hall, Feb. 1, 1856, Appleton Oaksmith Papers, William R. Perkins Library, Duke University. McKeon demanded that the Accessory Transit Company itself take on the responsibility of inquiring into the intent of its Nicaragua-bound passengers. But he had no way of enforcing this order. As late as January 1857, federal authorities in New York were reported as being constrained

from making arrests because the filibusters did not even carry arms when they left the port. See *New York Herald*, Jan. 28, 1857, quoted in *Daily Alta California*, Feb. 27, 1857.

31. Ivor Debenham Spencer, *The Victor and the Spoils: A Life of William L. Marcy* (Providence: Brown Univ. Press, 1959), 371–72; William L. Marcy to Antonio José de Irisarri, Dec. 6, 1855, Manning, ed., *Diplomatic Correspondence*, 4:76–77; John F. Crampton to the Earl of Clarendon, Mar. 3, 1856, in Bourne and Watt, eds., *British Documents*, 4:384.

32. *Baltimore Sun*, May 16, 1856; May, *Southern Dream*, 99–102; William L. Marcy to George M. Dallas, June 16, 1856, Manning, ed., *Diplomatic Correspondence*, 7:138–41; "Camden" letter, May 15, 1856 in *Philadelphia Public Ledger*, May 17, 1856; Brown, *Agents*, 325–43; Wilbur Devereux Jones, *The American Problem in British Diplomacy, 1841–1861* (Athens: Univ. of Georgia Press, 1974), 139–52; Spencer, *Marcy*, 371.

33. William L. Marcy to Appleton Oaksmith, Sept. 13, 1856, [William] L. Marcy to John H. Wheeler, Sept. 27, 1856, Manning, ed., *Diplomatic Correspondence*, 4:86, 87; *Washington Evening Star*, May 16, 1856. Oaksmith claimed that Pierce would have received him had not a "secret influence" been "brought to bear" upon the president at the last minute. Appleton Oaksmith to William Walker, Sept. 9, 1856, Oaksmith Papers.

34. John H. Wheeler to William L. Marcy, Sept. 30, 1856, Manning, ed., *Diplomatic Correspondence*, 4:573–74.

35. *New-York Daily Times*, May 10, 1856.

36. Department of State Circular, Sept. 18, 1857, Lewis Cass to Joseph M. Kennedy, Nov. 13, 1857, Cass to Franklin H. Clack, Nov. 13, 1857, Cass to F. H. Hatch, Nov. 13 (all telegrams), Isaac Toucey to Frederick Chatard, Oct. 2, 1857, Toucey to Hiram Paulding, Oct. 3, 1857, Cass to James Conner, Nov. 16, 1857, *House Ex. Doc.*, 35th Cong., 1st sess., no. 24:4–5, 22, 24; Toucey to John J. Almy, Oct. 3, 1857, Toucey to Joshua R. Sands, Nov. 16, 1857, Bauer, ed., *New American State Papers: Naval Affairs*, 2:166.

37. *William Walker and S. F. Slatter v. The United States*, Case #3811, RG 267, Supreme Court Appeals Case File, NA; Howell Cobb to Thaddeus Sanford, Nov. 27, Dec. 16, 1857; Lewis Cass to Franklin H. Clack, Nov. 19, 1857; Cass to Sanford, Dec. 2 (telegram), 16, 1857; Cass to Thomas J. Semmes, Dec. 14 (telegram), 16, 1857; Isaac Toucey to Charles H. A. Kennedy, Dec. 22, 1857; Cobb to H. Stuart, Dec. 26, 1857; Cass to the collectors of customs and district attorneys at New Orleans and Mobile, Jan. 2, 1858 (telegram), *House Ex. Doc.*, 35th Cong., 1st sess., no. 24:42, 25, 28, 44–45, 34, 35, 77, 46, 38.

38. May, *Southern Dream*, 114–26; Smith, *Presidency of James Buchanan*, 72–73; Karl Bermann, *Under the Big Stick: Nicaragua and the United States Since 1848* (Boston: South End Press, 1986), 89–91.

39. Thaddeus Sanford to Howell Cobb, Apr. 20, 1858; Cobb to Sanford, Apr. 29, 1858, *House Ex. Doc.*, 35th Cong., 2d sess., no. 25:3–4.

40. Thaddeus Sanford to Howell Cobb, Oct. 16, Nov. 9 (telegram and letter), Nov. 23 (telegram), 1858, ibid., 4–6, 15; Robert H. Smith to Jeremiah S. Black, Dec. 21, 1858, RG 60, Letters Received, Alabama, NA.

41. Howell Cobb to Thaddeus Sanford, Oct. 25, Nov. 13, 14 (telegram), Dec. 11, 1858, Sanford to Cobb, Nov. 23 (telegram), Dec. 1, 4, 5, 1858, *House Ex. Doc.*, 35th Cong., 2d sess., no. 25:5, 9–16, 18–20, 22.

42. Jeremiah S. Black to Thomas J. Semmes, A. J. Requier, Cade M. Godbold, and Joseph M. Kennedy, all dated Nov. 6, 1858 (letterbook copies), Black to Robert H. Smith, Nov. 12, 1858, Black to Henry C. Wilson, Dec. 4, 1858, RG 60, Letters Sent, General and Miscel-

laneous, M699, roll 5, NA; John A. Campbell to Black, Nov. 24, 1858, Jeremiah S. Black Papers, LC; Isaac Toucey to James M. McIntosh, Nov. 17, 1858, Bauer, ed., *New American State Papers: Naval Affairs*, 2:174.

43. John A. Campbell to Jeremiah S. Black, Nov. 22, 1858, Black Papers; Log of the *Robert McClelland*, Dec. 6, 1858, "Detention of the Sch 'Susan'" in "Extraordinary Operations & Legislation, 1790–1870," 259–62, RG 26, Department of Transportation of the United States Coast Guard, NA; Frederick Seymour to E. B. Lytton, Dec. 26, 1858, Great Britain, Foreign Office, F.O. 39/7, PRO, Consular Despatches from Honduras; Henry Wilson to Jeremiah S. Black, Dec. 4, 1858, Black to Robert H. Smith, Dec. 14, 1858, Smith to Black, Dec. 21, 1858, RG 60, Letters Received, Alabama, M699, roll 5, NA; Thaddeus Sanford to Howell Cobb, Jan. 11, 1859, Cobb to Sanford, Jan. 5, 1859, *House Ex. Doc.*, 35th Cong., 2d sess., no. 25:23. While the *Susan* and *Robert McClelland* were anchored next to each other, the U.S. collector and district attorney in Mobile and special counsel Smith responded to Captain Morrison's appeal by preparing affidavits for the arrest of every passenger aboard the *Susan*. But Marshal Cade M. Godbold delayed serving the warrants.

44. Alfred B. McCalmont to R. J. Requier, H. C. Miller, C. M. Godbold, and Joseph M. Kennedy, Aug. 18, 1859 (single letterbook copy of separate letters), M699, roll 5. See also Jeremiah S. Black to P. L. Solomon, Apr. 27, 1859; Black to Isaiah Rynders, Oct. 4, 1859 (telegram); Black to H. C. Miller, Oct. 4, 1859 (telegram); Black to Robert H. Smith, Oct. 5, 1859 (telegram), ibid.; Isaac Toucey to John C. Long, May 19, 1859; Toucey to Thornton A. Jenkins, May 25, 1859; Toucey to John C. Long, May 19, 1859; Toucey to William J. McCluney, June 3, 1859; Toucey to John N. Moffitt, Oct. 5, 1859; Bauer, ed., *New American State Papers: Naval Affairs*, 2:176, 177, 178; Howell Cobb to James Buchanan, Oct. 7, 1859, Ulrich Bonnell Phillips, ed., *The Correspondence of Robert Toombs, Alexander H. Stephens, and Howell Cobb*, 2 vols. (Washington, D.C.: American Historical Association, 1913), 2:447; Richardson, comp., *Messages*, 5:649.

45. John M. Clayton to Robert B. Campbell, June 1, 1850; Daniel Webster to Daniel M. Barringer, Nov. 26, 1851; William L. Marcy to Lorenzo Shepard, Apr. 12, 1855; Marcy to Augustus C. Dodge, May 1, 1855, Manning, ed., *Diplomatic Correspondence*, 11:78–79, 124–28, 210–14; James Buchanan to Romulus Saunders, June 17, 1848, Moore, ed. and comp., *Works of James Buchanan*, 8:90–102; John M. Clayton to Charles Morris, June 29, 1850, *Sen. Ex. Doc.*, 31st Cong., 2d sess., no. 41:4–6.

46. Lawrence Berry Washington to ?, July 28, 1851, Bedinger-Dandridge Family Papers, Duke University; William Walker to Callender Irvine Fayssoux, Jan. 5, 1858, Callender I. Fayssoux Collection of William Walker Papers, Latin American Library, Tulane University, New Orleans; William Walker, *The War in Nicaragua* (Mobile: Goetzel, 1860), 167–68; John S. Thrasher to James Johnston Pettigrew, Dec. 7, 1855, Pettigrew Family Papers, Southern Historical Collection, University of North Carolina, Chapel Hill. See also John A. Quitman to B. F. Dill, June 18, 1854 (draft), Quitman Papers, HU; F. Jones to Quitman, June 10, 1854, John S. Ford to Quitman, Aug. 12, 1854, F. R. Witter to Quitman, Oct. 17, 1854, Quitman Papers, MDAH; *Washington, D.C. The States*, Apr. 29, 1857; *Tuskegee (Alabama) Republican*, Dec. 30, 1858.

47. John A. Quitman to B. F. Dill, June 18, 1854 (draft), Quitman Papers, HU; Alexander Walker to A. G. Haley, June 15, 1854, Jefferson Davis Papers, LC; Alexander H. Stephens to Linton Stephens, Jan. 20, 1858, Alexander H. Stephens Papers, Southern Historical Collection, University of North Carolina; Augustus R. Wright to Frank [?], undated copy, Augustus R. Wright Papers, LC; *Tuskegee (Alabama) Republican*, Jan. 7, 1858; *Congressional Globe*, 34th Cong., 1st sess., appendix, 1295.

Chapter Two
"FREEDOM AND LIBERTY FIRST, AND THE UNION AFTERWARDS":
STATE RIGHTS AND THE WISCONSIN REPUBLICAN PARTY, 1854–1861

1. The *Milwaukee Sentinel*, Sept. 3, 1856, contains Bashford's speech.

2. For two recent historiographical essays on Civil War causation, see Eric Foner, "The Causes of the American Civil War: Recent Interpretations and New Directions," *Civil War History* 20 (Sept. 1974): 197–214, and Kenneth M. Stampp, "The Irrepressible Conflict," in *The Imperiled Union: Essays on the Background of the Civil War* (New York: Oxford Univ. Press, 1980), 191–245. Thomas J. Pressley's *Americans Interpret Their Civil War* (Princeton, N.J.: Princeton Univ. Press, 1954) remains a valuable guide to the various schools of thought.

3. David M. Potter, *The Impending Crisis, 1848–1861*, completed and edited by Don E. Fehrenbacher (New York: Harper & Row, 1976). Also see William E. Gienapp, *The Origins of the Republican Party, 1852–1856* (New York: Oxford Univ. Press, 1987), 357–65; and Arthur Bestor, "State Sovereignty and Slavery: A Reinterpretation of Proslavery Constitutional Doctrine, 1846–1860," *Journal of the Illinois State Historical Society* (Summer 1961): 117–80, esp. 122–27.

4. Potter, *The Impending Crisis*, 18–50.

5. Kenneth Stampp, "The Concept of a Perpetual Union," *Journal of American History* 64 (June 1978): 5–53; Major L. Wilson, "Liberty and Union: An Analysis of Three Concepts Involved in the Nullification Controversy," in *Essays on Jacksonian America*, ed. Frank Otto Gatell (New York: Oxford Univ. Press, 1970), 133–47; Paul C. Nagel, *One Nation Indivisible: The Union in American Thought, 1776–1861* (New York: Oxford Univ. Press, 1964).

6. Stampp, "The Concept of a Perpetual Union," 12–20; Nagel, *One Nation Indivisible*, 235–47; James M. Banner, *To the Hartford Convention: The Federalists and the Origins of Party Politics in Massachusetts, 1789–1815* (New York: Knopf, 1969), 117–20, 109–21, 294–350; Herman Belz, *A New Birth of Freedom: The Republican Party and Freedmen's Rights, 1861–1866* (Westport, Conn.: Greenwood, 1976), ix–xiv; Harold M. Hyman, *A More Perfect Union: The Impact of the Civil War and Reconstruction on the Constitution* (New York: Knopf, 1973), 3–16; Bestor, "State Sovereignty and Slavery," 136–40; Eric Foner, *Free Soil, Free Labor, Free Men: The Ideology of the Republican Party Before the Civil War* (New York: Oxford Univ. Press, 1970), 138–42.

7. Lewis Perry, *Radical Abolitionism: Anarchy and the Government of God in Antislavery Thought* (Ithaca, N.Y.: Cornell Univ. Press, 1973), 57–59, 181–82; Aileen S. Kraditor, *Means and Ends in American Abolitionism: Garrison and His Critics on Strategy and Tactics, 1834–1850* (New York: Pantheon, 1969), 198–203, 206–8, 213–15; Ronald G. Walters, *The Antislavery Appeal: American Abolitionism After 1830* (Baltimore: Johns Hopkins Univ. Press, 1976), 129–45.

8. *Southport (Wisconsin) Telegraph*, June 21, 1850, also Dec. 8, 1848; Michael J. McManus, "'A Redeeming Spirit Is Busily Engaged': Political Abolitionism and Wisconsin Politics, 1840–1861" (Ph.D. diss., University of Wisconsin, 1991), 13–14; Richard H. Sewell, *Ballots For Freedom: Antislavery Politics in the United States, 1837–1860* (New York: Norton, 1976), 80–106, 237; Foner, *Free Soil, Free Labor, Free Men*, 134–36, 209–10; Paul Finkelman, *An Imperfect Union: Slavery, Federalism and Comity* (Chapel Hill: Univ. of North Carolina Press, 1981), 159; David Herbert Donald, *Charles Sumner and the Coming of the Civil War* (New York: Knopf, 1960), 231–32; Perry, *Radical Abolitionism*, 158–87.

9. James Brewer Stewart, *Holy Warriors: The Abolitionists and American Slavery* (New York: Hill & Wang, 1976), 112–13.

10. The quotation is from the *Monroe (Wisconsin) Sentinel*, Feb. 21, 1855; Nagel, *One Nation Indivisible*, 123, 235–41; Rush Welter, *The Mind of America, 1820–1860* (New York: Columbia Univ. Press, 1975), 349–73; Foner, *Free Soil, Free Labor, Free Men*, 138–40, 209–10; James Brewer Stewart, "Abolitionists, Insurgents, and Third Parties: Sectionalism and Partisan Politics in Northern Whiggery, 1836–1844," in *Crusaders and Compromisers: Essays on the Relationship of the Antislavery Struggle to the Antebellum Party System*, ed. Alan M. Kraut (Westport, Conn.: Greenwood, 1983), 25–43; Herbert Ershkowitz and William G. Shade, "Consensus or Conflict? Political Behavior in the State Legislatures during the Jacksonian Era," *Journal of American History* 57 (Dec. 1971): 611–13; Gienapp, *The Origins of the Republican Party*, 446–47; Ray M. Shortridge, "The Voter Realignment in the Midwest During the 1850s," *American Politics Quarterly* 4 (Apr. 1976): 193–221; Leonard L. Richards, "The Jacksonians and Slavery," in *Antislavery Reconsidered: New Perspectives on the Abolitionists*, ed. Lewis Perry and Michael Fellman (Baton Rouge: Louisiana State Univ. Press, 1979), 99–118; John M. McFaul, "Expediency vs. Morality: Jacksonian Politics and Slavery," *Journal of American History* 61 (June 1975): 24–39.

11. Thomas D. Morris, *The Personal Liberty Laws of the North, 1780–1860* (Baltimore: Johns Hopkins Univ. Press, 1974); J. Mills Thornton III, *Politics and Power in a Slave Society: Alabama, 1800–1860* (Baton Rouge: Louisiana State Univ. Press, 1978), 415, 448. Actually, fourteen Northern states had some form of Personal Liberty Laws on their books in 1860, five of which had been enacted prior to 1850. Also see Foner, *Free Soil, Free Labor, Free Men*, 134–37.

12. Alice E. Smith, *The History of Wisconsin, Volume I: From Exploration to Statehood* (Madison: Univ. of Wisconsin Press, 1973), 467–73; Edward P. Alexander, "Wisconsin, New York's Daughter State," *Wisconsin Magazine of History* 29 (Sept. 1946): 11–30; Joseph P. Schafer, "The Yankee and the Teuton in Wisconsin," *Wisconsin Magazine of History* 6 (1922–23): 125–44, 261–79, 386–402; 7 (1923–24): 3–19, 148–71.

13. Whitney Cross, *The Burned Over District: The Social and Intellectual History of Enthusiastic Religion in Western New York, 1800–1850* (Ithaca, N.Y.: Cornell Univ. Press, 1950).

14. Lewis Gerteis, "Antislavery Agitation in Wisconsin, 1836–1848" (M.A. thesis, University of Wisconsin, 1966).

15. Sewell, *Ballots for Freedom*, 3–79; Foner, *Free Soil, Free Labor, Free Men*, 73–102; McManus, "'A Redeeming Spirit,'" 6–16.

16. Frederick J. Blue, *The Free Soil Party: Third Party Politics, 1848–1854* (Urbana: Univ. of Illinois Press, 1973), 104–51; McManus, "'A Redeeming Spirit,'" 76–110.

17. Sewell, *Ballots for Freedom*, 202–53; Gienapp, *The Origins of the Republican Party*, 37–67; McManus, "'A Redeeming Spirit,'" 111–279.

18. Gienapp, *The Origins of the Republican Party*, 69–102; Sewell, *Ballots for Freedom*, 254–91; Tyler Anbinder, *Nativism and Slavery: The Northern Know Nothings & the Politics of the 1850s* (New York: Oxford Univ. Press, 1992); Potter, *The Impending Crisis*, 145–265.

19. The *Madison Argus and Democrat*, Sept. 15, 1860, provides a levelheaded retrospective of Glover's capture and subsequent events. Also see Vroman Mason, "The Fugitive Slave Law in Wisconsin, with Reference to Nullification Sentiment," *State Historical Society of Wisconsin, Proceedings* (1895), 117–44; Joseph Schafer, "Stormy Days in Court—The Booth Case," *Wisconsin Magazine of History* 20 (1936): 89–110.

20. Thomas D. Morris, *Free Men All: The Personal Liberty Laws of the North, 1780–1861* (Baltimore: Johns Hopkins Univ. Press, 1974), 130–47.

21. Ibid.; *Wisconsin Argus*, Oct. 29, 1850; *Wisconsin Democrat*, Oct. 26, 1850; *Milwaukee*

Sentinel, Oct. 11, 12, 1850; *Wisconsin Free Democrat*, Oct. 26, 1850, Mar. 26, 1851. According to the 1850 federal census, fewer than seven hundred blacks resided in Wisconsin, about one hundred of whom lived in Milwaukee.

22. *Wisconsin Free Democrat*, Jan. 22, 1851; *Wisconsin Assembly Journal, 1853*, 719–32.

23. *Wisconsin Senate Journal, Appendix, 1851*, 39–49; *Senate Journal, 1851*, 17, 35, 51, 94, 134, 184–85, and *1852*, 273, 690; *Wisconsin Assembly Journal, 1851*, 252, 263, 429, 653.

24. *Argus and Democrat*, Sept. 18, 1860. Also see the *Evening Wisconsin*, Mar. 12, 1897, for a Milwaukee speech the senior Booth gave commemorating the event. Booth was owner and editor of the influential *Milwaukee Daily Free Democrat*, Wisconsin's leading antislavery newspaper. John Goadby Gregory, *History of Milwaukee, Wisconsin* (Chicago: Clarke, 1931), 746.

25. *Milwaukee Sentinel*, Mar. 13, 15, 17, 1854; *Milwaukee Daily Free Democrat*, Mar. 13, 1854. Also see Mason, "The Fugitive Slave Law in Wisconsin," 124–25.

26. *Milwaukee Sentinel*, Mar. 22, 23, 24, 1854.

27. More than three hundred delegates reportedly attended the meeting, which Booth had called. See the *Milwaukee Sentinel*, Apr. 14, 1854, for the resolutions adopted. Also see Mar. 14, 16, and 18, in which the *Sentinel* carried extended editorials on the threat the Fugitive Slave Act posed to individual freedom and state rights. Rufus King, grandson of the great Federalist leader, one of Wisconsin's leading Whigs, and an outspoken opponent of slavery, edited the *Sentinel*. On the intent of the Virginia and Kentucky Resolutions, see Adrienne Koch and Harry Ammon, "The Virginia and Kentucky Resolutions: An Episode in Jefferson and Madison's Defense of Civil Liberties," *William and Mary Quarterly* 5 (Apr. 1948): 145–76, and Bestor, "State Sovereignty and Slavery," 117–80, esp. 136–40.

28. "In Re Sherman Booth," *Wisconsin Reports (1854)*: 20. Other essays on the Glover Affair include Joseph Schafer, "Stormy Days in Court—The Booth Case," 89–110; Vroman Mason, "The Fugitive Slave Law in Wisconsin, with Reference to Nullification Sentiment," 117–44; Joseph A. Ranney, "'Suffering the Agonies of Their Righteousness': The Rise and Fall of the States Rights Movement in Wisconsin, 1854–1861," *Wisconsin Magazine of History* 67 (Winter 1991–92): 83–116.

29. "The Argument of Byron Paine, Esquire: Regarding the Unconstitutionality of the Fugitive Slave Act," *Wisconsin Miscellaneous Pamphlets* 27, 1–23.

30. "In Re Sherman Booth," *Wisconsin Reports (1854)*, 13–54, esp. 32–46.

31. *Milwaukee Sentinel*, July 20–25, 1854. A federal grand jury had issued a warrant for Booth's arrest on July 11 for violating the Fugitive Slave Law. The federal district court judge, Andrew G. Miller, waited until the state court decision before acting on the warrant.

32. "Ex Parte Sherman Booth," *Wisconsin Reports (1854)*, 134–44.

33. Ranney, "'Suffering the Agonies of Their Righteousness,'" 92–96, gives a good account of the trial and the actions of Judge Miller in the case.

34. *Milwaukee Sentinel*, Jan. 15, Feb. 6, 1855.

35. Morris, *Free Men All*, 167–85.

36. The opinions of Wisconsin's three supreme court justices can be followed in *Wisconsin Reports (1854)*, "In Re Sherman Booth," 13–54, for Smith's original decree, "In Re Sherman Booth," 54–134, for the decision of the full court in June 1854, and "In Re Booth and Rycraft," 144–97, for the February 1855 reaffirmation of the June ruling and the reversal of the federal court decision.

37. "In Re Sherman Booth," 72–86, "In Re Booth and Rycraft," 170–72. Don E. Fehrenbacher, *The Dred Scott Case: Its Significance in American Law and Politics* (New York: Oxford

Univ. Press, 1978), 43–47, and Paul Finkelman, "*Prigg v. Pennsylvania* and Northern State Courts: Antislavery Use of a Proslavery Decision," *Civil War History* 25 (Mar. 1979): 5–35, provide background and evaluations of *Prigg v. Pennsylvania*.

38. "In Re Sherman Booth," 54–71; "In Re Booth and Rycraft," 160–61.

39. Smith designed his opinion around Paine's defense, sustaining every one of his main positions, which embraced the Virginia and Kentucky Resolutions and quoted liberally from them. Paine, "Argument of Byron Paine," 2–3. Also see Paine to Charles Sumner, Jan. 12, 1856, Byron Paine Papers, in which he admits the influence of John C. Calhoun on his thinking. Also see Foner, *Free Soil, Free Labor, Free Men*, 135, and William W. Freehling, *Prelude to Civil War: The Nullification Controversy in South Carolina, 1816–1836* (New York: Harper & Row, 1965), 134–76, for the South Carolinian's theory.

40. "In Re Sherman Booth," 39–40; "In Re Booth and Rycraft," 177–79; Schafer, "Stormy Days in Court," 91–101.

41. "In Re Sherman Booth," 49–54, 97–134; Fehrenbacher, *The Dred Scott Case*, 43–47; Finkelman, "*Prigg v. Pennsylvania* and Northern State Courts," 5–14; Schafer, "Stormy Days in Court," 102–3.

42. "In Re Sherman Booth," 32–38, 90–91; "In Re Booth and Rycraft," 181–85. Also see the *Walworth County Independent*, in the *Wisconsin Daily Free Democrat*, June 19, 1854, for an elaboration of the theory of state "judicial nullification."

43. "In Re Sherman Booth," 86–92; "In Re Booth and Rycraft," 182–89.

44. *Walworth County Independent*, in the *Wisconsin Daily Free Democrat*, June 19, 1854; Potter, *The Impending Crisis*, 294–95; Morris, *Free Men All*, 174–75; Freehling, *Prelude to Civil War*, 159–73.

45. Bestor, "State Sovereignty and Slavery," 140–80; Freehling, *Prelude to Civil War*, 219–301.

46. Paine, "Argument of Byron Paine," 1–3; "In Re Booth and Rycraft," 188–89; A. D. Smith to William Cullen Bryant, Horace Greeley et al., published in the *Milwaukee Sentinel*, Mar. 27, 1857; Morris, *Free Men All*, 156–85.

47. "In Re Booth and Rycraft," 172–76; Koch and Ammon, "The Virginia and Kentucky Resolutions," 145–76; Bestor, "State Sovereignty and Slavery," 136–37; Potter, *The Impending Crisis*, 294–95.

48. Charles Sumner to Byron Paine, Aug. 8 and Dec. 28, 1854, Jan. 18, 1856, and Wendell Phillips to Paine, Nov. 24, 1854, all in the Byron Paine Papers; Greeley's editorial was reprinted in the *Milwaukee Sentinel*, July 17, 1854; letter of Judge A. D. Smith to William Cullen Bryant, Horace Greeley et al., printed in the *Milwaukee Sentinel*, Apr. 16, 1857; Schafer, "Stormy Days in Court," 92; Mason, "The Fugitive Slave Law in Wisconsin," 133.

49. Rufus King to William H. Seward, Feb. 11, 1855, William H. Seward Papers; *Janesville Gazette*, Feb. 3, 1855; *Milwaukee Sentinel*, Feb. 6, 1855; *Wisconsin State Journal*, Feb. 5, 1855; *Kenosha Tribune and Telegraph*, Feb. 8, 1855; *Portage Independent*, Mar. 4, 1855; *Walworth County Independent*, June 19, 1854; *Potosi Republican*, Feb. 17, 1855; *Monroe Sentinel*, Mar. 7, 14, 1855. These contain a sampling of Republican opinion. *The Milwaukee Morning News*, July 22, 1854, contains a representative Democratic response, which labeled the decision a threat to republicanism and to the Union.

50. The Senate race can be followed in the *Wisconsin Daily Free Democrat*, Dec. 22, 27, 1854, Jan. 11, 17, 22, 1855; the *Wisconsin State Journal*, Jan. 11, 30, 31, 1855; and the *Weekly Argus and Democrat*, Jan. 30, 1855.

51. Sherman Booth, recently discharged from jail, led the Free-Soil faction and reportedly

vowed that "no one but Durkee shall be elected" by the Republican coalition. The Free-Soilers looked to avenge Durkee's 1852 defeat for reelection to Congress, when a number of Whigs allegedly crossed party lines and helped to elect Durkee's Democratic opponent. For Booth's "dictation," see the *Weekly Argus and Democrat,* Jan. 30, 1855, and the *Wisconsin Daily Free Democrat,* Jan. 22, 1855. Byron Kilbourn to Horace Tenney, Dec. 15, 1854, Horace Tenney Papers, gives details on the efforts of Kilbourn, the Democratic nominee and a onetime Free-Soiler, to court his former allies; also see Rufus King to William H. Seward, Feb. 11, 1855, William H. Seward Papers, for King's report on the difficulty of reconciling the Free-Soilers, Whigs, and anti-Nebraska Democrats in the Republican coalition.

52. *Wisconsin State Journal,* Feb. 15, 1855; *Janesville Gazette,* Mar. 3, 1855.

53. *Wisconsin Daily Free Democrat,* Jan. 5, 15, 1857. On these dates Booth published a retrospective on the 1855 caucus meetings. Also see the Feb. 26, Mar. 2, 16, 1855 editions, the *Janesville Gazette,* Mar. 10, 14, 1855, and the *Mineral Point Tribune,* Mar. 14, 1855. For Cole's early support of the state rights position, see the *Milwaukee Sentinel,* July 22, 1854.

54. *Milwaukee Sentinel,* Apr. 21, 1855; *Janesville Gazette,* Apr. 14, 1855. More than 80 percent of the 1854 Democratic voters cast a ballot for Crawford; nearly 90 percent of the 1854 [Republican] electorate voted for Cole. The voting analysis relies on a statistical technique known as ecological regression, which provides estimates of individual voting behavior using aggregate data, in this case, county-level voting returns, including nonvoters. Ecological regression permits historians to calculate changes in a political party's constituency from one election to another and to measure the stand its voters took on specific questions. Gienapp, *The Origins of the Republican Party,* provides a more detailed technical description of ecological regression, as well as of one of its more effective uses. My dissertation, "A Redeeming Spirit is Busily Engaged,'" also explains the technique in greater detail, and comments on some of its more successful applications.

55. Michael Fellman, "Rehearsal for the Civil War: Antislavery and Proslavery at the Fighting Point, 1854–1856," in *Antislavery Reconsidered: New Perspectives on the Abolitionists,* ed. Lewis Perry and Michael Fellman (Baton Rouge: Louisiana State Univ. Press, 1979), 287–307; William E. Gienapp, "The Crime Against Sumner: The Caning of Charles Sumner and the Rise of the Republican Party," *Civil War History* 25 (Sept. 1979): 218–45.

56. McManus, "A Redeeming Spirit,'" 204–79. The Republicans dominated the Senate, 19 to 11, and the Assembly, 65 to 31.

57. Rublee edited the *Wisconsin State Journal,* King, the *Milwaukee Sentinel.* Both remained publicly uncommitted to any candidate; probably they were confident about Howe's prospects and did not want to stir up any intraparty feuds. The *Menasha Conservator,* Jan. 15, 29, 1857, carried information on the maneuvering by the candidates and their backers, as did the *Grant County Herald,* Jan. 24, 31, 1857, the *Daily Milwaukee News,* Jan. 24, Feb. 13, 1857, the *Wisconsin Daily Free Democrat,* Jan. 24, 1857, and the *Wisconsin Argus and Democrat,* Jan. 10, 1857. Edward D. Holton was the favorite of the state rights wing, but he, like Durkee, had Liberty party roots, and few believed that the party would elect another "original abolitionist." Holton himself was prepared to withdraw whenever the caucus settled on a candidate.

58. Sherman Booth to Samuel D. Hastings, Dec. 15, 1856, Samuel D. Hastings Papers; *Wisconsin Daily Free Democrat,* Dec. 22, 29, 1856, Jan. 24, 26, 1857.

59. *Wisconsin Daily Free Democrat,* Jan. 5, 1857, for Booth's report of the conversation with Howe, and Mar. 23, 1857. Before publishing the substance of the discussion, Booth read it back to Howe and obtained his agreement that it fairly represented his views. James L.

Sellers, "Republicanism and State Rights in Wisconsin," *Mississippi Valley Historical Review* 17 (1930): 213–29, recounts the episode; Ranney, "'Suffering the Agonies of Their Righteousness,'" 98–102.

60. *Menasha Conservator*, Jan. 8, 15, 1857; *Grant County Herald*, Jan. 24, 1857; *Racine Advocate*, Jan. 24, 1857; *Wisconsin Daily Free Democrat*, Jan. 14, 1857. The Democratic *Daily Milwaukee News*, Jan. 17, 1857, reported that Booth's manifesto against Howe gave the Republican legislators fits and effectively blew apart his coalition. George B. Smith, Diary entry, Jan. 16, 1857, George B. Smith Papers. Smith, also a Democrat, closely followed the controversy among Republicans in choosing a senator.

61. *Wisconsin State Journal*, Jan. 16, 1857; *Milwaukee Sentinel*, Jan. 19, 1857; *Wisconsin Daily Free Democrat*, Jan. 17, 1857.

62. Booth's *Wisconsin Daily Free Democrat*, Jan. 20, 1857, claimed that the caucus passed the resolutions by a 5 to 1 margin.

63. *Wisconsin State Journal*, Jan. 19, 1857.

64. This was a direct reference to South Carolina's controversial application of state rights and nullification doctrine in 1832–33.

65. *Wisconsin State Journal*, Jan. 20, 21, 1857, for the letter of Howe and the other minor candidates. The caucus had by this time declared Doolittle eligible for the seat.

66. Ibid., Jan. 22, 1857.

67. Moses M. Davis to John Fox Potter, Jan. 28, Feb. 22, 1857, John Fox Potter Papers; *Wisconsin Daily Free Democrat*, Jan. 24, 26, 1857; *Wisconsin State Journal*, Jan. 23, 24, 1857.

68. *Assembly Journal*, 1853, 97, 719–31, 1855, 48–50, 752–55, 1856, 228, 497; *Senate Journal*, 1853, 23, 76, 83, 213–16, 1855, 603, 749; *Weekly Wisconsin*, Jan. 26, Feb. 2, 16, 1853; *Wisconsin Free Democrat*, Apr. 2, 1853; *Milwaukee Sentinel*, Feb. 9, 1856; Morris, *Free Men All*, 163–64. On the one vote taken on a personal liberty proposal, in 1856, Republicans supported the measure by a 7 to 1 margin, while Democrats opposed it by a 3 to 1 margin.

69. *Senate Journal*, 166.

70. Ibid., 241–42.

71. *Assembly Journal*, 1857, 431–32, 439–40, 456–62, 486–87; George B. Smith, Diary, Feb. 17, 18, 19, 1857, Smith Papers; *Milwaukee Sentinel*, Feb. 21, 1857. Booth was actively lobbying the Assembly for the relief clause because the federal district court, in January 1857, had ordered his printing press and steam engine, valued at $3,000, to be sold at public auction in order to defray the expenses that Garland, Glover's alleged owner, had suffered for the loss of his slave. The property was purchased for $175, after which Booth sued for and received a writ of replevin, and had it returned pending the outcome of further court action. For Booth's travails, see his *Wisconsin Daily Free Democrat*, Feb. 23, 24, Apr. 6, 1857, June 28, 1858.

72. *Senate Journal*, 1857, 287, 290; *Assembly Journal*, 1857, 1183. Forty-six Assembly Republicans voted for the final bill and five opposed it. In the Senate, only three Republicans favored the relief provision.

73. *Milwaukee Sentinel*, Feb. 21, 1857; *Mineral Point Tribune*, Mar. 17, 1857; *Janesville Gazette*, Feb. 28, 1957. Timothy Howe to Horace Rublee, Apr. 5, 1857, Timothy Howe Papers; for the Democratic perspective, see the *Weekly Argus and Democrat*, Mar. 31, 1857, and the *Daily Milwaukee News*, Mar. 26, 1857.

74. The decision was handed down on Mar. 6, 1857, two days after the inauguration of the new president of the United States, James Buchanan.

75. Fehrenbacher, *The Dred Scott Case*; Potter, *The Impending Crisis*, 267–96. Congress had repealed the Missouri Compromise three years earlier in the Kansas-Nebraska Act.

76. *Milwaukee Sentinel*, Mar. 14, 1857; *Wisconsin State Journal*, June 4, 1857; *Portage City Record*, Oct. 27, 1858; *Wisconsin Daily Free Democrat*, Mar. 7, 1857; *Grant County Herald*, Mar. 24, 1857; Willet S. Main, Diary, Mar. 13, 17, 1857, Willet S. Main Papers.

77. *Mineral Point Tribune*, Mar. 31, 1857; *Grant County Herald*, Mar. 28, 1857; *Wisconsin State Journal*, Mar. 28, 1857; *Menasha Conservator*, Mar. 26, 1857; *Milwaukee Sentinel*, Mar. 24, 25, 1857; *Wisconsin Daily Free Democrat*, Mar. 23, 1857.

78. *Daily Milwaukee News*, Mar. 18, 26, 1857; *Weekly Argus and Democrat*, Mar. 10, 31, 1857.

79. Based on 1857 population estimates, about 54 percent of the estimated eligible voters turned out for the election. Presidential races drew by far the largest turnout from statehood in 1848 through 1860. The 1855 governor's contest had attracted about 52 percent of the eligible electorate, the highest turnout for a state contest before the 1857 judicial election.

80. *Wisconsin State Journal*, Apr. 8, 1857.

81. Timothy Howe to Horace Rublee, Apr. 5, May 17, 1857, Timothy Howe Papers; *Wisconsin State Journal*, Mar. 13, 1857.

82. Moses M. Davis to "My Dear Sir" (probably Byron Paine), Mar. ?, 1857, Moses M. Davis Papers; Timothy Howe To Horace Rublee, Apr. 3, 1857, Timothy Howe Papers; *Menasha Conservator*, Apr. 2, 23, May 2, 1857; *Wisconsin Daily Free Democrat*, Mar. 23, 27, 30, 1857.

83. *Wisconsin Daily Free Democrat*, Apr. 6, May 5, 11, 1857; *Kenosha Tribune and Telegraph*, May 14, 21, 1857; *Monroe Sentinel*, May 27, 1857.

84. *Wisconsin Daily Free Democrat*, June 17, 18, 1857; *Menasha Conservator*, June 25, July 7, 1857; *Wisconsin State Journal*, June 18, 1857; *Milwaukee Sentinel*, June 18, 1857.

85. *Milwaukee Sentinel*, June 18, 1857.

86. *Menasha Conservator*, June 25, 1857; *Wisconsin State Journal*, June 19, 1857; Moses M. Davis to John Fox Potter, July 3, 1857, John Fox Potter Papers; Timothy Howe to Horace Rublee, Aug. 14, 1857, Timothy Howe Papers.

87. Timothy Howe to Horace Rublee, Aug. 14, 1857, Timothy Howe Papers.

88. *Wisconsin Daily Free Democrat*, Aug. 27, 1857; *Wisconsin State Journal*, Sept. 2, 1857; *Milwaukee Sentinel*, Sept. 4, 5, 1857; *Baraboo Republic*, Sept. 10, 1857; *Monroe Sentinel*, Sept. 9, 1857; *Portage City Record*, Sept. 9, 1857; *Grant County Herald*, Sept. 12, 1857.

89. *Weekly Argus and Democrat*, Sept. 8, 1857. Howe was joined on the committee by two other Republicans known to be cool toward the state rights position and the Booth faction.

90. Timothy Howe to Horace Tenney, Mar. 27, 1859, Timothy Howe Papers; William Brisbane, Diary, Sept. 3, 1857, William Brisbane Papers; *Daily Argus and Democrat*, Sept. 3, 4, 1857; *Daily Wisconsin Patriot*, Sept. 5, 1857; *Wisconsin Daily Free Democrat*, Sept. 7, 10, 1857; *Wisconsin State Journal*, Sept. 4, 1857.

91. Moses M. Davis to John Fox Potter, Dec. 24, 1857, and A. A. Huntington to Potter, Mar. 27, 1857, both in the John Fox Potter Papers. Also see the *Milwaukee Sentinel*, Feb. 27, Mar. 4, 15, 27, 1858; *Monroe Sentinel*, Jan. 6, Feb. 13, 1858; *Portage City Record*, Dec. 23, 1857; *Kenosha Tribune and Telegraph*, Feb. 25, 1858; *Wisconsin Daily Free Democrat*, Feb. 8, Mar. 15, 1858.

92. "Badger" to the *Monroe Sentinel*, Feb. 10, 1858.

93. *Ableman v. Booth*, and *U.S. v. Booth*, 21 *Howard*, 506–26; Bestor, "State Sovereignty and Slavery," 136–42; Morris, *Free Men All*, 178–80.

94. *Ableman v. Booth*, and *U.S. v. Booth*, 522–26.

95. *Laws of Wisconsin*, 1859, 247–48, contains the joint resolution. For the legislative proceedings, see the *Assembly Journal*, 1859, 777–79, 863–65, and the *Senate Journal*, 1859, 749–50.

96. *Laws of Wisconsin*, 1859, 248. The legislature substituted only the words *positive defiance* for *nullification*.

97. *Kenosha Tribune and Telegraph*, Mar. 24, 1859; *Wisconsin Daily Free Democrat*, Mar. 21, 1859; *Milwaukee Sentinel*, Mar. 15, 1859; *Wisconsin State Journal*, Mar. 11, 1859; Timothy Howe to Horace Rublee, Mar. 24, 1859, Timothy Howe papers.

98. Richard N. Current, *The History of Wisconsin, Volume II: The Civil War Era, 1848–1873* (Madison: State Historical Society of Wisconsin, 1973), 244–50; *Wisconsin State Journal*, Aug. 4, 5, 1858; *Wisconsin Daily Free Democrat*, June 9, 10, 1858. An 1858 investigation by the Randall administration had uncovered widespread corruption, particularly among Democrats, although many Republicans also were implicated. The full report was published in 1858, but Smith denied the charges against him.

99. *Wisconsin State Journal*, Feb. 17, 21, Mar. 4, 1859; *Milwaukee Sentinel*, Feb. 18, 28, Mar. 7, 1859; *Wisconsin Daily Free Democrat*, Feb. 21, 22, 26, 28, Mar. 5, 1859; *Menasha Conservator*, Feb. 19, 26, Mar. 5, 12, 1859. Paine at first turned down the nomination, citing his close personal friendship with Smith, but he was prevailed upon after being informed that Smith would drop out of the race if the party chose him.

100. See the "Address to the Republican Electors of Wisconsin," authored by the editors of Wisconsin's three most influential newspapers, Horace Rublee, Rufus King, and Booth, in *Milwaukee Sentinel*, Mar. 9, 1859.

101. *Milwaukee Sentinel*, Mar. 24, 1859, contains Schurz's speech; in Carl Schurz to his wife, Apr. 15, 1859, *Speeches, Correspondence and Political Papers of Carl Schurz*, vol. 1, ed. Frederic Bancroft (New York: G. P. Putnam's Sons, 1913), Schurz writes about the warm reception that greeted his speech in the North.

102. *Milwaukee Sentinel*, Mar. 24, 1859. Schurz later claimed that this speech was the best received of any he ever gave, but after the war he did not include it among his published addresses because his views had changed. James L. Sellers, "Republicanism and State Rights In Wisconsin," *Mississippi Valley Historical Review* 16 (Sept. 1930): 227.

103. Nearly 65 percent of the eligible electorate turned out to vote. Paine received 62,755 votes, his Democratic opponent, 54,525. Estimated relationships between the 1859 gubernatorial and judicial races with the 1858 congressional contest, and the 1860 state supreme court election with the 1859 judicial and governor's elections, show a significantly less pronounced tendency of Republicans to cross over and vote for their opponents; my overall impression of the crossover from Paine to the Democratic candidate is that it was probably somewhat less than the table suggests. See McManus, "'A Redeeming Spirit,'" 431–33.

104. Timothy Howe to Horace Rublee, Mar. 24, 25, Apr. 3, 1859, Howe to John Tweedy, Apr. 11, 17, 1859, all in the Howe Papers. Also see the *Wisconsin State Journal*, Apr. 14, 1859, published by Howe's friend Rublee, which forthrightly admitted that most Republicans in Wisconsin endorsed the state rights position.

105. McManus, "'A Redeeming Spirit,'" 363–69, 378–81.

106. Edward Daniels to Horace Tenney, Mar. 5, 1859, Horace Tenney Papers; *Whitewater Register*, in the *Menasha Conservator*, Mar. 19, 1859, as well as the issues of Mar. 12 and 26.

107. McManus, "'A Redeeming Spirit,'" 382–83.

108. *Racine Advocate*, Apr. 27, 1859; *Portage City Record*, Apr. 4, 1860; *Wisconsin State Journal*, Apr. 19, 1859. Dixon had signed a public address endorsing ex-justice Crawford's reelection in 1855. For the address, see the *Mineral Point Tribune*, Feb. 15, 1855.

109. *Ableman v. Booth, Wisconsin Reports, 1860*, unpaginated; Ranney, "'Suffering the Agonies of their Righteousness,'" 107–8.

110. *Racine Advocate*, Dec. 21, 1859, Jan. 25, Mar. 28, 1860; *Wisconsin Daily Free Democrat*, Apr. 22, 29, Dec. 28, 1859; *Portage City Record*, Dec. 28, 1859, Jan. 4, Apr. 4, 1860; *Kenosha*

Telegraph, Feb. 9, 23, 1860. Dixon was appointed to serve out Whiton's term, which was scheduled to come to an end in April 1860.

111. *Wisconsin State Journal*, Jan. 20, 22, 27, 1860; *Milwaukee Sentinel*, Jan. 14, 19, 20, 30, 31, 1860; *Portage City Record*, Feb. 1, 8, 1860; *Baraboo Republic*, Jan. 19, 26, 1860; *Kenosha Telegraph*, Feb. 23, 1860; *Racine Advocate*, Jan. 18, 25, 1860.

112. *Wisconsin State Journal*, Mar. 2, 1860; *Milwaukee Sentinel*, Mar. 2, 1860; *Baraboo Republic*, Mar. 1, 1860; Carl Schurz to John Fox Potter, Apr. 12, 1860, John Fox Potter Papers. On behalf of Paine's candidacy in 1859, Rublee, King, and Booth, for the state Republican organization, had issued an unequivocal endorsement of state right principles. For the endorsement, see the *Milwaukee Sentinel*, Mar. 9, 1859.

113. *Milwaukee Sentinel*, Mar. 2, 1860. Two hundred thirty delegates were present at the convention, so Dixon's support, in spite of the efforts of Howe and other Republicans, was meager.

114. *Wisconsin State Journal*, Mar. 1, 1860; *Portage City Record*, Mar. 7, 1860; *Milwaukee Sentinel*, Mar. 2, 1860; *Racine Advocate*, Mar. 7, 1860.

115. C. L. Sholes to John Fox Potter, Mar. 10, 1860, John Fox Potter Papers; Moses M. Davis to John Fox Potter, Apr. 8, 1860, Moses M. Davis Papers; Mathilde Anneke to Fritz Anneke, July 4, 1860, Mathilde Anneke Papers; *Wisconsin State Journal*, Feb. 17, 1860; *Portage City Record*, Mar. 7, 21, 1860; *Milwaukee Sentinel*, Jan. 19, 1860; *Oconto Pioneer*, Feb. 4, 1860.

116. Carl Schurz to his Wife, Mar. 2, 1860, *Speeches, Correspondence and Political Papers of Carl Schurz*, 108–9; C. L. Sholes to John Fox Potter, Mar. 10, 1860, John Fox Potter Papers. George M. Paul to Elisha Keyes, Mar. 24, 1860, A. L. Hayes to Keyes, Mar. 25, 1860, Moses M. Strong to Keyes, Mar. 26, 1860, Samuel C. Bean to Keyes, Mar. 26, 1860, all in the Elisha Keyes Papers, and Keyes to George Paul, Mar. 25, 1860, George M. Paul Papers, show the effort of Democrats and Republicans to work on Dixon's behalf. *Milwaukee Sentinel*, Mar. 12, 1860; *Wisconsin State Journal*, Mar. 8, 1860; *Portage City Record*, Feb. 1, 1860.

117. Henry J. Paine to John Fox Potter, Mar. 12, 1860, John Fox Potter Papers; *Racine Advocate*, Mar. 14, 1860; *Wisconsin Daily Free Democrat*, Mar. 6, 8, 1860; *Kenosha Telegraph*, Mar. 8, 1860; *Grant County Herald*, Mar. 17, 1860.

118. A. Scott Sloan to Elisha Keyes, Mar. 6, 1860, Elisha Keyes Papers; *Wisconsin State Journal*, Mar. 15, 17, 1860, contains Sloan's March 6 letter to his brother. Also see the *Wisconsin Daily Free Democrat*, Mar. 17, 1860; *Grant County Herald*, Mar. 24, 1860.

119. Charles Durkee to Moses M. Davis, Apr. 11, 1860, Moses M. Davis Papers; Moses M. Davis to John Fox Potter, Apr. 8, 1860, Carl Schurz to John Fox Potter, Apr. 12, 1860, John Fox Potter Papers; *Racine Advocate*, Apr. 18, 1860; *Grant County Herald*, Apr. 4, 1860.

120. Bestor, "State Sovereignty and Slavery," 136–40; Belz, *A New Birth of Freedom*, 113–82.

Chapter Three

AGING STATESMEN AND THE STATESMANSHIP OF AN EARLIER AGE: THE GENERATIONAL
ROOTS OF THE CONSTITUTIONAL UNION PARTY

1. Washington correspondence, *Philadelphia Journal*, reprinted in *Washington Daily National Intelligencer*, Dec. 26, 1859. *The New York Express*, Dec. 22, 1859, also contains details of this meeting. For background, see John Burgess Stabler, "A History of the Constitutional Union Party, A Tragic Failure" (Ph.D. diss., Columbia University, 1954), 312–18. An earlier version of this essay was presented at the annual meeting of the American Historical Asso-

ciation, San Francisco, Jan. 9, 1994. I wish to thank Daniel Crofts, Phyllis Field, and Michael Morrison for their comments and assistance.

2. The convention proceedings can be followed in the files of the *Baltimore American*, May 9–11, 1860; William B. Hesseltine, ed., *Three Against Lincoln: Murat Halstead Reports the Caucuses of 1860* (Baton Rouge: Louisiana State Univ. Press, 1960), 118–40; Stabler, "History of the Constitutional Union Party," chap. 11; and Donald Walter Curl, "The Baltimore Convention of the Constitutional Union Party," *Maryland Historical Magazine* 67, no. 3 (Fall 1972): 254–77.

3. *New York Daily Tribune*, May 11, 1860.

4. *New York Herald*, May 9, 1860.

5. Crittenden to Washington Hunt, Washington, D.C., Apr. 25, 1860, John Jordan Crittenden Papers, Library of Congress (hereafter Crittenden MSS, LC).

6. Speech in Philadelphia, May 12, 1860, reported in *Philadelphia Inquirer*, reprinted in *New York Daily Tribune*, May 14, 1860.

7. See, for example, the *Nashville Republican Banner*, Jan. 25, 1860; *Baltimore American*, Jan. 23, May 11, 1860, and an undated excerpt in *New York Daily Tribune*, May 21 (quotation); *Baltimore Clipper*, n.d., extract in ibid., May 21, 1860.

8. Allan Nevins, *The Emergence of Lincoln*, 2 vols. (New York: Scribner's, 1950), 2:262. See also Reinhard H. Luthin, *The First Lincoln Campaign* (Cambridge, Mass.: Harvard Univ. Press, 1944), 119, for a similar analysis. "If the Constitutional Union Party was to have succeeded in its mission to save the Union, it needed strong, dynamic, and visionary leadership. Instead it was presided over by the same men who had staged the decline of the old Whig party," Donald Walter Curl observes. "Baltimore Convention," 277.

9. David Potter, *The Impending Crisis, 1848–1861*, completed and edited by Don E. Fehrenbacher (New York: Harper & Row, 1976), 417; James McPherson, *Battle Cry of Freedom: The Civil War Era* (New York: Oxford Univ. Press, 1988), 221.

10. See three articles by John Vollmer Mering: "The Slave-State Constitutional Unionists and the Politics of Consensus," *Journal of Southern History* 43, no. 3 (Aug. 1977): 395–410; "Allies or Opponents? The Douglas Democrats and the Constitutional Unionists," *Southern Studies* 23, no. 4 (Winter 1984): 376–85; "The Constitutional Union Campaign of 1860: An Example of the Paranoid Style," *Mid-America* 60 (1978): 101; and Thomas B. Alexander, "The Civil War as Institutional Fulfillment," *Journal of Southern History* 47, no. 1 (Feb. 1981): 20.

11. V. O. Key, *Politics, Parties, and Pressure Groups*, 5th ed. (New York: Thomas Crowell, 1959), 255; W. D. Burnham, *Critical Elections and the Mainsprings of American Politics* (New York: Norton, 1970), 28n.18.

12. The only book-length study of the party is Stabler, "History of the Constitutional Union Party"; see also Albert D. Kirwan, *John J. Crittenden: The Struggle for Union* (Lexington: Univ. of Kentucky Press, 1962); Joseph Parks, *John Bell of Tennessee* (Baton Rouge: Louisiana State Univ. Press, 1950); Carl N. Degler, *The Other South: Southern Dissenters in the Nineteenth Century* (New York: Harper & Row, 1974), 99–123; and the articles by Mering, cited above. Daniel Crofts, *Reluctant Confederates: Upper South Unionists in the Secession Crisis* (Chapel Hill: Univ. of North Carolina Press, 1989), 37–89, 104–29, has an able analysis of the election of 1860 and its consequences for Unionists in the border South. Tyler Anbinder, *Nativism and Slavery: The Northern Know Nothings & the Politics of the 1850s* (New York: Oxford Univ. Press, 1993), chap. 10, discusses the American party influence on Northern Bell support. There is no modern study of the 1860 campaign; see Emerson D. Fite, *The Presidential Campaign of 1860* (New York: Macmillan, 1911); Ollinger Crenshaw, *The Slave States in*

the Presidential Election of 1860 in *The Johns Hopkins University Studies in Historical and Political Science*, ser. 63, no. 3 (1945).

13. Although Gienapp's data reveal a strong Republican tilt among younger and new voters, the converse is not necessarily true. There is as yet no clear evidence that older and more experienced voters inclined toward Bell. Age effects are masked, if they are present, at the aggregate level. William Barney has found evidence of a slight difference in age and political experience among Bell and Breckinridge leaders in Alabama. See Barney, *The Secessionist Impulse: Alabama and Mississippi in 1860* (Princeton, N.J.: Princeton Univ. Press, 1974), 95–96.

14. On new voters, see the estimates in Thomas Alexander, "Voter Partisan Constancy in Presidential Elections," in *Essays on Antebellum Politics, 1840–1860*, ed. Stephen Maizlish and John Kushma (College Station: Texas A&M Univ. Press, 1982), 88, table 12.

15. On age consciousness, see Howard P. Chudacoff, *How Old Are You? Age Consciousness in American Culture* (Princeton, N.J.: Princeton Univ. Press, 1989), 8–27.

16. William E. Gienapp, *The Origins of the Republican Party, 1852–1856* (New York: Oxford Univ. Press, 1987), 435–37; William E. Gienapp, "'Politics Seem to Enter Into Everything,'" in *Essays on Antebellum Politics*, ed. Maizlish and Kushma, 59–64; Christine B. Williams, "A Socialization Explanation of Political Change," in *The Electorate Reconsidered*, ed. John C. Pierce and John L. Sullivan (Beverly Hills, Calif.: Sage, 1980), 111–34; Paul R. Abrahamson, *Generational Change in American Politics* (Lexington, Mass.: Lexington Books, 1975); Paul Allen Beck, "A Socialization Theory of Partisan Realignment," in *The Politics of Future Citizens: New Dimensions in the Political Socialization of Children*, ed. Richard G. Niemi (San Francisco: Jossey-Bass, 1974), 199–219; Samuel P. Huntington, "Generations, Cycles, and Their Role in American Development," in *Political Generations and Political Development*, ed. Richard J. Samuels (Lexington, Mass.: Lexington Books, 1976), 9–28; and W. Phillips Shively, "The Relationship Between Age and Party Identification: A Cohort Analysis," *Political Methodology* 6 (1979): 437–46. For a discussion of historical applications, see Alan B. Spitzer, "The Historical Problem of Generations," *American Historical Review* 78, no. 5 (Dec. 1973): 1353–85; Morton Keller, "Reflections on Politics and Generations in America" in *Generations*, ed. Stephen R. Graubard (New York: Norton, 1979), 123–31; William Strauss and Neil Howe, *Generations: A History of America's Future* (New York: William Morrow, 1991). For applications to the Civil War era, see, for example, Daniel Eleazar, *Building Toward Civil War: Generational Rhythms in American Politics* (Lanham, N.Y.: Madison Books, Center for the Study of Federalism, 1992); George Forgie, *Patricide in the House Divided: A Psychological Portrait of Lincoln and His Age* (Chapel Hill: Univ. of North Carolina Press, 1979); and Reid Mitchell, *The Vacant Chair: The Northern Soldier Leaves Home* (New York: Oxford Univ. Press, 1992).

17. Marvin Rintala, "Political Generations," in International *Encyclopedia of the Social Sciences*, ed. David Sills (New York: Macmillan, 1968), 6:93: "A political generation is seen as a group of individuals who have undergone the same basic historical experiences during their formative years [17–25]. Such a generation would find political communication with earlier and later generations difficult, if not impossible."

18. Spitzer, "Historical Problem of Generations," 1385; Rintala, "Political Generations"; Julian Marias, *Generations: A Historical Method*, trans. Harold C. Raley (University, Ala.: Univ. of Alabama Press, 1970), 13–14; Huntington, "Generations, Cycles," 11; Keller, "Reflections," 123. For a more searching and informative discussion of these difficult issues than is sketched here, see Samuels, ed., *Political Generations and Political Development*, passim.

19. Pauline Maier, *The Old Revolutionaries: Political Lives in the Age of Samuel Adams* (New York: Knopf, 1980), esp. 269–94; Merrill Peterson, *The Great Triumvirate: Webster, Clay, and Calhoun* (New York: Oxford Univ. Press, 1987); William R. Taylor, *Cavalier & Yankee: The Old South and the American National Character* (New York: Harper & Row, 1961), esp. 23–36. Robert Beisner, *Twelve Against Empire: The Anti-Imperialists, 1898–1900* (New York: McGraw-Hill, 1968), 136–37, 186–211, applies generational themes to the debate over expansion in the late nineteenth century.

20. Forgie, *Patricide*, 9–12; Mitchell, *Vacant Chair*, 115–34; Robert E. May, "Young American Males and Filibustering in the Age of Manifest Destiny: The United States Army as a Cultural Mirror," *Journal of American History* 78, no. 3 (Dec. 1991): 857–86; Merle Curti, "Young America," *American Historical Review* 32 (Oct. 1926): 34–49; Donald S. Spencer, *Louis Kossuth and Young America: A Study of Sectionalism and Foreign Policy, 1848–1852* (Columbia: Univ. of Missouri Press, 1977), 11–14; Robert Fogel, "Modeling Complex Dynamic Interactions: Role of Intergenerational, Cohort, and Period Processes and of Conditional Events in the Political Realignment of the 1850s," NBER Working Paper No. 12 (Chicago, 1990).

21. Holman Hamilton, *Prologue to Conflict: The Compromise of 1850* (New York: Norton, 1966), 40, notes that more than half the representatives in the Thirty-first Congress were novices; 44 percent of them would not return in the next Congress. For more on this, see Allan G. Bogue, *The Congressman's Civil War* (Cambridge, Mass.: Harvard Univ. Press, 1989), 10–12. Eleazar, *Building Toward Civil War*, 163–91, tries unsuccessfully to link the ebb and flow of age cohorts in the census figures to a generational pattern in prewar politics.

22. Mitchell, *Vacant Chair*.

23. Peter Knupfer, "The Scholarly Consensus on American Third Parties: The Constitutional Union Party as a Test Case," paper presented at annual meeting, Social Science History Association, Chicago, Nov. 5, 1992. Group cohesion among Whigs is not a prominent theme in studies of the Whig party, in contrast to studies of the Democrats. See, for instance, Daniel Walker Howe, *The Political Culture of the American Whigs* (Chicago: Univ. of Chicago Press, 1979) as opposed to Jean H. Baker, *Affairs of Party: The Political Culture of the Mid-nineteenth Century Democrats* (Ithaca, N.Y.: Cornell Univ. Press, 1984). As Howe has pointed out, Whig reluctance is too easily labeled antipartyism; it could in fact be owing simply to the extrinsic sources of political socialization (third parties, evangelical movements), the later organization, and the early demise of the party; Howe, "The Evangelical Movement and Political Culture in the North during the Second Party System," *Journal of American History* 77, no. 4 (Mar. 1991): 1224n.19.

24. Dale Baum, *The Civil War Party System: The Case of Massachusetts, 1848–1876* (Chapel Hill: Univ. of North Carolina Press, 1984), argues that the Republicans suffered serious erosions of their voting base by 1876, but does not offer a socialization explanation for this change. Perhaps the most vigorous advocate of Democratic constancy is Thomas B. Alexander, who measures party development by the relationship of the Democrats to their challengers. See Alexander, "Voter Partisan Constancy."

25. Williams, "Socialization Explanation"; Beck, "Socialization Theory"; Michael F. Holt, *Political Parties and American Political Development from the Age of Jackson to the Age of Lincoln* (Baton Rouge: Louisiana State Univ. Press, 1992), 248–56.

26. *New York Express*, Dec. 2, 1859.

27. Buchanan, *Mr. Buchanan's Administration on the Eve of the Rebellion* (1866), in *The Works of James Buchanan: Comprising his Speeches, State Papers, and Private Correspondence*, ed.

John Bassett Moore, 12 vols. (1908–11; rpt. New York: Antiquarian, 1960), 12:70.

28. Seward speech in Springfield, Mass., Sept. 23, 1848, reported in *New York Daily Tribune*, Sept. 30, 1848. Wilson McCarey Williams, "Parties as Civic Associations," in *Party Renewal in America: Theory and Practice*, ed. Gerald Pomper (New York: Praeger, 1980), 51–68. The stabilizing effect of party development before the Civil War is a prominent theme in the large literature on parties in Jacksonian America. The most forceful statement of this argument is in two works by Joel Silbey: *The Partisan Imperative, The Dynamics of American Politics Before the Civil War* (New York: Oxford Univ. Press, 1985) and *The American Political Nation, 1838–1893* (Stanford, Calif.: Stanford Univ. Press, 1991). Recently, historians have come to see the development of national political parties as part of a great organizing process in response to the sweeping economic and social changes wrought by the market revolution. See Howe, "Evangelical Movement," and Donald B. Cole, *The Presidency of Andrew Jackson* (Lawrence: Univ. of Kansas Press, 1993), chap. 11.

29. See ABJ, "Party Spirit," in the *New York Journal of Commerce*, Apr. 5, 1858; and *Hartford Evening Press*, Oct. 25, 1860, in *Northern Editorials on Secession*, 2 vols., ed. Howard Cecil Perkins (New York: Appleton-Century Co., 1942), 1:60–61, for typical expressions of this theme.

30. Quoted in *Baltimore American*, Jan. 23, 1860.

31. John Higham, *From Boundlessness to Consolidation: The Transformation of American Culture* (Ann Arbor: Univ. of Michigan Press, 1969), 22–23; Paul Nagel, *One Nation Indivisible: The Union in American Thought, 1776–1861* (New York: Oxford Univ. Press, 1964), 82–124; Peter Knupfer, "Crisis in Conservatism: Northern Unionism and the Harpers Ferry Raid," in *His Soul Goes Marching On: Reactions to John Brown and the Harpers Ferry Raid*, ed. Paul Finkelman (Charlottesville: Univ. of Virginia Press, 1994), 119–48, and the sources cited in note 67, page 147.

32. Anbinder argues that youthfulness was not a unique characteristic of the Northern Know Nothings, *Nativism and Slavery*, 40–42. But cf. Hendrik Booraem, *The Formation of the Republican Party in New York: Politics and Conscience in the Antebellum North* (New York: New York Univ. Press, 1983), 244n.44 (I am grateful to Bruce Levine for this reference); George Haynes, "A Chapter from the Local History of Knownothingism," *New England Magazine* 21 (1896): 82–96; Michael F. Holt, "The Politics of Impatience: The Origins of Know Nothingism," *Journal of American History* 60 (Sept. 1973): 309–31.

33. McPherson, *Battle Cry of Freedom*, 221; Gienapp, "'Politics,'" 59–64; Gienapp, "Who Voted for Lincoln?" in *Abraham Lincoln and the American Political Tradition*, ed. John L. Thomas (Amherst: Univ. of Massachusetts Press, 1986), 75–77; Glenn C. Howland, "Organize! Organize! The Lincoln Wide Awakes in Vermont," *Vermont History* 48, no. 1 (Winter 1980): 28–32; on the advantages of Lincoln's inexperience and freshness, see *New York Daily Tribune*, May 23, 1860.

34. *New York Daily Tribune*, May 5, 1860.

35. "In anciently inhabited countries," Lincoln remarked in February 1859, "the dust of ages—a real downright old-fogyism—seems to settle upon, and smother the intellects and energies of man." Second Lecture on Inventions, delivered to the Phi Alpha Society of Illinois College in Jacksonville; later delivered in Decatur and Springfield, in *Collected Works of Abraham Lincoln*, ed. Roy Basler (New Brunswick, N.J.: Rutgers Univ. Press, 1953), 3:356–63, at 363.

36. Forgie, *Patricide*, 243–81.

37. *New York Daily Tribune*, May 9, 1850.

38. *Hartford Evening Press*, Oct. 25, 1860, in Perkins, ed., *Northern Editorials*, 1:60–61.

39. See, for example, the editorial, May 19, 1860, and extracts in *New York Daily Tribune*, May 21, 1860, from *Newark Daily Advertiser* and *Newark Mercury*.

40. Speech to the Richmond Agricultural Society, Oct. 18, 1859, in the *Washington Daily National Intelligencer*, Nov. 5, 1859.

41. *New York Express*, Dec. 14, 1859, discussing the Fillmorite *Buffalo Commercial Advertiser*'s reaction to a recent meeting of American party editors seeking to reorganize their party.

42. *New York Express*, Oct. 26, 1859.

43. Anbinder, *Nativism and Slavery*, overstates the antislavery inclinations of nativists, an interpretation reinforced by the exclusion of border-state nativist strongholds like Baltimore from his study. On the affinity between urban commercial interests and the Union movement, see Philip Foner, *Business & Slavery: The New York Merchants & the Irrepressible Conflict* (Chapel Hill: Univ. of North Carolina Press, 1941).

44. Charles Royster, *The Destructive War: William Tecumseh Sherman, Stonewall Jackson, and the Americans* (New York: Knopf, 1991), 40–41.

45. Report of speech and meeting, *Washington Daily National Intelligencer*, Dec. 2, 1859.

46. Amos A. Lawrence to John Jordan Crittenden, Boston, Mar. 30, 1860, Crittenden MSS, LC. "You are the 'link between the past and the present' in our Senate," one admirer wrote him in 1858, "for the mighty Websters & Clays, of the other day, were your friends & compeers," in Brainerd Williamson to Crittenden, Philadelphia, Mar. 20, 1858, ibid.; see also M. B. Franklin to Crittenden, Franklin, N.H., Mar. 3, 1858, and John Thompson et al., Philadelphia Committee, to Crittenden, Apr. 8, 1858, ibid.

47. Kirwan, *John J. Crittenden*, 346–65.

48. Organizational matters can be followed in Kirwan, *John J. Crittenden*, 346–65, Stabler, "Constitutional Union Party," chap. 12, and in the files of the *New York Express* and *Washington Daily National Intelligencer*.

49. Joseph Fitz Randolph to John Jordan Crittenden, Trenton, N.J., Jan. 30, 1860, Crittenden MSS, LC; see also Samuel Smith Nicholas to John Jordan Crittenden, Louisville, Ky., Feb. 2, 1860, in ibid.; Nevins, *Emergence*, 2:280–82.

50. Charles Magill Conrad to John Jordan Crittenden, New Orleans, Apr. 19, 1860, Crittenden MSS, LC.

51. See James Collins to John Jordan Crittenden, New Albany, Ind., Feb. 2, 1860, Crittenden MSS, LC.

52. See John Jordan Crittenden to W. M. Smallwood, Jno P. Bowman Esqrs, Frankfort?, Sept. 1860, Crittenden MSS, LC.

53. Rives to John J. Crittenden, Castle Hill, Va., May 5, Jan. 9, 1860, Crittenden MSS, LC.

54. John Bell to Boteler, Nashville, July 2, 1860 (part of a letter finished on July 30), A. R. R. Boteler Papers, Special Collections, Perkins Library, Duke University (hereafter Boteler Papers).

55. See circular letter to "National Union Men of the City and State of New York," [Jan. 15, 1860], Millard Fillmore Papers, State University of New York-Oswego (hereafter Fillmore MSS); report of Union meeting in New York City, *Washington Daily National Intelligencer*, Dec. 21, 1859.

56. Nicholas to Crittenden, Louisville, Ky., Feb. 2, 1860, Crittenden MSS, LC.

57. "Address of the National Union Men," Fillmore MSS, SUNY-Oswego.

58. See "Americus," *Washington Daily National Intelligencer*, printed Feb. 18, 20, 26, 1850,

for a good statement of these conservative themes; Clay's speech to Kentucky legislature, Nov. 15, 1850, reported in ibid., Nov. 27, 1850.

59. Kirwan, *John J. Crittenden*, 350.

60. Pechin to Boteler, Philadelphia, Nov. 19, 1859, Boteler Papers; Pechin to Crittenden, Philadelphia, Dec. 22, 1859, Crittenden MSS, LC.

61. Holt, *Political Parties*, 251.

62. J. Mills Thornton, *Politics and Power in a Slave Society: Alabama, 1800–1860* (Baton Rouge: Louisiana State Univ. Press, 1978), xxi. A similar generational theme was evident among the Gold Democrats of 1896. See Philip R. VanderMeer, "Political Crisis and Third Parties, The Gold Democrats of Michigan," *Michigan Historical Review* 15 (Fall 1989): 61–84.

Chapter Four

BLACKFACE MINSTRELSY AND THE CONSTRUCTION OF RACE
IN NINETEENTH-CENTURY AMERICA

1. A pioneering and still powerful analysis of the Enlightenment-era scientific construction of race is Philip D. Curtin, *The Image of Africa: British Ideas and Action, 1780–1850* (Madison: Univ. of Wisconsin Press, 1964), particularly 28–52 and 363–87.

2. Portions of the Linnaean classification system are reproduced and discussed in Winthrop D. Jordan, *White Over Black: American Attitudes Toward the Negro, 1550–1812* (Chapel Hill: Univ. of North Carolina Press, 1968), 220–21; see also, Curtin, *The Image of Africa*, 37–38.

3. A. Hunter Dupree, *Asa Gray, 1810–1888* (Cambridge, Mass.: Harvard Univ. Press, 1959), 135, 151–53, 217–20, 228–29; Edward Lurie, *Louis Agassiz: A Life in Science* (Chicago: Univ. of Chicago Press, 1960); see also George M. Fredrickson, *The Black Image in the White Mind: The Debate on Afro-American Character and Destiny, 1817–1914* (New York: Harper and Row, 1971), 75–76.

4. [Chauncey Wright,] *Philosophical Discussion By Chauncey Wright. With a Biographical Sketch of the Author by Charles Eliot Norton* (1877; rpt. New York: Burt Franklin, 1971), 226–27, 416; Dupree, *Gray*, 246–47, 289, 296, 313; see also Gray's essays on Darwin in *Atlantic Monthly* 6 (July, Aug., and Oct. 1860).

5. The general significance of theatricality in social representation can only be suggested here. The topic is framed and explored in Richard Sennett, *The Fall of Public Man* (New York: Knopf, 1977); Jean-Christophe Agnew, *Worlds Apart: The Market and the Theater in Anglo-American Thought, 1550–1750* (Cambridge, Mass.: Harvard Univ. Press, 1986); and David Marshall, *The Figure of Theater: Shaftesbury, Defoe, Adam Smith and George Eliot* (New York: Columbia Univ. Press, 1986).

6. The impact of the market revolution is stressed in Charles Sellers, *The Market Revolution: Jacksonian America, 1815–1846* (New York: Oxford Univ. Press, 1991), particularly 3–35.

7. On the growth of popular theater and the unpredictability of audiences, see Noah M. Ludlow, *Dramatic Life as I Found It* (St. Louis, 1880), particularly 427–29, 478–79; and Sol Smith, *Theatrical Management in the West and South for Thirty Years* (1868; rpt. New York: B. Blom, 1968), particularly 13–27.

8. For a number of examples of blackface in English low comedy, see Hans Nathan, *Dan Emmett and the Rise of Early Negro Minstrelsy* (Norman: Univ. of Oklahoma Press, 1962), 3–31. On the British blackface tradition generally, see George F. Rehin, "Harlequin Jim Crow: Continuity and Convergence in Blackface Clowning," *Journal of Popular Culture* 9 (Winter

1975): 682–701; and Alan Brody, *The English Mummers and Their Plays: Traces of Ancient Mystery* (Philadelphia: Temple Univ. Press, 1970), esp. 25 and fig. 8. For suggestive comments on the transmission of these and the Morris dance blackface tradition across the Atlantic, see Adam Lively, "Fisticuffs," *London Review of Books* 16 (Mar. 10, 1994): 16. On the history of public masquerade and popular disorder in the United States, see Paul A. Gilje, *The Road to Mobocracy: Popular Disorder in New York City, 1763–1834* (Chapel Hill: Univ. of North Carolina Press, 1987), 16–19, 34; Susan G. Davis, *Parades and Power: Street Theatre in Nineteenth-Century Philadelphia* (Philadelphia: Temple Univ. Press, 1986), particularly 77; and David R. Roediger, *The Wages of Whiteness: Race and the Making of the American Working Class* (London: Verso Books, 1991), 100–111.

9. *The Irishman in London. A Farce, In Two Acts* (New York: Samuel French, n.d.), in the Gundlach Collection of Prompt Books, Theatre Programs Collection, Missouri Historical Society, St. Louis, Mo.

10. *The Forest Rose* is reprinted in Richard Moody, ed., *Dramas from the American Theatre, 1762–1909* (New York: Houghton Mifflin, 1966), 155–74.

11. Joe Cowell, *Thirty Years Passed Among the Players in England and America* (1844; rpt. Hamden, Conn.: Harper and Brothers, 1979), 77–78.

12. William J. Mahar, "Black English in Early Blackface Minstrelsy: A New Interpretation of the Sources of Minstrel Show Dialect," *American Quarterly* 37 (Summer 1985): 260–85; Smith, *Theatrical Management*, 138.

13. "Backside Albany" (New York: Thomas Birch, 1837), Sheet Music Filed for Copyright, 1820–1860, Music Division, Library of Congress, Washington, D.C.

14. Playbills, Apr. 9, 1831, Harvard Theatre Collection, Harvard University, Cambridge, Mass. (hereafter cited as HTC).

15. "Coal Black Rose" (New York: Firth and Hall, n.d.) in Minstrel Sheet Music Collection, HTC.

16. *Oh! Hush! Or, The Virginny Cupids! An Operatic Olio* (New York: Samuel French, n.d.) in Houghton Library, Harvard University.

17. John William Ward, *Andrew Jackson Symbol for an Age* (New York: Oxford Univ. Press, 1953), 13–16.

18. Louisville *Public Advertiser*, Nov. 17, 1829.

19. Ibid., Nov. 7, 14, 17, 1829; Mar. 11 and Dec. 31, 1830.

20. Ibid., May 21 and June 8, 1830.

21. *Washington, D.C. Globe*, Jan. 22, 1833 (advertising Rice's performance on January 23).

22. *Washington, D.C. Globe*, Jan. 26, 1833.

23. "Gumbo Chaff" (Baltimore: G. Willig, Jr., n.d.); "Gombo Chaff" (Baltimore: J. Cole and Son, 1834). Both copies are in the Minstrel Sheet Music Collection, HTC.

24. "Clare de Kitchen" (Boston: C. Bradlee, n.d.), Minstrel Sheet Music Collection, HTC.

25. Dena Epstein, *Sinful Tunes and Spirituals: Black Folk Music to the Civil War* (Urbana: Univ. of Illinois Press, 1977), 141–44.

26. For roughly similar English folk song lyrics in America, see Cecil J. Sharp and Maud Karpeles, collectors, *Eighty English Folk Songs from the Southern Appalachians* (Cambridge, Mass.: Harvard Univ. Press, 1968), 25, 95.

27. Emma Jones Lapsansky, "'Since They Got Those Separate Churches': Afro-Americans and Racism in Jacksonian Philadelphia," *American Quarterly* 32 (Spring 1980): 64–68, quotation at 65; see also Elizabeth Johns, *American Genre Painting: The Politics of Everyday*

Life (New Haven, Conn.: Yale Univ. Press, 1991), 26, 34–35, 46–47, 63–64, 107.

28. "'Jim Crow' at the Royal Surrey Theatre" (London: Purday, n.d.), Minstrel Sheet Music Collection, HTC.

29. "'Jim Crow' at the Theatre Royal, Adelphi" ([London?]: D'Almaine and Co., [1836?]), Minstrel Sheet Music Collection, HTC.

30. "Long Time Ago" (Baltimore: John Cole, 1833), Minstrel Sheet Music Collection, HTC.

31. Front Street Theatre, Baltimore, playbill for Oct. 17, 1832, Playbill Collection, HTC.

32. On the role of sentimentality in blackface, see Eric Lott, *Love and Theft: Blackface Minstrelsy and the American Working Class* (New York: Oxford Univ. Press, 1993), particularly 169–233.

33. Quoted in Carl Wittke, *Tambo and Bones: A History of the American Minstrel Stage* (1930; rpt. New York: Greenwood, 1968), 31.

34. Undated clipping, Dan Bryant Clipping File, HTC. The clipping is the reminiscences, following Bryant's death, of early blackface acts by someone (perhaps a tavernkeeper) who had "always been fond of burnt-cork people. . . . So my place has always been a favorite resort for what one of the boys used to call 'the corkonians.'"

35. Playbill, New Theatre, Mobile, Feb. 24, 1841, reproduced in Nathan, *Dan Emmett*, 61. Nathan mistakenly reported that Diamond challenged only whites, to avoid confronting Juba. It is more likely that Diamond's challenge was designed to bring local blacks on the stage in a repetition of the Diamond-Juba challenge dance. But Sol Smith, Barnum's rival in New Orleans and the manager of the Mobile Theatre, charged that Barnum faked the wagers and the challenges and pitted Diamond against less talented blackface jig dancers. See Smith, *Theatrical Management*, 155.

36. Gerald Boardman, *The Oxford Companion to American Theatre* (New York: Oxford Univ. Press, 1984), 415; Pell Clipping File and Juba Playbills File, HTC.

37. Agnew, *Worlds Apart*, 97.

38. Lott, *Love and Theft*, 101.

39. Lawrence Levine, *Highbrow/Lowbrow: The Emergence of Cultural Hierarchy in America* (Cambridge, Mass.: Harvard Univ. Press, 1988).

40. In general, see Richard Moody, *The Astor Place Riot* (Bloomington: Univ. of Indiana Press, 1958). Iver Bernstein, in *The New York City Draft Riots: Their Significance for American Society and Politics in the Age of the Civil War* (New York: Oxford Univ. Press, 1990) compares the Astor Place Riot with the New York Draft Riot of 1863 and thereby places both upheavals in a broader social and political context.

41. David Grimsted, *Melodrama Unveiled: American Theatre and Culture, 1800–1850* (Chicago: Univ. of Chicago Press, 1968), 52–53; Smith, *Theatrical Management*, 209.

42. Bowery Theatre Playbills, HTC.

43. Playbill, St. Louis Theatre, Apr. 23, 1860, Theatre Programs Collection, Oversized Playbills, Missouri Historical Society, St. Louis, Mo.

44. Mobile Theatre Playbill, HTC; Boardman, *Oxford Companion to American Theatre*, 198.

45. C. Peter Ripley et al., eds., *The Black Abolitionist Papers*, vol. 5 (Chapel Hill: Univ. of North Carolina Press, 1992), 76.

46. Thomas Wentworth Higginson, *Army Life in a Black Regiment* (1870; rpt. New York: Collier Books, 1962), 212.

Chapter Five
WHO FREED THE SLAVES? EMANCIPATION AND ITS MEANING

1. An earlier version of this essay appeared in *Reconstruction* 4 (1994): 41–44. I would like to thank Susan O'Donovan, Steven Miller, and Leslie S. Rowland for their counsel in expanding it.

2. *Washington Post*, Dec. 30, 1992, also Jan. 1, 1993. Susan L. Cooper, Julie Nash, and the staff of the public affairs office of the National Archives graciously supplied copies of the exhibit's press clippings.

3. *New York Times*, Dec. 20, 1992; *Washington Post*, Dec. 30, 1992, Jan. 1, 1993; *Baltimore Sun*, Dec. 31, 1992.

4. Julius Lester, *Look Out, Whitey! Black Power's Gon' Get Your Mama!* (New York: Dial Press, 1968). "He probably did more to trick Negroes than any other man in history," observed Malcolm X. Quoted in Don E. Fehrenbacher, "Only His Stepchildren: Lincoln and the Negro," *Civil War History* 30 (1974): 298. Also see Lerone Bennett, Jr., "Was Abe Lincoln a White Supremacist?" *Ebony*, 23 Feb. 1968, 35–42.

5. *Washington Post*, Dec. 19, 1992; *USA Today*, Dec. 30, 1992; *Norfolk Virginian-Pilot and Ledger Star*, Jan. 1, 1993. For a view more in line with Julius Lester's, see the column by Michael Paul Williams in the *Richmond Times-Dispatch*, Jan. 4, 1993.

6. The other members of the panel were William Safire of the *New York Times*, Gabor S. Boritt of Gettysburg College, David Herbert Donald of Harvard University, and Leslie S. Rowland of the University of Maryland. McPherson had earlier presented his paper in October 1991 at the sixth annual Lincoln Colloquium in Springfield, Illinois. It was published as part of the colloquium's proceedings. (George L. Painter, ed., *Abraham Lincoln and the Crucible of War: Papers from the Sixth Annual Lincoln Colloquium* [n.p., n.d.], 59–69.) He subsequently published yet other versions in *Reconstruction* 2 (1994): 35–41 and another in the *Proceedings of the American Philosophical Society* 139 (1995): 1–10. He added further commentary on the controversy in an essay-review entitled "Liberating Lincoln," *New York Review of Books*, Apr. 21, 1994.

7. In retrospect, the exhibit was one of the first skirmishes in what soon became know as the culture war of the 1990s.

8. Vincent Harding, *There is a River: The Black Struggle for Freedom in America* (New York: Harcourt, Brace, Jovanovich, 1981).

9. Since most historical scholarship is carried on in the solitary artisan tradition, it is easy to exaggerate the numbers involved in collaborative historical research. Sad to say, "the largest scholarly enterprise on the history of emancipation" bears little resemblance to the Manhattan Project or major research projects in the social sciences. Since its inception in 1976, fewer than a dozen historians have been associated with the project—never more than five at any one time. Besides myself, the editors of the four volumes in print are Barbara Jeanne Fields, Thavolia Glymph, Steven Miller, Joseph P. Reidy, Leslie S. Rowland, and Julie Saville.

The project's main work has been published by Cambridge Univ. Press under the title *Freedom: A Documentary History of Emancipation*. Thus far four volumes are in print: *The Destruction of Slavery* (1985); *The Wartime Genesis of Free Labor: The Upper South* (1993); *The Wartime Genesis of Free Labor: The Lower South* (1991); and *The Black Military Experience* (1982). In 1992, The New Press published an abridgment of the first four volumes entitled *Free At Last: A Documentary History of Slavery, Freedom, and the Civil War*, and Cambridge has issued a volume entitled *Slaves No More*.

10. Barbara Jeanne Fields, "Who Freed the Slaves?" in *The Civil War: An Illustrated History*, ed. Geoffrey C. Ward with Ken Burns and Ric Burns (New York: Knopf, 1990), 178–81. One particularly unfortunate aspect of the debate is the tendency to divide the participants along racial lines and to identify black scholars as the proponents of the slave's agency. See McPherson, "Liberating Lincoln."

11. Robert F. Engs, "The Great American Slave Rebellion," quoted in McPherson, "Who Freed the Slaves?" *Colloquium*, 60.

12. Mark E. Neely, Jr., "Lincoln and the Theory of Self-Emancipation," in John Y. Simon and Barbara Hughett, eds., *The Continuing Civil War: Essays in Honor of the Civil War Round Table of Chicago* (Dayton, Ohio: Morningside, 1992), 47. As far as is known, Neely made no attempt to contact any member of the Freedmen and Southern Society Project or its publisher, Cambridge Univ. Press. If he had, he would have discovered that the earlier publication of *The Black Military Experience* had its origins in a crisis created by the Reagan administration, which threatened to eliminate funding of the project's chief sponsor, the National Historical Publications and Records Commission. In 1981, after spending some five years at the National Archives accumulating evidence for a documentary history of emancipation, the Freedmen and Southern Society Project appeared to be scheduled for dissolution. In an effort to present something before the project's demise, the editors—who had been working simultaneously on a number of volumes—focused their attention on the one nearest to completion, which happened to be the soldiers' story.

13. Richard Hofstadter, *The American Political Tradition and the Men Who Made It* (New York: Vintage, 1948), 132. Hofstadter's judgment has become something of a cliché. The vitality of Lincoln's prose is a rather superficial ground from which to condemn what was, after all, a legal document. The debate over the significance of the Emancipation Proclamation cannot stop with Hofstadter's description of the document.

14. U.S. War Department, *The War of the Rebellion: A Compilation of the Official Records of the Union and Confederate Armies*, 128 vols. (Washington, D.C.: GPO, 1880–1901), ser. 2, vol. 1, 750 (hereafter cited as *OR*). What drove these slaves to present themselves at Fort Pickens is, of course, not known. The most important source of information for slaves may well have been the slaveholders' own indiscriminate condemnation of abolitionists and black Republicans, among them Abraham Lincoln. In this sense, McPherson may indeed be right about Lincoln freeing the slaves.

15. See, for example, *The Wartime Genesis of Free Labor: The Upper South*, doc. 7.

16. The argument is fully explicated in *The Destruction of Slavery*.

17. Quoted in James M. McPherson, *What They Fought For, 1861–1865* (Baton Rouge, Louisiana State Univ. Press, 1994), 59.

18. Quoted in ibid., 60.

19. Edward McPherson, *The Political History of the United States of America during the Great Rebellion, 1860–1865*, 2d ed. (Washington, D.C.: Philip & Solomons, 1865), 249, 416.

20. *The Destruction of Slavery*, 275–76.

21. *Black Military Experience*, 85–86.

22. For the proposed amendment, see McPherson, *Political History of the United States*, 59; Abraham Lincoln, *Collected Works of Abraham Lincoln*, ed. Roy P. Basler, 9 vols. (New Brunswick, N.J.: Rutgers Univ. Press, 1953–55), 4:421–41.

23. Lincoln, *Collected Works*, 4:531–33, quotation on p. 532. Lincoln's concerns about the border states and their effects on the evolution of Federal policy is discussed in *The Destruction of Slavery*, chaps. 6–8. Also Barbara J. Fields, *Slavery and Freedom on the Middle Ground:*

Maryland during the Nineteenth Century (New Haven, Conn.: Yale Univ. Press, 1985); Charles L. Wagandt, *The Mighty Revolution: Negro Emancipation in Maryland, 1862–1864* (Baltimore: Johns Hopkins Univ. Press, 1964); William E. Parish, *Turbulent Partnership: Missouri and the Union, 1861–1865* (Columbia: Univ. of Missouri Press, 1963); Victor B. Howard, *Black Liberation in Kentucky: Emancipation and Freedom, 1862–1884* (Lexington: Univ. of Kentucky Press, 1983).

24. Louis S. Gerteis, *From Contraband to Freedman: Federal Policy toward Southern Blacks, 1861–1865* (Westport, Conn.: Greenwood, 1973), chap. 4; C. Peter Ripley, *Slaves and Freedmen in Civil War Louisiana* (Baton Rouge: Louisiana State Univ. Press, 1976); and especially Peyton McCrary, *Abraham Lincoln and Reconstruction: The Louisiana Experiment* (Princeton, N.J.: Princeton Univ. Press, 1978).

25. On the matter of Lincoln's lifelong connection to the idea of colonization and his principled commitment to the idea and his strategic use of it, see Michael Vorenberg, "Abraham Lincoln and the Politics of Black Colonization," *Journal of the Abraham Lincoln Association* 14 (1993): 23–45, which is both a summary of the state of scholarship on the matter and an argument that Lincoln's commitment to colonization changed over time and that the change was itself used in an effort to secure larger political goals, including emancipation. On the same point, see Jason H. Silverman, "'In Isles Beyond the Main': Abraham Lincoln's Philosophy on Black Colonization," *Lincoln Herald* 80 (1978): 115–22.

26. Lincoln, *Collected Works*, 5:29–31, 317–19. There has been much nonsense written about Lincoln's views on race, some writers praising him as a farseeing egalitarian and some dismissing him as a white bigot who embodied the racist views of most white Americans. Many of the same conclusions are reached by George M. Fredrickson, "A Man But not a Brother: Abraham Lincoln and Racial Equality, *Journal of Southern History* 41 (1975): 39–58, and Fehrenbacher, "Only His Stepchildren." Also valuable is Arthur Zilversmit, "Lincoln and the Problem of Race: A Decade of Interpretations," *Papers of the Abraham Lincoln Association* 2 (1980): 22–45.

27. *U.S. Statutes at Large*, 12 (Washington, D.C.: GPO, 1863): 1267–68.

28. Lincoln, *Collected Works*, 5:317–19, quotation on p. 318.

29. Lincoln's executive order, dated July 22, 1862, was promulgated to the armies in the field by a War Department order dated August 16. *OR*, ser. 3, 2:397.

30. As Lincoln later put it, "No human power can subdue this rebellion without using the Emancipation lever as I have done." Lincoln, *Collected Works*, 7:499–502, 506–8, quotation on p. 507.

31. Lincoln, *Collected Works*, 5:344–46, quotation on p. 346; also 350–51, quotation on p. 350.

32. Lincoln, who had declared in his second annual message to Congress, "I cannot make it better known than it already is, that I strongly favor colonization," never made another public appeal for the scheme. Fehrenbacher, "Only His Stepchildren," 308.

33. At times, McPherson appears to argue that the preeminence of Lincoln's role in the process of emancipation derived from the simple fact that he was the Republican candidate, wartime president, and commander in chief of the Union army, for freedom could not be achieved without Southern secession, civil war, and Union victory. If that is the pith of the case, it is easy enough to concede. Indeed, the first sentence of *The Black Military Experience* asserts: "Freedom came to most American slaves only through force of arms."

34. Although he makes no case for the slaves' role in emancipation, Don Fehrenbacher reaches a similar conclusion respecting Lincoln's role. "Emancipation itself, as [Lincoln] vir-

tually acknowledged, came out of the logic of events, not his personal volition, but the time and manner of its coming were largely his choice." "Only His Stepchildren," 306.

35. Lincoln, *Collected Works*, 7:499–502, 506–8, quotation on p. 507.

36. "I barely suggest for your private consideration," Lincoln wrote to the Unionist governor of Louisiana in March 1864, "whether some of the colored people may not be let in [to the suffrage]—as, for instance, the very intelligent, and especially those who have fought gallantly in our ranks. They would probably help," he added, "in some trying times to come, to keep the jewel of liberty within the family of freedom." Lincoln, *Collected Works*, 7:243.

37. If there is a tendency in one brand of social history to emphasize the agency of the disfranchised, there is a similar tendency in one brand of political history to emphasize the omnipotence and clairvoyance of the great leader. The hero sees farthest, first. While combating the former fallacy, McPherson succumbs to the latter. From the beginning of the war, McPherson maintains, "Lincoln demurred from turning the war for Union into a war for slavery because the war for Union united Northern people while premature emancipation would divide them and lose the war." Lincoln, in other words, understood the Civil War as a struggle for emancipation from the beginning. He waited, however, for the right moment to spring the news on those not quite as farseeing. "With an acute sense of timing," McPherson continues, "Lincoln first proclaimed emancipation only as a *means* to win the war (to gain moderate and conservative support) and ultimately as an *end*—to give America 'a new birth of freedom,' as Lincoln said at Gettysburg."

38. *USA Today*, Dec. 30, 1992.

Chapter Six
QUANDARIES OF COMMAND: ULYSSES S. GRANT AND BLACK SOLDIERS

1. George W. Williams, *A History of the Negro Troops in the War of the Rebellion, 1861–1865* (New York: Harper and Brothers, 1888); Dudley Taylor Cornish, *The Sable Arm: Negro Troops in the Union Army, 1861–1865* (New York: W. W. Norton, 1966 [1956]); Ira Berlin, Joseph P. Reidy, and Leslie S. Rowland, eds., *Freedom: A Documentary History of Emancipation, 1861–1867*, 4 vols. to date (Cambridge, Eng.: Cambridge Univ. Press, 1982–90), ser. 2, *The Black Military Experience*; and Joseph T. Glatthaar, *Forged in Battle: The Civil War Alliance of Black Soldiers and White Officers* (New York: Free Press, 1990). One earlier historian who did weave the story of the black soldier into his larger account was Bruce Catton. See, for example, *A Stillness at Appomattox* (Garden City, N.Y.: Doubleday, 1953).

2. On Grant and black soldiers, see Howard C. Westwood, *Black Troops, White Commanders, and Freedmen During the Civil War* (Carbondale: Southern Illinois Univ. Press, 1992), chap. 2; Brooks D. Simpson, *Let Us Have Peace: Ulysses S. Grant and the Politics of War and Reconstruction, 1861–1868* (Chapel Hill: Univ. of North Carolina Press, 1991), chaps. 2–5, passim; Arthur Zilversmit, "Grant and the Freedmen," in *New Perspectives on Race and Slavery in America: Essays in Honor of Kenneth M. Stampp*, ed. Robert H. Abzug and Stephen E. Maizlish (Lexington: Univ. Press of Kentucky, 1986), chap. 7.

3. James G. Wilson, *The Life and Campaigns of General Ulysses S. Grant* (New York, 1885), 105.

4. John Eaton, *Grant, Lincoln, and the Freedmen* (New York: Longman and Green, 1907), 15.

5. Halleck to Grant, Mar. 30, 1863, John Y. Simon et al., eds., *The Papers of Ulysses S. Grant* (Carbondale: Southern Illinois Univ. Press, 1967–), 8:93; Stanton to Thomas, Mar. 25, 1863,

The War of the Rebellion: A Compilaton of the Official Records of the Union and Confederate Armies,
128 vols. (Washington, D.C.: GPO, 1880–1901), ser. 3, 3:100–101.

6. Simpson, *Let Us Have Peace*, 40; Army of the Tennessee, General Orders No. 25, Apr.
22, 1863, *Papers of Grant*, 8:94.

7. Grant to Halleck, Apr. 19, 1863, *Papers of Grant*, 8:91–92; Grant endorsements of Apr.
23 and 27 quoted in ibid., 8:94; Grant to Thomas, July 11, 1863, ibid., 9:23–24; Grant to
Lincoln, Aug. 23, 1863, ibid., 9:196; Westwood, *Black Troops, White Commanders, and Freedmen*, 210.

8. Theodore S. Bowers to James B. McPherson, July 22, 1863, *Papers of Grant*, 9:112;
Grant to Halleck, July 24, 1863, ibid., 9:110; Berlin, *Freedom: The Black Military Experience*,
484–85; Louis S. Gerteis, *From Contraband to Freedman: Federal Policy toward Southern Blacks,
1861–1865* (Westport, Conn.: Greenwood, 1973), 122.

9. Grant to Thomas, June 16, 1863, *Papers of Grant*, 8:328; Grant to Julia Dent Grant,
July 1, 1863, ibid., 8:454.

10. Elias K. Owen to David D. Porter, June 16, 1863, and Porter to Grant, June 19, 1863,
Papers of Grant, 8:401; Grant to Taylor, June 22, 1863, ibid., 8:400–401; Taylor to Grant, June
27, 1863, and Grant to Taylor, July 4, 1863, ibid., 8:468–69.

11. Wilson, *Life and Campaigns of Grant*, 105; Grant to Halleck, July 24, 1863, *Papers of
Grant*, 9:110.

12. Grant to Stanton, July 20, 1864, *Papers of Grant*, 11:284; Grant to Sherman, Mar. 4,
1864, ibid., 10:190; Grant to Banks, Mar. 31, 1864, ibid., 10:243; Grant to Sherman, Apr. 4,
1864, ibid., 10:255.

13. Grant to Burnside, May 11, 1864, ibid., 10:423; Grant to Stanton, July 15, 1864, ibid.,
11:250; Grant to Butler, June 17, 1864, ibid., 11:68–69; Grant to Meade, June 19, 1864, ibid.,
11:82; Grant to Halleck, June 23, 1864, ibid., 11:112.

14. Grant to Meade, July 26, 1864, ibid., 11:321. See Henry Pleasants, Jr., *The Tragedy of the
Crater* (Eastern National Park and Monument Association, 1975 [1938]).

15. Grant, Testimony Before the Joint Committee on the Conduct of the War, Dec. 20,
1864, *Papers of Grant*, 13:140.

16. Grant to Meade, Aug. 1, 1864, ibid., 11:369; Grant to Halleck, Aug. 1, 1864, ibid., 11:361;
Theodore S. Bowers to James H. Wilson, Aug. 1, 2, 1864, ibid., 11:363; Grant, Testimony
before the Joint Committee on the Conduct of the War, Dec. 20, 1864, ibid., 13:138–42.

17. Butler to Grant, Aug. 19, 1864, ibid., 12:41–42; Cornish, *Sable Arm*, 279–81; Richard J.
Sommers, *Richmond Redeemed: The Siege at Petersburg* (Garden City, N.Y.: Doubleday, 1981),
passim, esp. p. 75.

18. Grant to Sherman, Apr. 15, 1864, *Papers of Grant*, 10:285; Lee to Grant, Oct. 1, 1864,
and Grant to Lee, Oct. 2, 1864, ibid., 12:258; Lee to Grant, Oct. 3, 1864, and Grant to Lee,
Oct. 3, 1864, ibid., 12:263.

19. Lee to Grant, Oct. 19, 1864, ibid., 12:324–26; Grant to Lee, Oct. 20, 1864, ibid.,
12:323–25.

20. Sherman to Grant, Dec. 31, 1864, ibid., 13:171; Stanton to Grant, Jan. 5, 1865, ibid.,
13:238; Grant to Halleck, Jan. 1, 1865, ibid., 13:200–201; Grant to Stanton, Jan. 6, 1865, ibid.,
13:237–38. For a detailed discussion of Sherman's position on black soldiers, see Michael Fellman,
Citizen Sherman (New York: Random House, 1995), 155–69.

21. Grant to Halleck, Jan. 24, 1864, and Halleck to Grant, Jan. 25, 1864, ibid., 10:59; Grant
to Stanton, Nov. 15, 1864, ibid., 12:418; Butler to Rawlins, Nov. 30, 1864, and Grant's approval,

ibid., 13:39; Grant to Ord, Apr. 6, 1865, ibid., 14:357.

22. S. M. Bowman to William T. Sherman, Feb. 7, 1865, Sherman Papers, Library of Congress; Augustus Chetlain, *Recollections of Seventy Years* (Galena, Ill., 1899), 100; Tyler Dennett, ed., *Lincoln and the Civil War in the Diaries and Letters of John Hay* (New York: Dodd, Mead, 1939), 242; Robert Hutchins, ed., *Letters from Lloyd Lewis* (Boston: Little, Brown, 1950), 49.

23. Theodore S. Bowers to Edward O. C. Ord, Apr. 16, 1865, *Papers of Grant*, 14:408.

24. Grant to Julia Dent Grant, Apr. 16, 1865, ibid., 14:396. Grant planned to send Ord to Charleston, South Carolina.

25. Bernarr Cresap, *Appomattox Commander: The Story of General E. O. C. Ord* (San Diego, Calif.: A. S. Barnes, 1981), 220–21; R. J. M. Blackett, ed., *Thomas Morris Chester: Black Civil War Correspondent* (Baton Rouge: Louisiana State Univ. Press, 1989), 332.

26. Halleck to Grant, Apr. 29, 1865, *Papers of Grant*, 14:438.

27. Grant to Halleck, Apr. 30, 1865, ibid., 14:438; Simpson, *Let Us Have Peace*, 103–4; Glatthaar, *Forged in Battle*, 219.

28. Blackett, *Thomas Morris Chester*, 364–65; Committee of Richmond Blacks to Andrew Johnson, June 10, 1865, in LeRoy P. Graf et al., eds., *The Papers of Andrew Johnson* (Knoxville: Univ. of Tennessee Press, 1967–), 8:211.

29. Robert M. Zalimas, "Black Union Soldiers in the Postwar South, 1865–1866" (M.A. thesis, Arizona State University, 1993), 106.

30. Arney R. Childs, ed., *The Private Journal of Henry William Ravenel, 1859–1887* (Columbia, S.C.: Univ. of South Carolina Press, 1947), 24; Alfred R. Wynne to Andrew Johnson, Sept. 8, 1865, Hiram Gamage to Johnson, Oct. 30, 1865, and Asa W. Messenger to Johnson, Jan. 9, 1866, *Papers of Johnson*, 9:50–51, 305, 584.

31. Zalimas, "Black Union Soldiers in the Postwar South," 86; James M. Howry to Johnson, Nov. 8, 1865, *Papers of Johnson*, 9:357–58.

32. Zalimas, "Black Union Soldiers in the Postwar South," 100–101.

33. Hans L. Trefousse, *Andrew Johnson: A Biography* (New York: W. W. Norton, 1989), 341.

34. Johnson to Thomas, Sept. 4, 1865, *Papers of Johnson*, 9:26; Thomas to Johnson, Sept. 7, 9, 1865, ibid., 9:41, 57; Thomas to Johnson, Sept. 18, 1865, Johnson Papers, Library of Congress. In *The United States Army and Reconstruction, 1865–1877* (Baton Rouge: Louisiana State Univ. Press, 1965), 50–53, James Sefton comes close to adopting Johnson's perspective in his discussion of the use of black soldiers on occupation duty.

35. Harvey M. Watterson to Andrew Johnson, June 20, 1865, in Brooks D. Simpson, LeRoy P. Graf, and John Muldowny, eds., *Advice After Appomattox: Letters to Andrew Johnson, 1865–1866* (Knoxville: Univ. of Tennessee Press, 1987), 50; John Dawson et al. to Andrew Johnson, [August] 1865, Johnson Papers, Library of Congress; Thomas J. Rawls to Johnson, Sept. 12, 1865, *Papers of Johnson*, 9:74; John Martin to Johnson, May 28, 1865, ibid., 8:126.

36. Stanton to Johnson, Aug. 21, 1865, Stanton Papers, Library of Congress; Abel Alderson to Johnson, Dec. 3, 1865, *Papers of Johnson*, 9:459.

37. Meade to Stanton, Sept. 20, 1865, in Simpson et al., *Advice After Appomattox*, 231; Thomas to Johnson, Sept. 9, 1865, Johnson Papers, Library of Congress.

38. Grant to Edwin M. Stanton, May 31, 1865, *Papers of Grant*, 15:499. Grant to Stanton, July 1, 1865, ibid., 15:550; Zalimas, "Black Union Soldiers in the Postwar South," 47; Grant to Theodore S. Bowers, July 31 and Sept. 8, 1865, *Papers of Grant*, 15:290, 581; Sheridan to John A. Rawlins, Oct. 24, 1865, and Rawlins to Sheridan, Oct. 26, 1865, ibid., 16:447. The directive

not to sell black soldiers their weapons was not implemented widely; eventually Grant revoked it. See endorsements by Theodore S. Bowers, Feb. 28, 1866, and John G. Foster, Mar. 12, 1866, on Charles H. Van Wyck to ?, Feb. 18, 1866, all ibid.

39. Grant to George H. Thomas, Nov. 4, 1865, *Papers of Grant*, 15:390; Grant to George G. Meade, Nov. 6, 1865, ibid., 15:398; Grant to John Pope, Oct. 14, 1865, ibid., 15:337–38; Pope to Grant, Oct. 10, 26, 1865, ibid., 15:338, 340; Grant to William T. Sherman, Oct. 31, 1865, ibid., 15:377; Grant to William Henry Seward, Nov. 10, 1865, ibid., 15:413.

40. Benjamin Perry (South Carolina) to Johnson, Aug. 10, 25, and Sept. 23, 1865, *Papers of Johnson*, 8:558, 651; 9:124; William Sharkey (Mississippi) to Johnson, Aug. 25 and 28, 1865, ibid., 8:653, 666; William G. Brownlow (Tennessee) to Johnson, Aug. 31, 1865, ibid., 8:686; William Holden (North Carolina) to Johnson, Aug. 10, 1865, ibid., 8:556; J. Madison Wells (Louisiana) to Johnson, Oct. 20, 1865, ibid., 9:262; Charles Jenkins (Georgia) to Johnson, Jan. 1, 1866, ibid., 9:557–58; Petition to Grant, Oct. 30, 1865, *Papers of Grant*, 15:610.

41. Simpson, *Advice After Appomattox*, 207–11; Grant to Johnson, Dec. 18, 1865, ibid., 212–14.

42. Grant to Andrew Johnson, Dec. 18, 1865, ibid., 212–14.

43. Schurz to Johnson, Aug. 29, 1865, ibid., 113–14.

44. Simpson, *Let Us Have Peace*, 122–28.

45. Grant to Andrew Johnson, Feb. 9, 1866, *Papers of Grant*, 16:52–53; Grant, endorsement of Jan. 9, 1866, on Robert M. Patton to George H. Thomas, Dec. 30, 1865, ibid., 16:54; Grant to Johnson, Feb. 17 and Mar. 14, 1866, ibid., 16:69, 114; Blacks of Apalachicola, Florida, to Grant, Jan. 31, 1866, ibid., 16:445–46; Ely S. Parker to Theodore S. Bowers, Jan. 27, 1866, ibid., 16:459.

46. James M. Chambers to Johnson, Feb. 15, 1866, *Papers of Johnson*, 10:96–97; Charles J. Jenkins to Johnson, Feb. 15, 1866, ibid., 10:101. On Feb. 14, 1866, Grant forwarded to Johnson the reports of two staff officers, Ely S. Parker and Cyrus B. Comstock, describing continued resistance to the imposition of federal authority and the mistreatment of and violence against blacks. He also forwarded statistics on interracial violence. See Simpson, *Let Us Have Peace*, 127–32; *Papers of Grant*, 16:458–61.

47. Grant to William T. Sherman, Mar. 3, 14, 1866, *Papers of Grant*, 16:93, 117; Grant to Philip H. Sheridan, Mar. 19, 29, 1866, ibid., 16:122, 116; Grant to Stanton, Mar. 14, 1866, ibid., 16:115.

48. Grant to George H. Thomas, Mar. 28, 1866, ibid., 16:139–41.

49. George Stoneman to Grant, May 12, 1866, ibid., 16: 235–36.

50. Grant to Edwin M. Stanton, July 7, 1866, ibid., 16:233–34.

51. Grant to Edwin M. Stanton, May 16, 1866, ibid., 16:199–201; Grant to Philip H. Sheridan, Dec. 31, 1866, ibid., 16:583.

52. Grant to Edwin M. Stanton, Oct. 20, 1865, ibid., 15:359; Grant to Henry Wilson, Jan. 12, 1866, ibid., 16:11.

53. Sefton, *Army and Reconstruction*, 96–97, cites circumstances in which black soldiers served in the South; Henry Wilson to Grant, July 28, 1866, and Grant to Edwin M. Stanton, Aug. 2, 1866, *Papers of Grant*, 16:274–75.

54. See Brooks D. Simpson, "Butcher? Racist? An Examination of William S. McFeely's *Grant: A Biography*," *Civil War History* 33 (Mar. 1987): 63–83, esp. pp. 73–83, on Grant's racial attitudes.

Chapter Seven
QUARREL FORGOTTEN OR A REVOLUTION REMEMBERED?
REUNION AND RACE IN THE MEMORY OF THE CIVIL WAR, 1875–1913

1. John R. Gillis, "Memory and Identity: The History of a Relationship," in *Commemorations: The Politics of National Identity*, ed. John R. Gillis (Princeton, N.J.: Princeton Univ. Press, 1994), 5.

2. Natalie Zemon Davis and Randolph Starn, Introduction to special issue on "Memory and Counter-Memory," *Representations* 26 (Spring 1989): 2. There are many theoretical works that discuss social memory as a matter of cultural conflict. Some places to start are Maurice Halbwachs, *On Collective Memory*, trans. and intro. Lewis A. Coser (Chicago: Univ. of Chicago Press, 1992); David Thelen, ed., *Memory in American History* (Bloomington: Univ. of Indiana Press, 1991); Michael Kammen, *Mystic Chords of Memory: The Transformation of Tradition in American Culture* (New York: Knopf, 1991), 3–14; Friedrich Nietzsche, *On the Advantage and Disadvantage of History for Life*, intro. Peter Preuss (Indianapolis: Hackett, 1980); Peter Burke, "History as Social Memory," in *Memory: History, Culture, and the Mind*, ed. Thomas Butler (London: Basil Blackwell, 1989), 97–113; Pierre Nora, "Between Memory and History: Les Lieux de Mémoire," *Representations* 26 (Spring 1989): 7–25; Barry Schwartz, "The Social Context of Commemoration: A Study in Collective Memory," *Social Forces* 67 (Dec. 2, 1982): 374–402; Eric Hobsbaum and Terrence Ranger, eds., *The Invention of Tradition* (Cambridge, Eng.: Cambridge Univ. Press, 1983); David Lowenthal, *The Past Is a Foreign Country* (Cambridge, Eng.: Cambridge Univ. Press, 1985), pts. 2 and 3; Charles S. Maier, *The Unmasterable Past: History, Holocaust, and German National Identity* (Cambridge, Mass.: Harvard Univ. Press, 1988); Benedict Anderson, *Imagined Communities: Reflections on the Origin and Spread of Nationalism* (London: Verso, 1991), 187–206; and the many rich essays in Gillis, ed., *Commemorations: The Politics of National Identity*.

3. Episode 9, "The Better Angels of Our Nature," *The Civil War*, produced and directed by Ken Burns (Washington, D.C.: WETA Television). Fields is quoting from Faulkner's *Absalom, Absalom!*

4. John Hope Franklin, "A Century of Civil War Observances," *Journal of Negro History* 47 (Apr. 1962): 98, 105. On the Civil War Centennial from a black perspective, also see J. A. Rogers, "Civil War Centennial, Myth and Reality," *Freedomways* 3 (Winter 1963): 7–18.

5. Richard Slotkin, "'What Shall Men Remember?': Recent Work on the Civil War," *American Literary History* 3 (Spring 1991): 13; Chamberlain is quoted in *The Civil War*, episode 9; Howells is quoted in Allan Gurganus, *Oldest Confederate Widow Tells All* (New York: Ivy Books, 1984), epigraph. For a trenchant recent critique of the "master narrative" of American history rooted in the idea of "automatic progress," see Nathan Irvin Huggins, "The Deforming Mirror of Truth," introduction to new edition, *Black Odyssey: The African-American Ordeal in Slavery* (New York: Vintage, 1990).

6. For a similar critique of the PBS film series, one that argues effectively that Burns employed an American "family" metaphor as the overall framework, see Bill Farrell, "All in the Family: Ken Burns's The Civil War and Black America," *Transition: An International Review* 58 (1993): 169–73.

7. Nina Silber, *The Romance of Reunion: Northerners and the South, 1865–1900* (Chapel Hill: Univ. of North Carolina Press, 1993), 3.

8. Daniel Aaron, *The Unwritten War: American Writers and the Civil War* (New York: Knopf, 1973), 328; W. E. B. Du Bois, *The Souls of Black Folk*, Signet edition (1903; reprint, New York: Signet, 1969), 54, 78.

9. Anderson, *Imagined Communities*, 3, 201.

10. Alain Locke, "The New Negro," in *The New Negro*, Atheneum edition, ed. Alain Locke (1925; reprint, New York: Atheneum, 1968), 4, 16.

11. On nostalgia as a psychological and social phenomenon, see Jean Starobinski, "Nostalgia," *Diogenes* 14 (Summer 1966): 80–103; and Renato Rosaldo, "Imperialist Nostalgia," *Representations* 26 (Spring 1989): 107–22.

12. Frederick Douglass, "The Color Question," July 5, 1875, Frederick Douglass Papers, Library of Congress (hereafter LC), reel 15. On this stage of Reconstruction, see William Gillette, *The Retreat from Reconstruction, 1869–1879* (Baton Rouge: Louisiana State Univ. Press, 1979).

13. John Hope Franklin, "The Birth of a Nation: Propaganda as History," reprinted from the *Massachusetts Review*, 1979, in John Hope Franklin, *Race and History: Selected Essays, 1938–1988* (Baton Rouge: Louisiana State Univ. Press, 1989), 10–23; Ralph Ellison, "Going to the Territory," address given at Brown University, Sept. 20, 1979, reprinted in Ralph Ellison, *Going to the Territory* (New York: Vintage, 1986), 124. On Dixon's significance, see Joel Williamson, *The Crucible of Race: Black-White Relations in the American South Since Emancipation* (New York: Oxford Univ. Press, 1984), 140–76.

14. On the turn in American cultural attitudes in the 1880s, see Gerald Linderman, *Embattled Courage: The Experience of Combat in the Civil War* (New York: Free Press, 1987), 266–97; Gaines M. Foster, *Ghosts of the Confederacy: Defeat, the Lost Cause, and the Emergence of the New South* (New York: Oxford Univ. Press, 1987), 63–162; Paul M. Gaston, *The New South Creed: A Study in Southern Myth-Making* (New York: Knopf, 1970); Silber, *Romance of Reunion*, 93–123; and Kammen, *Mystic Chords*, 91–116. On the dynamics of black thought, see August Meier, *Negro Thought in America, 1880–1915: Racial Ideologies in the Age of Booker T. Washington* (Ann Arbor: Univ. of Michigan Press, 1970), 3–82.

15. Alexander Crummell, *Africa and America: Addresses and Discourses* (1891; rpt. New York: Atheneum, 1969), iii, 14, 18, 13. I am indebted to Robert Gooding-Williams for bringing Crummell's speech to my attention. On Crummell, see Wilson J. Moses, *Alexander Crummell: A Study of Civilization and Discontent* (New York: Oxford Univ. Press, 1990); and Alfred A. Moss, Jr., *The American Negro Academy: Voice of the Talented Tenth* (Baton Rouge: Louisiana State Univ. Press, 1981), 19–34, 53–62. Crummell was the founder of the American Negro Academy.

16. See David W. Blight, "For Something Beyond the Battlefield: Frederick Douglass and the Memory of the Civil War," *Journal of American History* 75 (Spring 1989): 1156–78; and John David Smith, *An Old Creed for the New South: Proslavery Ideology and Historiography, 1865–1918* (Westport, Conn.: Greenwood, 1985), 287–88.

17. Frederick Douglass, "Speech at the Thirty-Third Anniversary of the Jerry Rescue," 1884, Frederick Douglass Papers, LC, reel 16.

18. Frederick Douglass, "Thoughts and Recollections of the Antislavery Conflict," speech undated, but it is at least from the early 1880s; "Decoration Day," speech at Mt. Hope Cemetery, Rochester, N.Y., May 1883; and "Address Delivered on the 26th Anniversary of Abolition in the District of Columbia," Apr. 16, 1888, Washington, D.C., all in Frederick Douglass Papers, LC, reel 15.

19. On white racial thought, see George M. Fredrickson, *The Black Image in the White Mind: The Debate on Afro-American Character and Destiny, 1817–1914* (New York: Harper & Row, 1971), 228–82; and Williamson, *Crucible of Race*, 111–323.

20. Paul B. Barringer, "The American Negro, His Past and Future" (address delivered Feb. 20, 1900, Charleston, S.C.; copy in Widener Library, Harvard University). On Barringer, see Williamson, *Crucible of Race*, 177; Fredrickson, *Black Image in the White Mind*, 252–53; and Smith, *Old Creed for the New South*, 286. Barringer was a leader of the University of Virginia faculty from 1896 to 1903, and later a founder of Virginia Polytechnic Institute.

21. Fredrickson, *Black Image in the White Mind*, 320–22. On the role of white supremacy in the development of a historiographical consensus, see Smith, *Old Creed for the New South*, 103–96, 239–77.

22. See Moses, *Crummell*, 226–28; William S. McFeely, *Frederick Douglass* (New York: Norton, 1991), 238–304; and David W. Blight, *Frederick Douglass' Civil War: Keeping Faith in Jubilee* (Baton Rouge: Louisiana State Univ. Press, 1989), 189–245.

23. Other such comparisons of black intellectuals and competing conceptions of memory might involve Booker T. Washington and his various critics, historian George Washington Williams and activist Ida B. Wells-Barnett, A.M.E. Church Bishop Henry McNeal Turner and historian-activist Archibald Grimke. The list could be much longer. On W. E. B. Du Bois in this regard, see David W. Blight, "W. E. B. Du Bois and the Struggle for American Historical Memory," in *History and Memory in Afro-American Culture*, ed. Genevieve Fabre and Robert O'Meally (New York: Oxford Univ. Press, 1994), 45–71.

24. See David Glassberg, *American Historical Pageantry: The Uses of Tradition in the Early Twentieth Century* (Chapel Hill: Univ. of North Carolina Press, 1990); T. J. Jackson Lears, *No Place of Grace: Antimodernism and the Transformation of American Culture, 1880–1920* (New York: Pantheon, 1981), 97–138; Wallace E. Davies, *Patriotism on Parade: The Story of Veterans' and Hereditary Organizations in America, 1783–1900* (Cambridge, Mass.: Harvard Univ. Press, 1955); and Kammen, *Mystic Chords*. On the development of patriotism and nationalism, see John Bodnar, *Public Memory, Commemoration, and Patriotism in the Twentieth Century* (Princeton, N.J.: Princeton Univ. Press, 1992).

25. *Fiftieth Anniversary of the Battle of Gettysburg: Report of the Pennsylvania Commission*, Dec. 31, 1913 (Harrisburg, Pa.: n.p., 1915), 39–41. Every state did not participate in providing funds for veteran transportation, especially some in the South and Southwest. On commemorations at Gettysburg over the years, also see Edward Tabor Linenthal, *Sacred Ground: Americans and Their Battlefields* (Urbana: Univ. of Illinois Press, 1991), 89–126; John S. Patterson, "A Patriotic Landscape: Gettysburg, 1863–1913," *Prospects* 7 (1982): 315–33.

26. *Fiftieth Anniversary of the Battle of Gettysburg*, 31, 36–37. The Pennsylvania Commission's report contained dozens of photographs, with one compelling scene after another of the spirit of reconciliation as well as of the generational transmission of national memory. In a few of these photographs one sees black laborers and camp workers, constructing the tents, serving as bakers, or passing out blankets and mess kits. Nowhere is there any photograph of a black veteran.

27. Ibid., 6, 39–41, 49–51, 53, 57–58. Paul Connerton, *How Societies Remember* (New York: Cambridge Univ. Press, 1989); and Alan Trachtenberg, *The Incorporation of America: Culture and Society in the Gilded Age* (New York: Hill & Wang, 1982); *Philadelphia Inquirer*, July 6, 1913. An essay might be written on the "scientific management" and efficiency aspects of the Gettysburg reunion alone. For understanding the Gettysburg community's extraordinary

preparation for the reunion, I have relied in part on the *Gettysburg Compiler*, March-July, 1913, microfilm copy at the Gettysburg National Military Park.

28. *Fiftieth Anniversary of the Battle of Gettysburg*, 6, 25; Walter H. Blake, *Hand Grips: The Story of the Great Gettysburg Reunion of 1913* (Vineland, N.J.: n.p., 1913), 66–67.

29. For the Boy Scouts and the suffragists at the reunion, see *Washington Post*, June 28, 30, 1913; *New York Times*, July 1, 1913; and *Fiftieth Anniversary of the Battle of Gettysburg*, 49–51. On the notion of "sites" of memory, see Nora, "Between Memory and History."

30. The Mann speech is reprinted in *Fiftieth Anniversary of the Battle of Gettysburg*, 144, 174–76; Wilson's speech in Arthur Link, ed., *The Papers of Woodrow Wilson*, vol. 28 (Princeton, N.J.: Princeton Univ. Press, 1978), 23.

31. *Louisville Courier-Journal*, July 4, 1913; Ernest Renan, "What is a Nation," in *Nation and Narration*, trans. Martin Thom, ed. Homi K. Bhabha (London: Routledge, 1990), 11, 19.

32. Oliver Wendell Holmes, "A Soldier's Faith," an address delivered on Memorial Day, May 30, 1895, at a meeting called by the graduating class of Harvard University, in *Speeches of Oliver Wendell Holmes, Jr.* (Boston: Little, Brown, 1934), 56–66; *Fiftieth Anniversary of the Battle of Gettysburg*, 176. On the role of language in the creation of nationalisms, see Anderson, *Imagined Communities*, 154.

33. Garry Wills, *Lincoln at Gettysburg: The Words that Remade America* (New York: Simon and Schuster, 1992), 38, 40; Link, ed., *Papers of Woodrow Wilson* 28:24–25. On the Wilson administration and racial segregation, see Henry Blumenthal, "Woodrow Wilson and the Race Question," *Journal of Negro History* 48 (Jan. 1963): 1–21; and Williamson, *Crucible of Race*, 358–95. On the 1912 election and Wilson's Progressivism in relation to race, see Nell Irvin Painter, *Standing at Armageddon: The United States, 1877–1919* (New York: Norton, 1987), 268–72.

34. See Foster, *Ghosts of the Confederacy*, 7–8. Foster avoids the term *myth* in favor of *tradition*. Also see Alan T. Nolan, *Lee Considered: General Robert E. Lee and Civil War History* (Chapel Hill: Univ. of North Carolina Press, 1991). Nolan comfortably uses the term *myth*. Distinctions between these slippery terms are important, but *myth* seems to be an appropriate terminology in this instance. On the idea of myth for historians, there are many good sources, but see Richard Slotkin, *The Fatal Environment: The Myth of the Frontier in the Age of Industrialization, 1800–1890* (New York: Atheneum, 1985), 1–48; Warren I. Susman, *Culture as History: The Transformation of American Society in the Twentieth Century* (New York: Pantheon, 1973), 7–26; and Kammen, *Mystic Chords*, esp. p. 431–71.

35. Burke, "History as Social Memory," 106; Connerton, *How Societies Remember*, 22–25, 28–31. Connerton's anthropological analysis of commemorative rituals is provocative and useful, but the content and the form, the meaning and the performance, must be examined with equal vigor. On commemorations, also see Schwartz, "The Social Context of Commemoration," and the many essays in Gillis, ed., *Commemorations*.

36. *Washington Post*, June 30, 1913. The *Post* also took direct aim at Progressive reformers in the context of the nationalism expressed at Gettysburg. *New York Times*, July 1–4, 1913; *The Outlook* 104 (July 12, 1913): 541, 554–55, 610–12.

37. *Times* (London), July 4, 1913; *Cincinnati Enquirer*, July 6, 1913; *San Francisco Examiner*, July 4, 1913; *Charleston News and Courier*, July 1, 1913; *Brooklyn Daily Eagle*, July 2, 1913.

38. *Baltimore Afro-American Ledger*, July 5, 1913.

39. See Williamson, *Crucible of Race*, 364–95. Booker T. Washington, *New York Times*, Aug. 18, 1913, quoted in Blumenthal, "Woodrow Wilson and the Race Question," 8. An especially interesting counterattack on Wilson administration segregation policies in 1913 is

Oswald Garrison Villard's "Segregation in Baltimore and Washington," an address delivered to the Baltimore branch of the National Association for the Advancement of Colored People, Oct. 20, 1913, copy in Widener Library, Harvard University. Villard had been a friend and supporter of Wilson's, and was then national chairman of the NAACP. The central figure in the NAACP's often successful resistance to Wilson administration segregation schemes was Archibald Grimke, the branch director for Washington, D.C. On Grimke's role in the 1913 disputes, see Dickson D. Bruce, Jr., *Archibald Grimke: Portrait of a Black Independent* (Baton Rouge: Louisiana State Univ. Press, 1993), 184– 200. It is also interesting to note that in the NAACP's monthly, *Crisis*, editor W. E. B. Du Bois made no mention whatsoever of the Gettysburg reunion. Instead, he wrote a celebration of the 54th Massachusetts black regiment, including a full-page photograph of the Shaw/54th Memorial in Boston. See *Crisis* 5–8 (July 1913): 122–26.

40. *Washington Bee*, May 24, June 7, 1913.

41. Paul H. Buck, *The Road to Reunion, 1865–1900* (New York: Random House, 1937), 126, 319, 308–9. The term *miracle* was frequently used in reviews of Buck's book as a means of referring to the triumph of sectional reconciliation. Arthur Schlesinger, Sr., also used the term on the jacket of the original edition. Among the many letters Buck received about his book was one from Margaret Mitchell, author of *Gone With the Wind*, which had just won the Pulitzer Prize for literature the year before. "I am sure your wonderful book, 'The Road to Reunion,' wrote Mitchell, "has never had as interested a reader as I. I am especially sure that no reader took greater pleasure in the Pulitzer award than I. My sincere congratulations to you." Margaret Mitchell Marsh (Mrs. John R. Marsh) to Paul Buck, May 10, 1938, in Buck's "Scrapbook" collection of reviews, commemorating his Pulitzer Prize, Paul Buck Papers, Harvard University Archives. *Atlanta Constitution*, July 2, 1913.

42. Friedrich Nietzsche, *The Birth of Tragedy* (1872; Garden City, N.Y.: Anchor Books, 1956), 136; C. Vann Woodward, *The Strange Career of Jim Crow* (New York: Oxford Univ. Press, 1955), viii; Kammen, *Mystic Chords*, 37; W. E. B. Du Bois, *Black Reconstruction in America, 1860–1880* (New York: Atheneum, 1935), 714, 717, 723, 725. It is worth pointing out here, of course, that 1913 was also the fiftieth anniversary of emancipation, an event much commemorated in black communities, popular culture, pageants, poetry, song, and literature. The U.S. Congress also held hearings in order to plan an official recognition of emancipation. Du Bois testified before a Senate committee on Feb. 2, 1912. See hearings, "Semicentennial Anniversary of Act of Emancipation," Senate Report no. 31, 62d Cong., 2d sess. Du Bois wrote and helped produce, under the auspices of the NAACP, a pageant, "The Star of Ethiopia," which was performed in 1913, 1915, and 1916. See Glassberg, *American Historical Pageantry*, 132–35; and William H. Wiggins, Jr., *O Freedom!: Afro-American Emancipation Celebrations* (Nashville: Univ. of Tennessee Press, 1987), 49–78. Also see Blight, "W. E. B. Du Bois and the Struggle for American Historical Memory."

43. Huggins, "Deforming Mirror of Truth," *Black Odyssey*, xliv.

CONTRIBUTORS

IRA BERLIN received his Ph.D. from the University of Wisconsin–Madison in 1970 and is Professor of History at the University of Maryland. He is the founder and former director of the Freedmen and Southern Society Project, an editor of *Freedom: A Documentary History of Emancipation,* and the author of *Slaves Without Masters: The Free Negro in the Antebellum South,* as well as of numerous other studies of the American South.

DAVID W. BLIGHT received his Ph.D. from the University of Wisconsin–Madison in 1985 and is Associate Professor of History and Black Studies at Amherst College. He is the author of *Frederick Douglass' Civil War: Keeping Faith in Jubilee* (1989) and editor of *When This Cruel War is Over: The Civil War Letters of Charles Harvey Brewster* (1992) and *Narrative of the Life of Frederick Douglass, An American Slave* (1993).

LOUIS SAXTON GERTEIS received his Ph.D. from the University of Wisconsin–Madison in 1969 and is Professor of History at the University of Missouri–St. Louis. He is the author of *From Contraband to Freedman* (1973) and *Mortality and Utility in American Antislavery Reform* (1987). He is currently working on a study of democracy and race in nineteenth-century America.

PETER KNUPFER received his Ph.D. from the University of Wisconsin–Madison in 1988 and is Associate Professor of History at Kansas State University. He is the author of *The Union as It Is: Constitutional Unionism and Sectional Compromise, 1848–1861* (1991) and, more recently, of "Crisis in Conservatism: Northern Unionism and the Harpers Ferry Raid," in *His Soul Goes Marching On: Responses to John Brown and the Harpers Ferry Raid* (1995). He is currently working on a study of the election of 1860.

MICHAEL J. McMANUS received his Ph.D. from the University of Wisconsin–Madison in 1991 with a dissertation on the Republican party and antislavery politics in Wisconsin before the Civil War. He is an owner-partner in an investment and insurance planning firm in Madison, Wisconsin.

ROBERT E. MAY received his Ph.D. from the University of Wisconsin–Madison in 1969 and is Professor of History at Purdue University. He is the author of *The Southern Dream of a Caribbean Empire, 1854–1861* (1973) and *John A. Quitman: Old South Crusader* (1985), and the editor of *The Union, the Confederacy, and the Atlantic Rim* (1995).

BROOKS D. SIMPSON received his Ph.D. from the University of Wisconsin–Madison in 1989 and is Associate Professor of History and Humanities at Arizona State University. Among his books are *Let Us Have Peace: Ulysses S. Grant and the Politics of War and Reconstruction, 1861–1868* (1991) and *The Political Education of Henry Adams* (1996).

A SELECTED BIBLIOGRAPHY
ON POLITICS, THE UNION,
EMANCIPATION, & ITS AFTERMATH
IN THE CIVIL WAR ERA

Works cited in this bibliography are drawn particularly from the essays in this volume, but are also intended as a selective guide to the major themes addressed by the book as a whole.

Aaron, Daniel. *The Unwritten War: American Writers and the Civil War.* New York: Knopf, 1973.

Abrahamson, Paul R. *Generational Change in American Politics.* Lexington, Mass.: Lexington Books, 1975.

Agnew, Jean-Christophe. *Worlds Apart: The Market and the Theater in Anglo-American Thought, 1550–1750.* Cambridge: Harvard University Press, 1986.

Anbinder, Tyler. *Nativism and Slavery: The Northern Know Nothings and the Politics of the 1850s.* New York: Oxford University Press, 1992.

Baker, Jean H. *Affairs of Party: The Political Culture of the Mid-Nineteenth Century Democrats.* Ithaca: Cornell University Press, 1984.

Belz, Herman. *A New Birth of Freedom: The Republican Party and Freedmen's Rights, 1861–1866.* Westport, Conn.: Greenwood Press, 1976.

Berlin, Ira. "Emancipation and Its Meaning in American Life." *Reconstruction* 2 (1994): 41–44.

Berlin, Ira, Leslie S. Rowland, and Steven F. Miller. *Slaves No More: Three Essays on Emancipation and the Civil War.* New York: Cambridge University Press, 1992.

Berlin, Ira, Barbara J. Fields, Steven F. Miller, Joseph P. Reidy, Leslie S. Rowland, eds. *Free At Last: A Documentary History of Slavery, Freedom, and the Civil War.* New York: New Press, 1992.

Berlin, Ira, et al., eds. *The Black Military Experience.* Vol. 1 of *Freedom: A Documentary History of Emancipation,* 2d ser. Cambridge: Cambridge University Press, 1982.

————. *The Destruction of Slavery.* Vol. 1 of *Freedom: A Documentary History of Emancipation,* 1st ser. New York: Cambridge University Press, 1985.

————. *The Wartime Genesis of Free Labor: The Lower South.* Vol. 3 of *Freedom: A Documentary History of Emancipation,* 1st ser. Cambridge: Cambridge University Press, 1991.

————. *The Wartime Genesis of Free Labor: The Upper South.* Vol. 2 of *Freedom: A Documentary History of Emancipation,* 1st ser. Cambridge: Cambridge University Press, 1993.

Bernstein, Iver. *The New York City Draft Riots: Their Significance for American Society and Politics in the Age of the Civil War.* New York: Oxford University Press, 1990.

Blackett, R. J. M., ed. *Thomas Morris Chester: Black Civil War Correspondent.* Baton Rouge: Louisiana State University Press, 1989.

Blight, David W. *Frederick Douglass' Civil War: Keeping Faith in Jubilee.* Baton Rouge: Louisiana State University Press, 1989.

Blue, Frederick J. *The Freesoil Party: Third Party Politics, 1848–1854.* Urbana: University of Illinois Press, 1973.

Bodnar, John. *Public Memory, Commemoration, and Patriotism in the Twentieth Century.* Princeton: Princeton University Press, 1992.

Brown, Charles H. *Agents of Manifest Destiny: The Lives and Times of the Filibusters.* Chapel Hill: University of North Carolina Press, 1980.

Buck, Paul H. *The Road to Reunion, 1865–1900.* New York: Random House, 1937.

Burnham, Walter D. *Critical Elections and the Mainsprings of American Politics.* New York: Norton, 1970.

Crofts, Daniel. *Reluctant Confederates: Upper South Unionists in the Secession Crisis.* Chapel Hill: University of North Carolina Press, 1989.

Curtin, Philip D. *The Image of Africa: British Ideas and Actions, 1780–1850.* Madison: University of Wisconsin Press, 1964.

Davis, David Brion, *The Slave Power Conspiracy and the Paranoid Style.* Baton Rouge: Louisiana State University Press, 1969.

Davis, Susan G. *Parades and Power: Street Theater in Nineteenth Century Philadelphia.* Philadelphia: Temple University Press, 1986.

Dillon, Merton L. *The Abolitionists: The Growth of a Dissenting Minority.* DeKalb: Northern Illnois University Press, 1974.

Donald, David Herbert. *Lincoln.* New York: Simon and Schuster, 1995.

Du Bois, W. E. B. *Black Reconstruction: An Essay Toward a History of the Part Which Black Folk Played in the Attempt to Reconstruct Democracy in America, 1860–1880.* New York: Atheneum, 1935.

Fehrenbacher, Don E. *The Dred Scott Case: Its Significance in American Law and Politics.* New York: Oxford University Press, 1978.

Fellman, Michael. *Citizen Sherman.* New York: Random House, 1995.

Fields, Barbara J. *Slavery and Freedom on the Middle Ground: Maryland During the Nineteenth Century.* New Haven: Yale University Press, 1985.

Finkelman, Paul. *An Imperfect Union: Slavery, Federalism, and Comity.* Chapel Hill: University of North Carolina Press, 1981.

Foner, Eric. "The Causes of the American Civil War: Recent Interpretations and New Directions." *Civil War History* 20 (September 1974): 197–214.

———. *Free Soil, Free Labor, Free Men: The Ideology of the Republican Party Before the Civil War.* New York: Oxford University Press, 1970.

———. *Reconstruction: America's Unfinished Revolution, 1863–1877.* New York: Harper & Row, 1988.

Forgie, George. *Patricide in a House Divided: A Psychological Portrait of Lincoln and His Age.* Chapel Hill: University of North Carolina Press, 1979.

Foster, Gaines M. *Ghosts of the Confederacy: Defeat, the Lost Cause, and the Emergence of the New South.* New York: Oxford University Press, 1987.

Franklin, John Hope. *The Emancipation Proclamation.* Garden City, N.Y.: Doubleday, 1963.

Fredrickson, George M. *The Black Image in the White Mind: The Debate on Afro-American Character and Destiny, 1817–1914.* New York: Harper & Row, 1971.

Freehling, William W. *Prelude to Civil War: The Nullification Controversy in South Carolina, 1816–1836.* New York: Harper & Row, 1965.

Gerteis, Louis S. *From Contraband to Freedman: Federal Policy Toward Southern Blacks, 1861–1865.* Westport, Conn.: Greenwood Press, 1973.

Gienapp, William E. *The Origins of the Republican Party, 1852–1856.* New York: Oxford University Press, 1987.

Glatthaar, Joseph T. *Forged in Battle: The Civil War Alliance of Black Soldiers and White Officers.* New York: Free Press, 1990.

Grimsted, David. *Melodrama Unveiled: American Theater and Culture, 1800–1850.* Chicago: University of Chicago Press, 1968.

Higginson, Thomas Wentworth. *Army Life in a Black Regiment.* 1870. Reprint, New York: Collier Books, 1962.

Holt, Michael F. *Political Parties and American Political Development From the Age of Jackson to the Age of Lincoln.* Baton Rouge: Louisiana State University Press, 1992.

Horsman, Reginald. *Race and Manifest Destiny: The Origins of American Racial Anglo-Saxonism.* Cambridge: Harvard University Press, 1981.

Howard, Victor B. *Black Liberation in Kentucky: Emancipation and Freedom, 1862–1884.* Lexington: University of Kentucky Press, 1983.

Howe, Daniel Walker. *The Political Culture of the American Whigs.* Chicago: University of Chicago Press, 1979.

Huggins, Nathan I. *Black Odyssey: The African-American Ordeal in Slavery.* New York: Vintage, 1990.

Hyman, Harold M. *A More Perfect Union: The Impact of the Civil War and Reconstruction on the Constitution.* New York: Knopf, 1973.

Kammen, Michael. *Mystic Chords of Memory: The Transformation of Tradition in American Culture.* New York: Knopf, 1991.

Knupfer, Peter B. *The Union As It Is: Constitutional Unionism and Sectional Compromise, 1787–1861.* Chapel Hill: University of North Carolina Press, 1991.

Kraditor, Aileen S. *Means and Ends in American Abolitionism: Garrison and His Critics on Strategy and Tactics, 1834–1850.* New York: Pantheon, 1969.

Kraut, Alan M., ed. *Crusaders and Compromisers: Essays on the Relationship of the Antislavery Struggle to the Antebellum Party System.* Westport, Conn.: Greenwood Press, 1983.

Levine, Lawrence W. *Highbrow/Lowbrow: The Emergence of Cultural Hierarchy in America.* Cambridge: Harvard University Press, 1988.

Linderman, Gerald. *Embattled Courage: The Experience of Combat in the Civil War.* New York: Free Press, 1987.

Linenthal, Edward T. *Sacred Ground: Americans and Their Battlefields.* Urbana: University of Illinois Press, 1991.

Litwack, Leon F. *Been in the Storm So Long: The Aftermath of Slavery.* New York: Knopf, 1979.

Lott, Eric. *Love and Theft: Blackface Minstrelsy and the American Working Class.* New York: Oxford University Press, 1993.

Maizlish, Stephen, and John Kushma, eds. *Essays on Antebellum Politics, 1840–1860.* College Station: Texas A&M University Press, 1982.

May, Robert E. *The Southern Dream of a Caribbean Empire, 1854–1861.* Baton Rouge: Louisiana State University Press, 1973.

McFeely, William S. *Frederick Douglass.* New York: Norton, 1991.

———. *Grant: A Biography.* New York: Norton, 1981.

McManus, Michael J. "'A Redeeming Spirit is Busily Engaged': Political Abolitionism and Wisconsin Politics, 1840–1861." Ph. D. dissertation, University of Wisconsin, 1991.

McPherson, James M. *Battle Cry of Freedom: The Civil War Era.* New York: Oxford University Press, 1988.

———. *The Negro's Civil War: How American Negroes Felt and Acted During the War for the Union.* New York: Vintage, 1965.

————. *The Struggle for Equality: Abolitionists and the Negro in the Civil War and Reconstruction.* Princeton: Princeton University Press, 1964.

————. "Who Freed the Slaves?" *Reconstruction* 2 (1994): 35–41.

Morgan, Lynda. *Emancipation in Virginia's Tobacco Belt, 1850–1870.* Athens: University of Georgia Press, 1992.

Morris, Thomas D. *The Personal Liberty Laws of the North, 1780–1860.* Baltimore: Johns Hopkins University Press, 1974.

Nagel, Paul C. *One Nation Indivisible: The Union in American Thought, 1776–1861.* New York: Oxford University Press, 1964.

Perry, Lewis. *Radical Abolitionism: Anarchy and the Government of God in Antislavery Thought.* Ithaca: Cornell University Press, 1973.

Perry, Lewis, and Michael Fellman, eds. *Antislavery Reconsidered: New Perspectives on the Abolitionists.* Baton Rouge: Louisiana State University Press, 1979.

Potter, David M. *The Impending Crisis, 1848–1861.* New York: Harper & Row, 1976.

Quarles, Benjamin. *The Negro in the Civil War.* Boston: Little, Brown, 1953.

Ripley, C. Peter. *Slaves and Freedmen in Civil War Louisiana.* Baton Rouge: Louisiana State University Press, 1976.

Ripley, C. Peter, et al., eds., *The Black Abolitionist Papers.* 5 vols. Chapel Hill: University of North Carolina Press, 1985–1992.

Roediger, David R. *The Wages of Whiteness: Race and the Making of the American Working Class.* London: Verso Books, 1991.

Samuels, Richard J., ed. *Political Generations and Political Development.* Lexington, Mass.: Lexington Books, 1976.

Sellers, Charles. *The Market Revolution: Jacksonian America, 1815–1846.* New York: Oxford University Press, 1991.

Sewell, Richard H. *Ballots for Freedom: Antislavery Politics in the United States, 1837–1860.* New York: Oxford University Press, 1976.

————. *A House Divided: Sectionalism and the Civil War, 1848–1865.* Baltimore: Johns Hopkins University Press, 1988.

————. *John P. Hale and the Politics of Abolition.* Cambridge: Harvard University Press, 1965.

Silber, Nina. *The Romance of Reunion: Northerners and the South, 1865–1900.* Chapel Hill: University of North Carolina Press, 1993.

Silbey, Joel. *The Partisan Imperative: The Dynamics of American Politics Before the Civil War.* New York: Oxford University Press, 1985.

Simpson, Brooks D. *America's Civil War.* Wheeling, Ill.: Harlan Davidson, 1996.

————. *Let Us Have Peace: Ulysses S. Grant and the Politics of War and Reconstruction, 1861–1868.* Chapel Hill: University of North Carolina Press, 1991.

Simpson, Brooks D., et al. *Advice After Appomattox: Letters to Andrew Johnson, 1865–66.* Knoxville: University of Tennessee Press, 1987.

Smith, John David. *An Old Creed for the New South: Proslavery Ideology and Historiography, 1865–1918.* Westport, Conn.: Greenwood Press, 1985.

Stampp, Kenneth M. *The Imperiled Union: Essays on the Background of the Civil War.* New York: Oxford University Press, 1980.

Stewart, James Brewer. *Holy Warriors: The Abolitionists and American Slavery.* New York: Hill and Wang, 1976.

Thelen, David, ed. *Memory in American History.* Bloomington: Indiana University Press, 1991.

Thomas, John L., ed. *Abraham Lincoln and the American Political Tradition.* Amherst: University of Massachusetts Press, 1986.

Toplin, Robert Brent, ed. *Ken Burns's The Civil War: Historians Respond.* New York: Oxford University Press, 1996.

Vorenberg, Michael. "Abraham Lincoln and the Politics of Black Colonization." *Journal of the Abraham Lincoln Association* 14 (1993): 23–45.

Walters, Ronald G. *The Antislavery Appeal: American Abolitionism After 1830.* Baltimore: Johns Hopkins University Press, 1976.

Wiggins, William H. *O Freedom!: Afro-American Emancipation Celebrations.* Nashville: University of Tennessee Press, 1987.

Williams, George W. *A History of the Negro Troops in the War of the Rebellion, 1861–1865.* New York: Harper and Brothers, 1888.

Williamson, Joel. *The Crucible of Race: Black-White Relations in the American South Since Emancipation.* New York: Oxford University Press, 1984.

Wittke, Carl. *Tambo and Bones: A History of the American Minstrel Stage.* New York: Greenwood Press, 1968.

INDEX

Union & Emancipation
was designed and composed
in 10½-point Adobe Caslon leaded 2½ points
on a Gateway 486 PC using PageMaker 5.0
by Will Underwood at The Kent State University Press;
printed by sheet-fed offset lithography
on 50-pound Glatfelter Natural Smooth acid-free stock,
notch case bound over 88-point binder's boards
in Arrestox B cloth with Rainbow endpapers,
and wrapped with dust jackets printed
in three colors on 100-pound enamel stock
finished with matte film lamination
by Braun-Brumfield, Inc.;
and published by
The Kent State University Press
KENT, OHIO 44242